JEWISH AND CHRISTIAN TEXTS IN CONTEXTS AND RELATED STUDIES

38

Executive Editor
James H. Charlesworth

Editorial Board of Advisors
Motti Aviam, Michael Davis, Casey Elledge, Loren Johns, Amy-Jill Levine,
Lee McDonald, Lidia Novakovic, Gerbern Oegema, Henry Rietz, Brent Strawn

The Samaritans

Étienne Nodet, OP

Translated by Sr Pascale-Dominique Nau, OP

t&tclark
LONDON • NEW YORK • OXFORD • NEW DELHI • SYDNEY

T&T CLARK
Bloomsbury Publishing Plc
50 Bedford Square, London, WC1B 3DP, UK
1385 Broadway, New York, NY 10018, USA
29 Earlsfort Terrace, Dublin 2, Ireland

BLOOMSBURY, T&T CLARK and the T&T Clark logo are trademarks of
Bloomsbury Publishing Plc

First published in 2022 as *Les Samaritains* by Les Éditions du Cerf

First published in Great Britain 2023
Paperback edition published in 2025

Copyright © Les Éditions du Cerf 2022
English translation copyright © Sr Pascale-Dominique Nau, OP, 2023

Sr Pascale-Dominique Nau has asserted their right under the Copyright, Designs and Patents Act, 1988, to be identified as translator of this work.

All rights reserved. No part of this publication may be reproduced or transmitted in any form or by any means, electronic or mechanical, including photocopying, recording, or any information storage or retrieval system, without prior permission in writing from the publishers.

Bloomsbury Publishing Plc does not have any control over, or responsibility for, any third-party websites referred to or in this book. All internet addresses given in this book were correct at the time of going to press. The author and publisher regret any inconvenience caused if addresses have changed or sites have ceased to exist, but can accept no responsibility for any such changes.

A catalogue record for this book is available from the British Library.

A catalog record for this book is available from the Library of Congress.

ISBN: HB: 978-0-5677-0966-0
PB: 978-0-5677-0970-7
ePDF: 978-0-5677-0967-7
ePUB: 978-0-5677-0969-1

Series: Jewish and Christian Texts in Contexts and Related Studies, volume 38

Typeset by Deanta Global Publishing Services, Chennai, India

To find out more about our authors and books visit www.bloomsbury.com and sign up for our newsletters.

Contents

List of Figures	vi
Series Editor's Preface	vii
List of Abbreviations	xxiii
Introduction	1
1 Preliminaries: The Importance of the Samaritans	7
2 The Royal Period	49
3 The Shock of the Maccabean Crisis	71
4 The Persian Period	89
5 Pause	115
Appendix: Status Quæstionis	125
Index of Modern Authors	132
Index of References	137

Figures

1	Eastern and Hellenistic dynasties	4
2	The Tribes' territories according to SJ and Josephus	20
3	Judas' Judea	21
4	Joshua's final speech	22
5	Josephus largely follows the source of 1 Ezra	24
6	For Josephus, Nehemiah was neither a governor nor a reformer	27
7	Continuation and end of the reign of the Hasmonean high priest Simon	31
8	Colonists' loyalty or infidelity?	51
9	Conversion of settlers?	52
10	The high priests after the exile according to Josephus	78
11	High priests of Jerusalem in the Persian period	81
12	Enlarged Judea	82
13	The high priests until the exile	100
14	Some ways to situate Nehemiah and Sanballat	111

Series Editor's Preface

Those on the Holy Mountain Called Gerizim

Time to Honor the Ancient Samaritans

Why are the Samaritans too frequently portrayed as illegitimate descendants of the Abrahamic Covenant? This question bothers me as I came to appreciate the Samaritans long ago. That time was about the same period I appreciated many of the insights within early Judaism and the Dead Sea Scrolls. My admiration grew, as I studied the Samaritans, edited and published a citation of Deuteronomy in a Dead Sea Scroll that preserves a reading found in the Samaritan Pentateuch,[1] as well as studied and edited so-called Samaritan texts and references to the Samaritans in the *Old Testament Pseudepigrapha* (*OTP*). Some of this admiration went with me in the 1960s[2] when I visited Samaria and heightened my understanding and wonderment on Mount Gerizim. It was increased in 2010 when on Mount Gerizim the High Priest gave me the Samaritan Medal for Contributions to Peace and Scholarship. It was this long experience and perspective that guided me as I examined Nodet's latest work.

Étienne Nodet, OP, a distinguished professor in the *École biblique*, endeavors to repair a historical injustice by which the Samaritans are assumed to be a degraded form of Judaism. This pejorative estimation of the Samaritans seems to have originated during the time of the prophet Nehemiah in the fifth century BCE. Judean Jews refused to allow the "Samaritans" to help in rebuilding the Temple in Jerusalem. The hatred was inflamed during the time of John Hyrcanus (ruler of Judea from 135/134 BCE to 104 BCE) who demolished the Samaritan Temple on the holy mountain called "Gerizim" near the end of the second century BCE (perhaps in 128). This rejection of the Samaritans was well known to Jesus from Nazareth. According to Luke, Jesus sought to portray a Samaritan as more compassionate and faithful to God than a Jerusalem priest and Levite. The account appears in the *Parable of the Good Samaritan*.

In this well-constructed parable, in Luke 10, Jesus describes a Samaritan, who in contrast to the admired priest and Levite did not pass by "on the other side" of the road to avoid contamination. The Samaritan "was moved with pity" (Σαμαρίτης δέ

---

[1] James H. Charlesworth, "An Unknown Dead Sea Scrolls Fragment of Deuteronomy XXVII 4-6," *The Samaritan News* 1019–20 (August 8, 2008), pp. 64–8. Charlesworth, "What is a Variant? Announcing a Dead Sea Scrolls Fragment of Deuteronomy," *MAARAV* 16.2 (2009), pp. 201–12, Plate IX and X. Charlesworth, "The Discovery of an Unknown Dead Sea Scroll: The Original Text of Deuteronomy 27?" *Ohio Wesleyan Magazine*, July 2012. Charlesworth, "An Unknown Dead Sea Scroll and Speculations Focused on the *Vorlage* of Deuteronomy 27:4," in: . Frey and E. E. Popkes (eds.), *Jesus, Paulus und die Texte von Qumran* [H-W Kuhn Festschrift], WUNT 2. Reihe 390, Tübingen: Mohr-Siebeck, 2014, pp. 393–414.

[2] In the fall of 1968, I served on Mount Gerizim as area supervisor (ASOR).

τις ὁδεύων ἦλθεν κατ' αὐτὸν καὶ ἰδὼν ἐσπλαγχνίσθη). The Samaritan, ostracized by Jesus' Galilean and Judean contemporaries, went to the wounded and bleeding man; he "bandaged his wounds, having poured oil and wine on them. Then he put him on his own animal, brought him to an inn, and took care of him. The next day he took out two denarii, gave them to the innkeeper, and said, 'Take care of him; and when I come back, I will repay you whatever more you spend.'" This well-known parable has one main focus: be a helpful neighbor to all who may need you.

A disturbing question remains but is too often not asked: Why would a Galilean Jew, like Jesus, create a parable that celebrated "a certain Samaritan" to perform healing and turn his back on robbers who might be lurking behind rocks? Surely, we are hearing the inclusive mission of Jesus (go into all the villages; cf. Mk 6:8, Mt. 9:35, Lk 4:43-44; see esp. Lk 9:52 and 17:11).

Nodet's research represents his own focus and exploration of the issues related to the Samaritans. Unlike too many biblical scholars he is not seeking to find and follow the footprints of previous experts. Neither he nor I would expect all readers uncritically to follow his explanations. He and I expect his approach will generate fresh reflections on the long and rich history of the Samaritans and a renewed appreciation of them.

At the outset, Nodet accurately clarifies that the area formed by Galilee, Samaria, and Judea corresponds roughly to Canaan at the time of Joshua when the twelve tribes entered what they assumed was "the Holy Land." Then "the Holy Land" was the area between the Jordan and the Mediterranean. Both Samaritans and Jews affirm the same "Holy Land" and worship One God affirmed as YHWH and deem sacred the Pentateuch given by the One God through Moses to Israel (which will obtain different meanings). According to the author of Acts, Peter and John undertook a special mission to Samaria to confirm Samaritans who had already been baptized by Philip. Recall Acts 8:

> Now when the apostles at Jerusalem heard that Samaria had accepted the word of God, they sent Peter and John to them. The two went down and prayed for them that they might receive the Holy Spirit (for as yet the Spirit had not come upon any of them; they had only been baptized in the name of the Lord Jesus). Then Peter and John laid their hands on them, and they received the Holy Spirit. (Acts 8:14-17; NRSV)

This passage is informative of very early Christian traditions for two main reasons. First, Peter and John "went down" to them, those in Samaria; at that time, when one left Jerusalem, one always went "down" (even if moving north) because of the holiness of Jerusalem. Second, to "accept the word of God" meant more than baptism; that could confuse Jesus' Movement with that of his cousin, John the Baptism. One must also "receive the Holy Spirit."

Hatred of Samaritans Before and During Early Judaism and Christian Origins

Many traditions castigate the Samaritans, rejecting their monotheism and asserting their heresy. In some apocryphal and pseudepigraphic texts the Samaritans are vilified.

Jews claimed that those who castigated Samaritans were those "whose mind poured forth wisdom." In the Jewish layer of the *Testaments of the 12 Patriarchs* the "Jews" circumcise and then massacre the Samaritans. Recall also the epilogue in *Sirach* 50:

> Two nations my soul detests,
> and the third is not even a people:
> Those who live in Seir, and the Philistines,
> and the foolish people that live in Shechem.
>
> Instruction in understanding and knowledge
> I have written in this book,
> Jesus, the son of Eleazar son of Sirach of Jerusalem,
> whose mind poured forth wisdom.

This evaluation dates from the second century BCE, the time of John Hyrcanus, and represents the opinion of many of the established priests and scholars centered in Jerusalem who rejected the "Israelites" on Mount Gerizim. They are detested, not really "a people," and are "foolish."

This name "Samaritan" has more than one meaning; here it denotes those who settled in Samaria and worshipped on Mount Gerizim. No one knows when the schism between the Samaritans and Jerusalemites began. According to the author of 2 Kings 17, the Samaritan sect arose from the mixing of cultures following Israel's defeat by Assyria in 721 BCE. The king of Assyria removed the Israelites from the Holy Land and repopulated the area with foreigners from Babylon, Cuthah,[3] and other nations. This tradition is clearly earlier than the tensions under Nehemiah and the obvious schism under the Hasmoneans like John Hyrcanus.[4] His obliterations of the Samaritan Temple help explain two subsequent horrors.

The hatred between Jews and Samaritans is evident when a group of Samaritans desecrated the Jerusalem Temple in approximately 6 CE by spreading human bones within the Temple porches and sanctuary during Passover. The Samaritan hatred of Jews who worshipped in the Jerusalem Temple is also placarded by the massacre of Galilean pilgrims who were slaughtered in about 52 CE, as they moved southward to Jerusalem (cf. Lk 9:51-53).

Herod the Great seems to have diverse feelings about those in Samaria (and many others, especially those in his family). He was married to Miriam there, but he expanded and refurbished the Jerusalem Temple and made it one of his most prized achievements. He orchestrated many aspects of the Temple, its larger size, and its prominence and beauty. A stone that weighs over 500 tons has been detected and studied on a lower course of the western wall. Herod's builders placed it there.

---

[3] "Cuthah" is today Tall Ibrāhīm. It was an ancient city in Mesopotamia; it was located north of Kish in what is now south-central Iraq. Cuthah was despised by those who honored YHWH because the inhabitants were devoted to the cult of Nergal, the god of the underworld.

[4] Alan D. Crown, ed., *The Samaritans*, Tübingen: Mohr-Siebeck, 1989. Crown, "Redating the Schism between the Judaeans and the Samaritans," *The Jewish Quarterly Review* 82 (July/October 1991), pp. 17–50. I am indebted to Alan D. Crown for his knowledge of the Samaritans.

The ignorance and even denigration of Samaritans today, after more than 2,000 years, is caused by many factors. The self-isolation, unique celebration of Passover,[5] and strict intermarriage of the Samaritans are factors. And the intermittent Samaritan "hatred" seems tainted by the Hasmonean wars, Josephus, early Judaism, rabbinic literature, and the much earlier eventual Jewish rejection of those in Samaria. According to the Jewish position regarding the Samaritans in the *Babylonian Talmud*, those who worship on Gerizim can be forgiven when they deny the sacredness of Gerizim, affirm the holiness of Jerusalem, and believe in the resurrection of the dead (*b.Kuthim* 2.7).

I guess all scholars throughout most areas of our globe should now be accustomed, and horrified, by the lack of knowledge about history. As the great philosophers have warned us, anyone who is oblivious of past errors is bound to repeat many of them. Samaritan history is not taught in universities, seminaries, or rabbinic schools. Almost all experts I know lament the loss of historiography in American institutions but not in some universities in Europe and Israel.

Ignorance and categorization of Samaritans as "defiled" appear in the present. Some authors presently contend that in 721 BCE, when northern Israel fell to the Assyrians, many Israelites were transported to Assyria. Some remained in the Land and "intermarried with foreigners planted there by the Assyrians. These half-Jewish, half-Gentile people became known as the Samaritans. To the Jews, a Samaritan was more revolting than a Gentile (pagan); Samaritans were half-breeds who defiled the true religion."[6] Even gracious authors can be misinterpreters and transmit old errors.

Nodet's penetrating analysis of all sources, archaeological and literary (despite the paucity and lateness of Samaritan sources), highlights the similarities between the Samaritans and the Jews. Nodet is correct to note that the Samaritans cherish "a holy place, a succession of high priests up to the present day, little *diaspora* and customs derived from the Pentateuch."

Despite the opinions of too many scholars, I agree with Nodet that it is impossible to consider the religion of the Samaritans as deriving from Judaism. Along with Moses Gaster, John Macdonald, and other specialists on the Samaritans, Nodet perceives that the Samaritans are basically the descendants of the ancient Kingdom of Israel. Nodet knows the recent excavations on Mount Gerizim disclosed a large sanctuary that was established at least by the end of the fifth century BCE, and that is prior to the establishment of "Judaism" in Judah. With boldness, Nodet claims: "Now, this discovery has given rise to renewed studies on the origin of this almost marginal entity. Nevertheless, the view that it is a degraded form of Judaism remains prevalent, for the decisive element—which is generally underestimated—is the significance of the reforms of Ezra and Nehemiah."[7] Many will await with anticipation to learn what Nodet has perceived.

---

[5] Now, the Samaritans continue to slaughter the Passover lambs in deep pits on Mount Gerizim.
[6] See Alyssa Roat, "The Samaritans: Hope from the History of a Hated People," *Bible/Bible Studies*, February 10, 2020. My source is the article on the web, and I may not have all the particulars.
[7] See the notes to his chapters.

A More Positive Appreciation of the Samaritans

Mount Gerizim and the region defined by the Samaritans held the blessed Mountain Gerizim. According to the author of Deuteronomy, the Israelites, when they entered the Holy Land, "Canaan," they selected Gerizim for the mountain to offer to YHWH blessings for the successful trip from Egyptian bondage to a "land flowing with milk and honey."

As is widely known, the biblical canon preserves two distinct attitudes of the Samaritans. Some passages laud the Israelites living in Samaria; they antedate the Jews in Judea and represent the area that is north of Judea and south of Galilee. Note Ezek. 16:46, "Your elder sister is Samaria, who lived with her daughters to the north of you." Recall Ezek. 16:51, which tends to praise the Samaritans in a condemnation of those in and around Judea: "Samaria has not committed half your sins; you have committed more abominations than they, and have made your sisters appear righteous by all the abominations that you have committed."

Obviously, the Samaritans defend a markedly different position than the one summarized first. They claim to originate from the Jewish tribes of Ephraim and Manasseh who remained in Samaria after the Assyrian conquest of 721 BCE. The New Testament gospels attest to the antiquity of the Samaritans; recall what a Samaritan woman by Jacob's well in Samaria asked Jesus: "Are you greater than our father Jacob, who gave us [this] well; and he and his sons and his flocks drank from it?" (μὴ σὺ μείζων εἶ τοῦ πατρὸς ἡμῶν Ἰακώβ, ὃς ἔδωκεν ἡμῖν τὸ φρέαρ καὶ αὐτὸς ἐξ αὐτοῦ ἔπιεν καὶ οἱ υἱοὶ αὐτοῦ καὶ τὰ θρέμματα αὐτοῦ; Jn 4:12).

The distinguished Israeli scholar (and beloved colleague), Shemaryahu Talmon, supported this interpretation. He judged the description of these Israelites in 2 Kgs 17:24 as "foreigners" to be tendentious. He also challenged us to perceive 2 Chron. 30:1 to confirm the hypothesis that most of the Jewish tribes of Ephraim and Manasseh remained in Samaria.[8] The Assyrian deportation in 721 BCE was only partial and certainly did not last long. A study of Syrian records indicates that Jeroboam's northern "Israel" was not totally deported (2 Chron. 34:9). Conceivably, Samaria after about 500 BCE consisted of Israelites who never left and returnees from Babylon. Perhaps, we should include a third group in Samaria; they would be some foreigners, who eventually affirmed the old faith of Israel. Syncretism and foreign elements filtered into the similar language in Israel to the north and in Judea to the south. But, up until the present century the Samaritans preserved a strict heritage, marrying only other Samaritans (but the practice led to the loss of intelligence).

Perhaps as a response to the venomous polemics emanating from Judea, the Samaritans claim the Jews are guilty of apostasy since the oldest and only holy site for worship and a temple is on the holy mountain of Gerizim. The Samaritans have been holding on to the claim that they are the true Israelites. While Jews for almost two millennia recognize all the books in the Hebrew Bible as sacred and divine, the Samaritans accept only the Pentateuch (the first five books). This position was not

---

[8] Shemaryahu Talmon, "Biblical Traditions in Samaritan History," in: Ephraim Stern and Hanan Eshel (eds.) *Sefer Ha-Shomronim*, Jerusalem: Ben Zvi Institute, 2002, pp. 25-7 (in Hebrew).

anathema to all Jews; it was shared by the Sadducees. We no longer can discern Jesus' canon of scripture; since he was a Galilean Jew and chose Jerusalem as the place to preach and sacrifice, he may have shared the canonical position of most pre-70 Jews (but we cannot be certain of what books were included or excluded before the so-called edits of Jamnia in the second century CE).

Though their name is similar to the city of Samaria, the Samaritans do not derive their name from this city. As the early scholars of the Church, notably Epiphanius of Salamis, Jerome, Eusebius, and Origen, professed the Samaritans took, and take, their name from the phrase "Keepers [of the Law]" (שמרים, shmrym in Hebrew and Samaritan, and in Arabic السامريون, perhaps al-Sāmiriyyūn). They refer to themselves as Shamerim (שָׁמֲרִים), and that term derives from the Semitic (Hebrew, Aramaic, and Samaritan) verb שמר , which means "to guard" and "to watch." Thus, the "Samaritans" believe that they are the "Guardians" or "Keepers" of the Law. They accept the Pentateuch given by the One God to Moses.[9]

The most ancient self-designation for Samaritans is an inscription found in the Samaritan Diaspora at Delos.[10] It dates from at least 150 BCE.[11] That inscription suggests that some Samaritans knew themselves as "Israelites," meaning the remnants of the north part of the Holy Land following the schism after Solomon. Today, I am told the Samaritans prefer to be known as "Israelite Samaritans."

According to Josephus (in *Wars* and in *Antiquities*) and the later Talmud (in Tosefta *Berakhot*), the "Samaritans" originated later, that is, to the time of the Babylonian captivity, and are signified as "Cuthites," that is, those who dwelt in Kutha, which today is in Iraq. Kutha (or Cuth) was one of the locales from which "Israelites" were exiled to Samaria (2 Kgs 17:24).

In present-day Hebrew, the term used for "the Samaritans" is *Shomronim* (שומרונים), which may mean "Samaritans" or more probably "inhabitants of Samaria." In antiquity, there were thousands of Samaritans, but so-called Christian and then Islamic wars, and intermarriage (and its horrors), reduced them to a small group living on Mount Gerizim and in Holon, in the southern portion of Tel Aviv.

Nodet knows the issues separating the Jews from the Samaritans; but he rightly calls for a reevaluation so that all forms of ancient "Israelite" religions that remain may be appreciated. Is Nodet not on target when he claims there is room for disagreement and

---

[9] Consult Benjamim Tsedaka and Sharon Sullivan, *The Israelite Samaritan Version of the Torah: First English Translation Compared with the Masoretic Version*, Grand Rapids (MI), Eerdmans Publishing, 2013. I am indebted to Tsedaka for many favors and trips to Mount Gerizim.

[10] L. Michael White, "The Delos Synagogue Revisited: Recent Fieldwork in the Graeco-Roman Diaspora," *Harvard Theological Review* 80.2 (1987), pp. 133–60. A Jewish community on Delos is mentioned in 1 Macc. 15:16-23; it is in a letter from Lucius Calpurnius Piso (140–139 BCE) and advocates protection of Jews as they were friends of Rome. Josephus records that during the reign of the Emperor Julius Caesar two Roman edicts protected the rights of Jews on Delos (*Ant.* 14.213-16 and 14.231-32).

[11] See Magnar Kartveit, *The Origin of the Samaritans*, Leiden: Brill, 2009. Kartveit, "Theories of the Origin of the Samaritans—Then and Now," *Religions* 10.12 (December 2019), pp. 1–14. Jonathan Bourgel, "The Samaritans During the Hasmonean Period: The Affirmation of a Discrete Identity?" *Religions* 10.11 (November 2019), pp. 1–21. B. Hensel, "On the Relationship of Judah and Samaria in Post-Exilic Times: A Farewell to the Conflict Paradigm," *Journal for the Study of the Old Testament* 44.1 (2019), pp. 19–42.

agreement? The Samaritans differed in the lauding of the only place to sacrifice and the appreciation of "the holy city." The Samaritans obviously hailed Gerizim as the only place to sacrifice to God. But, following Nodet's insights, let us appreciate that Jew and Samaritan shared a deep monotheism and one faith in the God of Abraham, Isaac, and Jacob. The Samaritan Pentateuch is ancient, and some of its divergent readings appear in some fragments found in the Qumran caves. but it is very similar to the so-called Masoretic text of the Middle Ages now used by Jews throughout the world (and also Christians in all countries).

On Mount Gerizim I was shown, among other claims, the site of Abel's first altar (Gen. 4:4), the location of Noah's sacrifice after the flood (8:20), the meeting place of Abraham and Melchizedek (Gen. 14:18), and the site of Isaac's sacrifice (Gen. 22). These claims represent the Samaritan understanding about their sacred mountain.

Nodet's Personal Methodology

Nodet is famous for not avoiding controversy and following the path he is convinced is indicated by the ancient sources, as is apparent in his earlier book in this series that I edit (*A Gate to Heaven*). That book helped us better appreciate the insights of the Qumran Essenes. The title of Nodet's previous book is apt, since the Qumran Essenes believed that they were "the Sons of Light" because their community was like an antechamber of heaven and that the Holy Spirit, a concept they developed, dwelt with them. Perhaps they imagined that the Holy Spirit *from* God left Jerusalem with them, when they abandoned the "Holy City," and lived in their *Yaḥad* near the western shores of the Dead Sea.

Among Nodet's controversial claims in this book is the following: "[W]hereas surrounding Mount Gerizim, their sacred mountain overlooking the ancient city of Shechem," the Samaritans "are in fact to this day the direct heirs of the ancient Israelites." Why is it controversial? In what specific ways does Nodet's position challenge contemporary views and open a gate so that Samaritans may once again be accepted as "People of YHWH's Covenant"? Let us ponder all such questions, and then answer.

In my preface to Nodet's *A Gate to Heaven* entitled "Diamonds Not Seen in Lanes Less Traveled," I clarified that Étienne Nodet, OP, has frequently taken the routes less traveled by authors who followed too closely their teacher's path. He has a creative mind, and his insights are clarions to regain the excitement of *viatori*—those who leave the classroom and wander among the cliffs and caves above the Essene headquarters at Qumran, looking for pieces of ancient pottery. Such inquisitor also may sit in a large cave and look down on the Jordan Valley, the Essene ruins and caves, and the path the Roman armies took as they moved southward to Qumran. I like Nodet's inquisitive demeanor; he explores areas of scholarship that remind me of the adventures of my youth, when I dove off the Florida coast at Delray Beach and explored tankers sunk by the Nazis.

Nodet's conclusion is obvious, thankfully, and he cuts through scholarly gibberish and leaves us with this conclusion:

> [It is not evident what] leads to firm conclusions, since it is not clear what made the Samaritans the heirs of the ancient kingdom of Israel. Moreover, the split from Judah and the Davidic dynasty seems more political than religious. If we move to a much later context, the separation between Jews and Samaritans was firm and long-standing at the time of the New Testament. Two episodes after the Maccabean crisis (167-164) lastingly established it: the destruction of the temple on Mount Gerizim by the Asmonaean high priest John Hyrcan, and a little earlier a litigation in Alexandria between Jews and Samaritans to determine which temple—Jerusalem or Gerizim—was the true one according to Scripture. However, before the crisis, there is evidence of the peaceful coexistence of these two temples.

Nodet's work is intermittently controversial. Given that all should not seek simply to agree with him, I find independent, but informed, searching all data and resources is the beating heart of advancing scholarship. His search for truth is refreshing and reminiscent of the Qumranites who brought to light the blindness of "the Sons of Darkness." One may also imagine the New Testament minds, Peter, James, John, and Paul, who boldly preached proclamations (*kerygma*) that were overwhelming new and creative. Likewise, the latter *Mishnah* and *Tosephta* are defined by contrasting opinions. Is it not almost always attractive to see scholars debating, intelligently and with maturity, what is historical? Should we not all agree that dialogue that seeks to avoid controversy is often meaningless? Do we not lose our way when we let the blind lead the blind?

Now, perhaps, it is time to focus on one controversial thought. Étienne Nodet writes that the Samaritans are "in fact to this day the direct heirs of the ancient Israelites." My problem is with "the direct heirs."

Mainline scholars (permit me for now to use this term) observe that about 721 BCE the Assyrians conquered the northern kingdom of Israel and took many groups to Assyria. According to ancient lore, the so-called "lost ten tribes" disappeared from history. One year earlier, Samaria was conquered by the Assyrians under the command of Shalmaneser V. According to the author of 2 Kings 17: "In the ninth year of Hoshea, the king of Assyria captured Samaria; and he carried the Israelites away to Assyria. The following year, in 701 BCE, the Assyrians attacked Judah to the south but could not capture Jerusalem."

Eventually, "the Israelites" were allowed to return to Samaria. Scholars debate whether all Israelites were deported to Assyria or whether those who remained continued as unassimilated "ancient Israelites"? Or had the Samaritans become categorically a mixed race? The prestigious Joachim Jeremias was persuaded that the Samaritans became a mixed race after 721 BCE;[12] Jacob Neusner showed that Jeremias was incorrect.[13] As you will see, Nodet provides his answer.

---

[12] Joachim Jeremias, "Σαμάρεια." In: Gerhard Kittel, Geoffrey William Bromiley, Gerhard Friedrich, and Ronald E. Pitkin (eds.), *Theological Dictionary of the New Testament*, Grand Rapids (MI), Eerdmans, 1964, vol. 7, pp. 88-94. Jeremias, *Jerusalem in the Time of Jesus: An Investigation into Economic and Social Conditions During the New Testament Period*, London, Fortress Press, 1969. Recent insights denigrate the claims of Joachim Jeremias.

[13] Jacob Neusner, "Review of Jerusalem in the Time of Jesus," *Journal of the American Academy of Religion* 39 (1971), pp. 201-3.

As we await to know how Nodet helps move forward the present arguments about the origin of the Samaritans and the rift with those in Judea, let me share the insight of Jonathan (Yonatan) Bourgel:

> While a great deal has been written in the attempt to delineate the circumstances of their "parting of the ways," most scholars now consider that this development was not the result of a single occurrence, a schism so to speak, but rather a gradual historical process extending over several centuries.
>
> In this regard, the Hasmonean period (167–63 BCE), during which an independent Jewish kingdom was established in the land of Israel, is commonly regarded as a decisive and formative moment, if not a definitive one, in the emergence of a self-contained Samaritan identity.[14]

Certainly, Shechem as well as its surroundings was a place of worship for those who exited Egypt under Moses and entered "the Promised Land" with Joshua. That was long before David chose Jerusalem as his "Holy City" about 1000 BCE. Did any Samaritan descend from these early followers of YHWH who helped Joshua conquer the Land? Obviously, we probably will never be able to answer all our questions, as we have entered the preliterary centuries of earliest Israel and names as well as perspectives change continuously.

After the defeat of the Jews in Palestine by the Romans in 70 CE, Josephus comprehended that the Samaritans claimed to be descendants of the early Israelites (*Ant.* 9:291, 11:341), but he also understood the Samaritans as a geographical group and a distinct ethnic group that were defined in contrast to the "Judeans" (*Ant.* 10:184, 17:20, 18:85). Obviously, Josephus's conflicted view of the Samaritans is not a reliable source for discerning their origin. Not geographical isolation but thought is the best way to comprehend how and in what ways the Samaritans preserved an ancient religion devoted to YHWH.[15]

On the holy mountain of Gerizim, I have explored the pits in which the Passover lambs are slaughtered today. Did the Samaritans ever have a building called "a temple"?[16]

---

[14] Bourgel, "The Samaritans During the Hasmonean Period: The Affirmation of a Discrete Identity?". As with main issues in history, Bourgel seems on target in arguing that the "Hasmoneans' attitude toward the Samaritans cannot simply be seen as one of hatred and rejection as is generally assumed." Complex historical events resist simple solutions. As we have learned that in antiquity "Jews" represented widely divergent perspectives, so we should not read Samaritan documents or reports about them with the presupposition that Samaritans expressed a unity and advocated one position. In contrast to Jews, Samaritans may be comprehended as distinct; but Samaritans compared with other Samaritans, some ancient and others recent, there are also differences. If Samaritans and Jews were so different, why did the authors of the *Mishna* find it incomprehensible to explain a difference?

[15] I am influenced by the research of Stewart Penwell, "Josephus on Samaritan Origins," *The Bible and Interpretation*, October 2019.

[16] I am indebted to Reinhard Pummer, "Was There an Altar or a Temple in the Sacred Precinct on Mt. Gerizim?" *Journal for the Study of Judaism* 47 (2016), pp. 1–21. Pummer summarizes the complex discussions; inter alia, he shows that the ancient Samaritan sources can be contradictory and have no consistent terminologies that help to distinguish between a house, a synagogue, an altar, or a temple. Sometimes the Samaritan sources refer to an "altar" and in the same text or another similar one to a roofed and walled building that is a temple.

Extensive excavations on Mount Gerizim were directed by Yitzhak Magen. He exposed the remains of a Samaritan Temple that he dates to the fifth century BCE and the time of Nehemiah.[17] Note his authoritative publications that correct Josephus's report that the Gerizim temple dates to the Greek period:

> The archaeological excavations at Mt. Gerizim proved unequivocally that the temple on the mount was built in the middle of the fifth century B.C.E., that is, most likely before Nehemiah's arrival in 445 B.C.E. The dating of the temple is based on the architecture that is dated with certainty to the Persian period, the carbon-14 tests that were conducted on hundreds of thousands of the bones of sacrifices from kosher animals that were discovered in the sacred precinct, and the pottery vessels and coins that are dated to the fifth century B.C.E. An additional temple was built over the first temple during the reign of Antiochus III, c. 200 C.E.[18]

Well known is the tradition that John Hyrcanus I (יוחנן הרקנוס; Ἰωάννης) was high priest and ruler of Judea from 135/134 BCE to 104 BCE; he never accepted the title "King."[19] During the time of Second Temple Judaism and his reign, Judeans experienced their last decades of freedom from Persians, Greeks, and Romans. He was succeeded as high priest by Alexander Jannaeus (103–76 BCE) who crucified perhaps 800 Pharisees. Jannaeus's reign was defined by cruelty and inhumanness; do not miss the account by Josephus, *Antiquities* 13 (my idiomatic rendering):

> While he [Jannaeus] was feasting with his concubines, in the sight of all [in] the city, he ordered about eight hundred of them (the Pharisees) to be crucified. And while they were still alive, he ordered the throats of their children and wives to be cut before their eyes. This was indeed by way of revenge for the injuries they had done him; which punishment yet was of an inhuman nature.

Jannaeus brutality was unlimited. In Ashkelon, he crucified eighty women, stripping them naked but making them face the wooden cross, for modesty, according to Josephus in *Wars* 1 (cf. 4QPesher Nahum 1:6-8).[20]

New Issues and Perplexing Questions

Shortly after the reign of Jannaeus, Pompey, and the Romans entered Jerusalem and the Temple. The rest is well-known history that placards the revolts of Jews in 66 CE

---

[17] Yitzakh Magen, "The Dating of the First Phase of the Samaritan Temple on Mt Gerizim in Light of Archaeological Evidence," in: Oded Lipschitz, Gary N. Knoppers, and Rainer Albertz (eds.), *Judah and the Judeans in the Fourth Century B.C.E.*, Winona Lake (IN), Eisenbrauns, 2007), pp. 157–212. Yitzkakh Magen, "Bells, Pendants, Snakes and Stones," *BAR*, November/December 2010. Magen's archaeological discoveries prove that the Samaritans are earlier and did not originate in the second century BCE.

[18] Yitzkakh Magen, "Dating of the Samaritan Temple on Mt. Gerizim," *BAR*, September 2013.

[19] The entry in Britannica needs to be corrected; it is "John Hyrcanus I King of Judaea." He was not a "king."

[20] According to *Mishnah Sanhedrin* 6, Simeon ben Shetah is the one who ordered the women to be crucified.

and the burning of many cities and towns in Galilee, then Jericho and Qumran, and finally the Temple in September 70 CE.

Less well known, and deserves focus, is the career of Vespasian. Disgraced because he had fallen asleep when Nero was singing, Vespasian was dispatched to Antioch. From there in 66 CE, he moved from Antioch to Akko-Ptolemais. Soon thereafter, he besieged Jotapata, which is on a high hill north of the Beit Netofa Valley (בקעת בית נטופה; cf. esp. Josephus, *Wars*, 3:141-288, 316–18). The collapsed walls and ruins remain as the Roman army left them. At Jotapata, Josephus, the leader of the revolt in Galilee, was taken prisoner by Vespasian and his son, Titus. After conquering Galilee, Vespasian and his massive army moved southward to Judea. In 68 CE, when Jerusalem was helpless and when Nero died almost everything related to the "Jewish War" was halted during the riotous brief times of the emperors Galba, Vitellius, and Otho. Eventually, Vespasian's troops saluted him as emperor in 69 CE, and while he was in Egypt the Roman Senate on 21 December 69 declared him emperor. Subsequently, Titus, Vespasian's son, conquered Judea and despite his instructions, the Temple was burned in 70 CE.

During the reign of John Hyrcanus, the Essenes, Sadducees, and Pharisees probably developed into identifiable religious groups. Within rabbinic literature, this high priest is often referred to as Yoḥanan Cohen Gadol (יוחנן כהן גדול) "John, the High Priest." Before 70 CE, many more "sects" or groups in the Land appeared; all long after the Samaritans populated Samaria.

What did John Hyrcanus I, the Hasmonean, destroy on Gerizim? About 110 BCE, John Hyrcanus did destroy the Samaritan Temple.[21] The first phase of the Samaritan Temple, a building, however, is dated now to the early Persian period and not to the Greek period, not during the time of Joshua or Solomon but to the time of Nehemiah, according to the excavations by Yitzhak Magen.[22]

Virtually no early literary evidence of the Samaritan Temple exists, and its archaeological remains were almost totally obliterated. First there was the destruction by Hyrcanus and later the construction of the *Church of Mary Theotokos* in the fifth century CE by Emperor Zeno (476–91). How reliable is the oral tradition that shaped the Samaritan compositions.

What is the earliest written historical account of the origin of the Samaritans? The earliest history of the Samaritan tradition is the *Kitab 'al-Ta'rikh* (كتاب التاريخ) compiled by Abu'l-Fath (أبو الفتح إبن أبي الحسن السامري), but this book dates from 1355 CE.[23] Moreover, many critics judge it to be unreliable and a "fictional" apology that derives from many earlier sources, some reliable, others oral, and many lost.

In some ways, I concur with Étienne Nodet that the Samaritans have an "Israelite" tradition; its oral base is ancient and cannot be dated. Does it antedate the founding of the Temple by Solomon in Jerusalem? Are some Samaritans the descendants of the Israelites who established the northern kingdom of Israel after the death of Solomon? What race do they represent? How may we now be certain of the blood line of the

---

[21] See Adele Berlin, *The Oxford Dictionary of the Jewish Religion* (Oxford: Oxford University Press, 2011), p. 330.
[22] Magen, *Judah and the Judeans in the Fourth Century B.C.E.*, pp. 157–93.
[23] See Kartveit, "Theories of the Origin of the Samaritans—Then and Now," 1–14.

Samaritans; they have for centuries been forced to marry only another Samaritan and now the sons of the high priest have low IQs (to be polite). How could we now, more than 3,000 years after Joshua entered the area of Shechem, discern "an ancient Israelite"? If mitochondrial DNA (mtDNA) of ancient bones is examined, we also must be convinced it was from a female Samaritan. Also, what would such research prove? Would not attention be drawn to the pre-Babylonian origin of the Samaritans?

By not agreeing always with Étienne Nodet of the *École biblique*, I may have pleased him when such apparent "rebuff" would have perturbed other experts. Étienne is certainly correct in asserting that the Samaritans must not be placarded "as a degraded form of Judaism." They antedated the concept of "Judaism," and they lived in the high mountains north of Judea and Jerusalem.

During Samaritan services one can feel that they worship the one true God, YHWH. The blood line of the Samaritans is probably closer to the ancient Israelites than is the bloodline of Jews today living in Jerusalem. They are either Ashkenazi, from central Europe,[24] or Sephardic, from Spain and northwest Africa. How can we today discern if anyone's blood line is purely Jewish?

Equally important is the question: "All not almost all of us bearers of Jewish blood?" Intermarriage was popular in many areas of Europe.

Most scholars of antiquity will laud Nodet for not seeking to follow the path of leading experts. He also does not begin with accustomed categories and moves easily from 300 BCE to 200 CE. His use of ancient sources in this study is superb and a model for other experts. He reminds me of a child's curiosity, as he explores texts before him, in the original languages, and does not begin with commentaries or published speculations. I often smile, maybe only inwardly, when I see a spark of enlightenment and enjoyment in his eyes.

Let us return to ancient times. About 67 CE, Samaritans collected on Mount Gerizim; that is shortly after the fall of Jotapata in Galilee. Vespasian and his troops, at that time, did not distinguish between Jews and Samaritans (and a similar perception is found in the *Mishnah*). Apparently, the Romans suspected a revolt on Gerizim; hence, Vespasian sent a tribune to quell a putative revolt. Unfortunately, the Roman's advance up Gerizim precipitated a massacre (Josephus, *War* 3:307-315).

Recall another, more famous, passage in Josephus about the Samaritans. They killed Galilean Jews who were traveling through Samaria to Jerusalem in order to celebrate in the Temple the Jewish festivals (*Ant.* 20). Evidently, Josephus, a Judean priest, considered the Samaritans as an ethnic group separate from the "Judeans" (see *Ant.* 10:184, 17:20, 18:85). Josephus, in the same publication, acknowledges that the Samaritans descended from the Israelites (*Ant.* 9:291, 11:341). Is it wise to unify all Josephus's references to the Samaritans, and is he an unbiased source?

Nodet's vision is both deep and panoramic. He claims that an overall sketch of "the Israelites" (broadly defined as those related to Abraham, Moses, and Joshua)

---

[24] Before the founding of Israel again in 1948, the Ashkenazi in Europe were an isolated population, with scarce intermarriage with other groups. They preserved many of the early Jewish traditions—perhaps not all the way back to pre-70 early Judaism—and they "ghettoized" themselves to preserve Judaism (shaped by rabbinic Judaism). Other groups of Jews who sought to keep Judaism "pure" were the Sephardic and also the Ethiopian Jews who claim to descend from King Solomon.

in the first century, before the destruction of Jerusalem in 70 CE, is focused on three sufficiently documented places: Alexandria in Egypt, Shechem in Samaria, and Jerusalem in Judea. Shechem became a Roman colony, *Flavia Neapolis* (Nablus), after the Jewish War that ended in 70 CE (except for those on Masada and in caves). Philo, the Samaritans, and those elsewhere in the Holy Land (the many sects, including the "Christians," and the earliest Rabbis of rabbinic literature) were grounded respectively in these three cities.

Philo knew Hebrew but expressed himself in Greek, preferring allegory to historiography to explain his Judaism. The Samaritans were defined by the oldest tradition; they witnessed to the earliest tradition that celebrated Joshua's conquest of the Land and focused on Shechem. The Samaritans and Rabbis chose different, but early, forms of Hebrew, with Aramaic nuances. The earliest Christians spoke Aramaic and a form of early Syriac and expanded around the world using Greek, and then Latin (and also Coptic, Syriac, Slavonics, and Armenian), as their chosen language. The source of Christian faith is almost always the Greek New Testament with all its challenging variants. The traditions in the Apocrypha, Pseudepigrapha, and other early texts often help explain comments and Jesus' sayings in the New Testament. Those in Ethiopia preserve many early Jewish compositions and cherish ancient texts over modern translations.

The Christians are defined by traditions and hopes founded in Jesus from Nazareth whom they hail as "the Messiah" (Jesus the Christ) and "the Son of God," an affirmation that has diverse meanings today. The early Jewish sects and groups disappeared sometime after about 70 CE except for the Samarians, Christians, and the Pharisees who tend to evolve into the Rabbis who were formed by old traditions preserved in Jerusalem and codified in Galilee.

Many readers may agree with me in hoping that the research of Nodet will shed clarifying light on the Samaritans. They have been vilified and despised. Perhaps we might together approximate a lost perspective, *mutatis mutandis*, whereby the שומרונים, the السامريون, are appreciated to be remnants of the ancient northern Kingdom of Israel, and "the House of Joseph," which includes the tribes of Ephraim and Manasseh. How would that renewed perspective harmonize with the appreciation of Jews, Christians, and Muslims—those who revere God's revelations in (or beginning in) the Abrahamic Covenant?

I appreciate the creative freedom grounded in faithfulness to *sacra scriptura* supported by Nodet's institution, the *École biblique* (EBAF), an alma mater for me and the location for the production of the early volumes of the "Dead Sea Scrolls" in DJDJ and then DJD. The EBAF is a Dominican institution that is faithful to the creeds and to a search for a better perception and articulation of the human search for faithfulness and truth. As for me, I find the *École* a delightful "home" in which I have completed numerous publications from 1968 to the present. It is a faith-centered scholarly community that is both challenging and stimulating. Many from around the world, including many Jewish *savants* in Jerusalem, find the *Ecole* one of the most replete libraries and a quiet setting for advanced research. I especially enjoy the spiritual services in the "Chapel" near where Steven, the first Christian martyr, was remembered to have been stoned.

References to Samaria and Samaritans are found in Matthew, Luke, John, and Acts. Why are the Samaritans not noted in the Gospel of Mark? Is that another indication that Mark was ignorant of Palestine and wrote in Rome, after Peter's martyrdom, and had no dialogue with Samaritans in Rome?

Many gifted scholars have published major tomes about the origin and history of the Samaritans; they are discussed in Nodet's following book. With you, I may wonder if Samaritan research is an area well researched, without presuppositions, as have the Sadducees, Pharisees, Essenes, Jesus' Movement, and other groups. My work on a Qumran manuscript that preserves a reading in the Samaritan Pentateuch (cited in note one) raises many questions. Was it an earlier reading in the Hebrew Bible and to what degree is the medieval Masoretic text a tradition that was significantly edited, that is, in what specific ways are variants in the Samaritan Pentateuch not "variants" but ancient readings? Finally, how massive was the Samaritan Temple at its final expansion; could it have been more impressive than the Temple built by Solomon?

Let us now remember the wise counsel of T. S. Eliot. This perspicacious poet, T. S. Eliot, shared a remarkable thought: "Only those who risk going too far can possibly find out how far one can go." In different ways, Christopher Columbus and Albert Einstein "set sail" on such "a wooden ship" but not commanded by Wynken, Blynken, and Nod, as in the poem by Eugene Field published in 1889. Glancing back on my life, I can perceive that inadvertently Eliot frequently directed my rudder. Does that admission not align me, at least a little bit, with Nodet? Has he, once again, not expressed himself clearly and churned up data for intense discussions?

For over sixty years, in more than fifteen countries, I have seen how engaging and informed debaters remove misunderstandings and bring us closer to the distant truth. Declarations remove us from the true and often untrodden path; interrogatives draw us closer to the far-off *via* to the beatific city.

Epilogos

In a second book now in preparation to appear in this same series, Nodet reflects on ancient Israelite (Samaritan) historiography. He points out that the Israelite history after the Pentateuch is given in two biblical blocks, which display a major contrast. The first is the collection of the books Joshua, Judges, 1-2 Samuel, and 1-2 Kings, also called the Former Prophets, which delineates after King Solomon a split between two rival kingdoms: Israel in the north, with ten or eleven of the twelve Israelite tribes, and Judah in the south around Jerusalem, with only the tribe of Judah and maybe little Benjamin. After several centuries, both kingdoms were defeated by major powers, who deported the populations: the northern tribes were taken in 722 BCE by the Assyrian king Sargon II; and later, the southern tribes were exiled in 587 by the Babylonian king Nebuchadnezzar.

The second block, which is made up of the books 1-2 Chronicles and Ezra-Nehemiah, has a larger historical perspective; for it begins with a brief synopsis from Adam and focuses on Judah as the true Israel. It manages such an approach in two different ways: The compilers of Chronicles rewrite the story from David down to the Judean exile and largely ignore the northern kingdom, while Ezra-Nehemiah strictly defines Israel as the repatriates from Babylonia so that the Israelite identity is given by a repatriated woman. Moreover, the authors of the second block try to present the postexilic reconstructions as a restoration of the preexilic era, but the facts are blurred and almost unintelligible.

In summation, the Hebrew Bible has sufficient elements to compile a story until the Babylonian Exile. Of course, there are the books of Esther and Daniel, but they do not focus upon and present a continuous story. The contrast just enunciated should entail a problem with the history of the Samaritans, since according to 2 Kings 17 (in the Hebrew Bible) they are the heirs of the settlers sent by the Assyrians after 722 BCE, and thus the "Samaritans" are described as a mixed race that observes essentially a corrupted "Yahwism." Is there additional, more reliable historical literary evidence?

Yes, Nodet points out that some Greek sources allow us to build a very different picture. While the present form of the Septuagint is a mixture of traditions it does intermittently present a favorable picture of the Samaritans: Note 2 Kings 17 (in the Septuagint):

And the king of the Assyrians commanded, saying:

Bring (some Israelites from) there (to Samaria), and let them go and dwell there, and they shall enlighten them (concerning) the judgment of the God of the Land. And they brought one of the priests whom they had removed from Samaria, and he settled in Bethel, and enlightened them how they should fear the Lord. (καὶ ἐνετείλατο ὁ βασιλεὺς Ἀσσυρίων λέγων Ἀπάγετε ἐκεῖθεν καὶ πορευέσθωσαν καὶ κατοικείτωσαν ἐκεῖ καὶ φωτιοῦσιν αὐτοὺς τὸ κρίμα τοῦ θεοῦ τῆς γῆς. καὶ ἤγαγον ἕνα τῶν ἱερέων, ὧν ἀπῴκισαν ἀπὸ Σαμαρείας, καὶ ἐκάθισεν ἐν Βαιθηλ καὶ ἦν φωτίζων αὐτοὺς πῶς φοβηθῶσιν τὸν κύριον.)

The antiquity of this report is indicated by many elements, especially its cryptic nature, requiring some words in the translation to be added. The context is also informative. Referring to those in Samaria, within an unedited mixture of early traditions, we find the following admiration of the Samaritans (οἱ Σαμαρῖται):

They have feared, and they have been doing according to their decrees and according to their judgment and according to the Law and according to the command that the Lord commanded to the descendants (sons) of Jacob (upon) whom he set his name (as) Israel. (καὶ κατὰ τὸν νόμον καὶ κατὰ τὴν ἐντολήν, ἣν ἐνετείλατο κύριος τοῖς υἱοῖς Ιακωβ, οὗ ἔθηκεν τὸ ὄνομα αὐτοῦ Ισραηλ). The Lord made with them a covenant, and he commanded them, saying, "Do not fear other gods and worship them. Do not serve them, and do not sacrifice to them. But the Lord who brought you up from the land of Egypt with great strength and with an upraised arm (καὶ ἐν βραχίονι ὑψηλῷ), fear him; also, worship and sacrifice to him. Keep the laws, the judgments, the Law, and the commands that he wrote for you to do all the days. Do not fear other gods. Do not forget the covenant (τὴν διαθήκην: הברית) that he made with you, and do not fear other gods. But rather, fear the Lord your God (τὸν κύριον θεὸν ὑμῶν φοβηθήσεσθε), and he will deliver you from all your enemies. (2 Kgs 17; the Septuagint)

Nodet adds that Flavius Josephus grasps the essence of the above excerpt and paraphrases his Hebrew Bible and shows that these "newcomers" (the Samaritans) "adopted a pure Yahwism, not contaminated by the idolatry of their original countries. Their position was similar to the story of Joshua 24, in which Joshua summons all the Israelites (those who had left Egypt) at Shechem, and, viewing them as newcomers just arriving from oriental countries, urges them to leave their idolatrous paganism and adopt pure Yahwism."

Nodet's thoughts are significant and represent the *Tendenzen* of 2 Kings 17. More valuable are his promptings to refocus on texts we may have not comprehended and must reexamine.

October 6, 2022
James H. Charlesworth
Princeton and Ramat HaSharon, Israel

Abbreviations

For abbreviations of journals and other common abbreviations, see:

Otto Leistner and Heike Becker, *Internationale Titelabkürzungen von Zeitschriften, Zeitungen, usw. International Title Abbreviations of Periodicals, Newspapers, etc.*, Osnabrück, Biblio-Verlag, 2 vols., ³1981.

Siegfried M. Schwertner, *Internationales Abkürzungsverzeichnis für Theologie und Grenzgebiete* (IATG3), Berlin/Boston, De Gruyter, ³2014.

1QH, 11QT …	Documents from the Qumran caves, published in the collection *Discoveries in the Judaean Desert*, Oxford University Press, 1955–2010.
Abel	Félix-Marie Abel, *Géographie de la Palestine* (EB), Paris, Gabalda, 2 vols., 1938.
ANET	James B. Pritchard (ed.), *Ancient Near Eastern Texts Relating to the Old Testament*, Princeton University Press, ³1969.
Ant.	Flavius Josephus, *Jewish Antiquities*.
Aristée	André Pelletier, *La Lettre d'Aristée à Philocrate* (SC 89), Paris, Cerf, 1962.
Arukh	Alexander Kohut, *Aruch completum*, 9 vols., ²1969.
BA	Marguerite Harl et al. (Dir.), *La Bible d'Alexandrie, LXX*, Paris, Cerf, 1986–.
CAp	Flavius Josephus, *Contra Apionem*, Loeb Classical Library, 1926; Collection Budé, 1930.
CD	*Document de Damas*, cf. André Dupont-Sommer, *L'Écrit de Damas*, in: André Dupont-Sommer and Marc Philonenko, *La Bible : Écrits intertestamentaires*, Paris, 1987, pp. 635–810.
Chron. Sam. II	John Macdonald, *The Samaritan Chronicle No. II (or: Sepher Ha-Yamim) from Joshua to Nebuchadnezzar* (BZAW, 107), Berlin, de Gruyter, 1969.
cor.	Correction(s).
Dict. Antiq.	Charles Daremberg, Édouard Saglio et al., *Dictionnaire des antiquités grecques et romaines*, Paris, Hachette, 1873–1919.
Field	Fridericus *Field*, *Origenis hexaplorum quae supersunt*, Oxford, Clarendon, 1875.

Geiger	Abraham Geiger, *Urschrift und Übersetzungen der Bibel in ihrer Abhängigkeit von der innern Entwicklung des Judenthums*, Breslau, 1857.
Ginzberg	Louis Ginzberg, *The Legends of the Jews*, Philadelphia, Jewish Publication Society, 7 vols., 1909–38.
Greek and Latin	Menahem Stern, *Greek and Latin Authors on Jews and Judaism*, Jerusalem, 3 vols., 1974–84.
ibn Ezra	Medieval commentator of the Hebrew Pentateuch, cf. *Miqraot Gedolot a. l.*
Jastrow	Marcus Jastrow, *Dictionary of Talmud Babli, Yerushalmi, Midrashic Literature and Targumim*, New York, 1903 (many reprints).
Jubilés	André Caquot, *Jubilés*, in: André Dupont-Sommer and Marc Philonenko (Dir.), *La Bible : écrits intertestamentaires*, Paris, 1987, pp. 635–810.
Lieberman I	Saul Lieberman, *Greek in Jewish Palestine*, New York, 1942.
Lieberman II	Saul Lieberman, *Hellenism in Jewish Palestine*, New York, 1950.
Life	Flavius Josephus, *Autobiography*.
Luc	Lucian recension of the LXX: Paul de Lagarde, *Librorum ueteris testamenti pars prior graece*, Göttingen, 1883.
LXX (A, B, S ...)	Text of the Septuagint, unless otherwise indicated, according to Alfred Rahlfs, *Septuaginta*, Stuttgart, 1935. The acronyms A, B, S, respectively, designate the Alexandrinus, the Vaticanus, and the Sinaiticus. (Transl. and comm. : cf. *Bible d'Alexandrie*.)
Meg Taan	*Megilat Ta'anit* (Scroll of Fasting), cf. Hans Lichtenstein, "Die Fastenrolle, eine Untersuchung zur jüdisch-hellenistischen Geschichte," *HUCA* (8–9), 1931-2; Vered Noam, *Megillat Ta'anit: Versions, Interpretation, History: With a Critical Edition*, Jerusalem, Yad Ben Zvi. 2003.
Mez	Adam Mez, *Die Bibel des Josephus, untersucht für Buch V-VII der Archäologie*, Basel, 1905.
Miqraot Gedolot	(Torah, Prophets and Writings with Targums and Traditional Jewish Commentaries), numerous editions since Daniel Bomberg, Venise, 1524-5.
Moore	George Foot Moore, *Judaism in the First Centuries of the Christian Era. The Age of Tannaim*, New York, 2 vols., 1927 (many reprints).
ms., mss	Manuscrit(s).
MT	Masoretic text (Hebrew Bible).
n., nn.	note, notes.
Naber	Flavii Iosephi, *Opera omnia* (ed. Samuel A. Naber). 7 vols., Berlin, 1885–95.

NH	Pliny the Elder, *Natural history*, Loeb Classical Library, 1966–79; Collection Budé, 1947–77.
Niese	Flavii Iosephi *Opera* (ed. Benedikt Niese), 7 vols., Berlin, 1885–95; (*ed. maior*).
Niese²	Flavii Iosephi *Opera* (ed. Benedikt Niese), 6 vols. Berlin, 1888–95; (*ed. minor*).
om.	omet(tent), omission.
Onom.	Erich Klostermann, *Eusebius Werke; III. Band, 1. Heft: Das Onomastikon der biblischen Ortsnamen*, Leipzig, 1904.
Praep. euang.	Karl Mras, *Eusebius Werke; VIII. Band: Die Praeparatio Euangelica*, Berlin, 1954–6.
Ps.-Philon	Pseudo-Philon, *Les Antiquités bibliques* (trad. par J. Cazeaux et al.), Paris, 1976, 2 vols.; English edition: M. R. James, *The Biblical Antiquities of Philo*. Prolegomenon by Louis H. Feldman, New York, Ktav, ²1971.
PW	*Paulys Real-Encyclopädie der klassischen Altertumswissenschaft*, hsgb. von G. Wissowa, Stuttgart, 1894–.
Rashi	Medieval commentator of the Babylonian Talmud and the Massoretic Bible, cf. *Miqraot Gedolot, a. l*, ou *b. . . ., a. l.*
Reinach	Théodore Reinach (Dir.), *Œuvres complètes de Flavius Josephus*, Paris, 1900–33.
Sam	The Samaritan Pentateuch, cf. August F. von Gall, *Der hebräischer Pentateuch der Samaritaner*, Giessen, 1914–18; Maurice Baillet, "Corrections à l'édition de von Gall du pentateuque samaritain", in: *Von Kanaan bis Kerala* (Festschrift van der Ploeg), AOAT 211 (1982), pp. 23–35.
Schürer-Vermes	Emil Schürer, *The History of the Jewish People in the Age of Jesus Christ*, English ed. by Geza Vermes et al., Edinburgh, T&T Clark, 1973–86.
SJ	Moses Gaster, "Das Buch Josua in hebräisch-samaritanischer Rezension," *Zeitschrift der Deutschen Morgenländischen Gesellschaft* 62 (1908), pp. 209–79 and 494–549. References according to *Chron. Sam. II.*
SOR Dov	B. Ratner, *Seder Olam Rabba. Die grosse Weltchronik*, Vilna, 1897; Luis Fernando Girón Blanc, Seder 'Olam Rabbah. El gran orden del universo : una cronología judía, Estella, Editorial Verbo Divino, 1996.
Strack	Hermann L. Strack and Günter Stemberger, *Einleitung in Talmud und Midrasch*, München, Beck, ⁷1982. Trad. franç. Paris, 1987.
Thackeray	Henry St. J. Thackeray, *Josephus: The Man and the Historian*, New York, 1929; trad. fr. Cerf, 2000.

Tosefta kifsh.	Saul Lieberman, *Tosefta ki-fshutah. A Comprehensive Commentary on the Tosefta*. New York, The Jew. Theol. Semin. of Amer., 8 vols., 1955–73.
VetLat	*Vetus Latina. Die Reste der altlateinischen Bibel, nach P. Sabatier neu gesammelt. . .*, Freiburg/B, Herder, 1949–
Vulg.	Jerome's Latin Vulgate, cf. *Biblia sacra iuxta latinam uulgatam uersionem ad codicum fidem, cura et studio monachorum sancti Benedicti*, Rome, 1927–.
War	Flavius Josephus, *The Jewish War against the Romans*.
Whiston	William Whiston, *The Works of Josephus, Complete and Unabridged*, New Updated Edition, Peabody, 1987 (with notes, dissertations, and index of the original Whiston 1736 and Niese's numbering).

Introduction

The aim of this study is to repair a historical injustice, which has presented the Samaritans' religion as a degraded form of Judaism, whereas surrounding Mount Gerizim, their sacred mountain overlooking the ancient city of Shechem, they are in fact to this day the direct heirs of the ancient Israelites.

What Happened?

The story of the Good Samaritan is so famous that the inn he found on the road down from Jerusalem to Jericho is still exists today. Yet when Jesus sent his disciples on a mission, he told them not to go to the Gentiles or to the Samaritans but only to "the lost sheep of the house of Israel." Samaria was conspicuous, even cumbersome, for it formed a kind of barrier between Jewish Galilee and Judea, while only the Jews were considered the rightful heirs of biblical Israel. "Salvation comes from the Jews," Jesus firmly told a Samaritan woman.

If we go further back, there is no doubt that the Hebrew Bible presents the Samaritans as foreign settlers who vaguely adopted the religion of Israel, while mixing it with their original paganism. Later, it is the Samaritans who oppose the return of the exiles to Jerusalem, although it is not clear why. On the one hand, before the exile, the North around Shechem took the name of kingdom of Israel, after Solomon and the splitting of his kingdom; but it is considered dissident, whereas the South around Jerusalem is only the kingdom of Judah; however, the latter claims to be the heir of David, the ancestor of the Messiah—and this is a lofty perspective. On the other hand, after the exile, the returning Jews only know Jerusalem and claim, together with Ezra and Nehemiah, that they alone are the true Israel.

Modern studies are mainly concerned with the Hebrew Bible, but when it comes to the Samaritans they stumble a bit, because it is obvious that their traditions, although poorly preserved, are strictly faithful to biblical monotheism, without any trace of syncretism. Now, to get a clearer view, a glance at recent archaeological work can be helpful, since we now know that at least since the fifth century there was a great sanctuary without idols at Gerizim; however, it will be above all necessary to consider Jewish sources that have come down to us only in Greek and been underestimated. Two salient facts can be indicated at the outset: on the one hand, at the time of the Maccabean crisis (167–164 BCE), the two temples of Jerusalem and Gerizim were equally honored by the Israelite nation without any apparent conflict; the definitive and brutal separation between the Samaritans and the Jews came later. On the other hand, Flavius Josephus, the only preserved first-century historian of Judea, provides—as if in spite of himself—elements that make it possible to give the Samaritans once again an honorable position in ancient Israelite history, even though he hates them and criticizes their versatility.

As an appetizer, an overall sketch of the Israelite reality at the beginning of our era can be situated around three sufficiently documented places: Alexandria of Egypt, Jerusalem, and Shechem, which became a Roman colony, *Flavia Neapolis* (Nablus), after the war of 70. The philosopher Philo, rabbinic Judaism, and the Samaritans are to be linked to these places, respectively; the first knew Hebrew but expressed himself in Greek, and the other two were attached to Hebrew with nuances of Aramaic.

Philo, a philosopher who was very sensitive to the practice of the Law, composed immense allegorical commentaries on the Pentateuch, but he seems to have known very little of the rest of the Bible and especially about Israelite history. For him, David was a poet, and Solomon a sage. He ignores the exile entirely and, on the contrary, rejoices that Jews have emigrated to many countries. Each one then has a homeland, where he was born, but he must regularly go on pilgrimage to the metropolis—that is to Jerusalem—and so to keep a keen sense of being a member of an international, or at least interregional, people, despite the differences of language and customs. Thus, when he returns home, he will be able to witness the one God, in the face of local idols. Following Aristotle, Philo believes that justice derived from the observance of unwritten customs is more valuable than obedience to written laws, because the latter is dictated by fear of sanctions. Moreover, he had no known Jewish posterity but was taken up by Christianity and even almost Christianized. One tradition goes as far as affirming that he met Peter in Rome; in fact, he went in 40 to try in vain to convince the emperor Caligula to give up his inept project of having his statue placed in the Temple of Jerusalem. (The emperor's assassination in early 41 put an end to the affair.)

Rabbinic Judaism, which developed after the disappearance of the Temple, knows the vast Hebrew Bible in three parts: the Law or Torah, the Prophets, and the Writings. It has the singularity of recognizing two fundamental sources of authority, both linked to Moses: the written Torah, which is essentially the Pentateuch, and the oral Torah, which is a collection of ancestral traditions. In practice, the latter took precedence over the written Torah, since they were binding under the penalty of law, unlike Philo's "unwritten laws." These traditions, recorded in collections of which the main one is the *Mishna*, are not in general a kind of jurisprudence complementing the written word, because they often oppose it. They are the heirs of the Pharisees and upstream of the ancient Babylonian customs. However, the sages of the second century did not want the existence of "two Toras" in tension, and to avoid this they tried to reduce the whole by presenting the oral traditions in the form of legal commentaries on the written word, by means of sometimes very subtle rules of interpretation. The literary result was called *Midrash Halakha*, a technical expression meaning that all precepts (*halakha*) can or must be extracted from Scripture (the *midrash*, resulting from research). Whereas Philo wrote books without any control over his readers, the sages favored orality—that is, the relationship of master to disciple, with an esoteric or even initiatory side. At the beginning, these traditions hardly entered the Greco-Latin sphere, and even complete rejection of the Mediterranean world was declared: "West of Tyra, they do not know Israel, nor their father who is in heaven."

As for the Samaritans, they never deviated from a pure Yahwism, despite some suspicions of biblical origin; however, in the course of history, they became almost evanescent. In particular, their literary traditions have remained very unstable, for they have never had a custom of study like that of the Jews. Their authorized Bible includes only the Hebrew Pentateuch, which contains some variants; notably, their Decalogue includes a precept mentioning the implementation of the Law at Gerizim, which reproduces a passage where Moses prescribes to the Israelites to write the Law on steles erected on that mountain, when they arrive in Canaan. According to other poorly preserved texts, the split among the Israelites occurred at the time when the priest Eli was at the sanctuary of Shiloh, for it was there that Samuel—who was later to anoint David as king of Judah and above all as founder of Jerusalem—grew up; hence, the irreducible divergence. We know a little more thanks to Christian and rabbinic sources. One of the most famous disciples of John the Baptist was Simon, a Samaritan who baptized in his own name and launched a vast movement, still very present in Rome a century later. As for the Jewish sages, while they do not spare their criticism of the Samaritans, there are at least two interesting concessions. On the one hand, it is admitted that Israel first received the Law in Hebrew letters, that is, in western Paleo-Hebrew, and then that, in Ezra's time, it was given to the Jews again, but in Aramaic characters from Babylonia (still in use today), while the ancient writing was left to the Samaritans (to this day). This suggests a perception that the Samaritans were local Israelites before Ezra, the prototype of the returnee from exile. On the other hand, in connection with a certain controversy, it is said that "in every precept that the Samaritans observe, they are more thorough than Israel," that is, "than the Jews." Clearly, even though the Samaritans are not part of Israel proper, their *biblical* accuracy is emphasized since they ignore the independent oral Torah.

There is thus a certain symmetry between the Samaritans in the North and Philo in the South, the latter representing the Jews of Egypt: complete authority of the Pentateuch, duly interpreted, but without that competing oral tradition that constitutes the singularity of rabbinic Judaism; Moses is the only true prophet, and Israelite history is largely ignored. In this respect, we must ask why the Samaritans lost sight of the prophets of the North, such as Elijah or Elisha. Why did the texts that present them acquire or retain authority only among the Jews, or Judeans?

The Stages of This Work

1. Preliminaries: The importance of the Samaritans in the time of Josephus and the New Testament. The area formed by Galilee, Samaria, and Judea corresponds approximately to Canaan at the time of Joshua, between the Jordan and the Mediterranean.
2. The founding account of 2 Kings 17: The Samaritans as descendants of the settlers sent by the Assyrians, who were initiated to a certain Yahwism after the

		Assyrians			
		Tiglath-Pileser III	745–727		
		Shalmaneser V	726–722		
		Sargon II	722–705		
		Sennacherib	705–681		
		Esarhaddon	680–669		
		Ashurbanipal	669–631		
		Sinsharishkun	627–612		
		Ashur-Uballit II	612–609		
		Neobabylonians			
		Nabopolassar	626–605		
		Nebuchadnezzar II	604–562		
		Amel-Marduk	561–556		
		Nabonidus	555–539		
		Achaemenides			
		Cyrus (Babylonia 539)	559–529		
		Cambyses	529–522		
		Darius I	521–486		
		Xerxes	485–465		
		Artaxerxes I L.manus	465–425		
		Darius II	425–405		
		Artaxerxes II Mnem.	405–359		
		Artaxerxes III Ochos	359–339		
		Darius III Codoman.	339–331		
		Macedonians			
Seleucids (Syria)		Alexander (Issos 333 BCE)	336–323	Lagides (Egypt)	
Seleucos I Nikator	301–281			Ptolemy Ier Lagos	301–282
Antiochus I Soter	281–262			Ptolemy II Philadelphus	282–246
Antiochus II Theos	262–246	Judaea		Ptolemy III Euergetes	246–222
Seleucos II Callinicus	246–225	(High priests, then kings)			
Seleucos III Soter	225–223	Onias A		Ptolemy IV Philop.	222–205
Antiochus III the Gr.	223–187	Simon the Just	(after 200 BCE)	Ptolemy V Épiph.	204–180
Seleucos IV Philop.	187–175	Onias B	until 175 BCE		
Antiochus IV Épiph.	175–164	Jason	175–173	Ptolemy VI Philom. . . .	
		(Onias C in Egypt)			
Antiochus V Eupator	163–162	Menelaus	173–162		
		(Judas Maccabeus	167–160)	(Cleopatra I Syra)	. . . 181–146
Démétrios I Soter	162–150	Alcimus	162–159		
Alexandre Balas	152–145	Jonathan (152)	50–144	Ptolemy VII	145–144
Démétrios II Nikator	145–140	Simon	144–135	Ptolemy VIII Physcon.	144–116
Tryphon (Diodotus)	142–138			Cleopatre II	124–116
Antiochus VII Sidetes	139–129	John Hyrcan	135–104	Ptolemy IX Lathyre[1]	118–109
Démétrios II Nikator	129–125	Aristobulus (king?)	104–103	Cleopatra III	127–101
Antiochus VIII Grip.	125–96			Ptolemy X Alex.	110–88
Antiochus IX Cyzic.	114–96	Alexander Jannaeus, king	103–76	Ptolemy IX Lathyros[2]	88–81
Antiochus X Eusebes	95–83	Alexandra, queen	76–67	Berenice III	81–80
Antiochus XII Dionys.	87–84				
Tigrane II the Great	83–67				
Defeated by Pompey, who created the province of Syria in 64 BCE (Triumvirats . . .)		Aristobulus II	67–63	Ptolemy XII Auletes	80–51
		Hyrcanus II	63–41		
		Antigonus, kings	41–37	Ptolemy XIII Theos	51–47
				Cleopatra VII	51–30
Auguste	de -31 à +14	Herod the Great, king (40)	37–4	*Then Roman domination*	

Figure 1 Eastern and Hellenistic dynasties.

fall of the kingdom of Israel (North) in 721 BCE. The latter had already been separated from Judah since the death of King Solomon.
3. Around the Maccabean crisis, a major event that founded the Hasmonean regime in Judea: The Samaritans then separated from the Jews; but before that there was a peaceful coexistence that is surprising, because it does not agree with the data on the Persian period before Alexander's conquest in 332 BCE.
4. In this Persian period, there were two phases of restoration after the exile: First, the temple in Jerusalem with the high priest Joshua, then a Babylonian-derived reform with Ezra and Nehemiah, the founders of Judaism. The local Israelites, including the Samaritans, opposed it in vain.

In fact, the study will highlight a contrast between the Samaritans and the Jews: the former, although poorly documented, are of immemorial local permanence, with a holy place, a succession of high priests up to the present day, little *diaspora*, and customs derived from the Pentateuch. On the contrary, the pillar of the formation of Judaism was the exile, which closed a quasi-mythical royal era, and after which, from a vast *diaspora*, there was a long, very complex period of refoundation, until the creation of a brilliant, conquering, and finally ephemeral Hasmonean state of Judaea. It is, hence, impossible to consider the religion of the Samaritans as deriving from Judaism. This is what they say about themselves, but only a minority of modern historians have partially agreed with them, in the name of their simplicity.[1] As it happens, fairly recent excavations have uncovered a large sanctuary on the summit of Gerizim that dates back to at least the fifth century. Now, this discovery has given rise to renewed studies on the origin of this almost marginal entity. Nevertheless, the view that it is a degraded form of Judaism remains prevalent, for the decisive element—which is generally underestimated—is the significance of the reforms of Ezra and Nehemiah. For this reason, a brief *status quæstionis* is given in the appendix,[2] after a sketch of the questions that remain unanswered (Figure 1).

NB. Only the principal rulers are indicated. In Judea, the titles "Onias A, B, C" replace "Onias II, III and V" of Josephus; cf. the explanation in Section 3.3.

---

[1] Hence, Moses Gaster, *The Samaritans: Their History, Doctrine and Literature*, London, British Academy, 1925, pp. 9–15, deems that they are the descendants of the ancient kingdom of Israel (North); John Macdonald, *The Theology of the Samaritans*, Philadelphia, Westminster, 1964, pp. 11–29, believes that Samaritanism and Judaism developed independently from the same matrix; Bernd Jørg Diebner, "Juda und Israel: Zur hermeneutischen Bedeutung der Spannung zwischen Judäa und Samarien für das Verständnis des TNK als Literatur," in: Martin Prudký (ed.), *Landgabe: Festschrift für Jan Heller zum 70. Geburtstag*, Praha, Oikúmené, 1995, pp. 86–132, concludes that Judah appropriated the name of Israel, which belonged to the northern kingdom and then to the Samaritans, by abuse of power.

[2] This study is a continuation of the recent work by Étienne Nodet, *La porte du ciel. Les esséniens, Qumrân et ensuite*, Paris, Cerf, 2016; some repetitions in bordering areas are unavoidable.

1

Preliminaries

The Importance of the Samaritans

Before examining the useful accounts of the Hebrew Bible, this chapter will present the other ancient sources on the Samaritans: the Samaritan documents themselves, the writings of Josephus, the New Testament; the rabbinic traditions, which are totally devoid of historical precision, will sometimes be consulted. As for modern discussions, they will be mentioned later, for they have been entirely renewed by the recent discovery of the ruins of an immense Samaritan sanctuary on Mount Gerizim[1] that dates back at least to the fifth century BCE.

1.1 Samaritan Traditions

In 2019, there were 820 Samaritans—a Hebrew name meaning "observant, guardians"— divided roughly into two communities of equal size: one in Nablus, near ancient Shechem, at the foot of the Gerizim; the other in Holon, on the outskirts of Tel Aviv.[2] They are certainly one of the smallest populations in the world, for in principle they practice endogamy, although unions with Jews are now tolerated in Israel. Yet, until the sixth century, they numbered several hundred thousand.[3] Their almost complete disappearance was mainly due to massive conversions to Christianity. Indeed, they were always linked to Mount Gerizim because of the pilgrimage obligation in their Decalogue; but from Constantine onward, the Christian presence became increasingly stronger in the country, with a proliferation of hermits and monasteries. Then in 380,

---

[1] Cf. Yitzhak Magen et al., *Mount Gerizim Excavations*, Jerusalem, Israel Antiquities Authority, 2 vol., 2004 and 2008. Cependant, Eusebius, *Onom.* pp. 64–5 (followed by St. Jerome and the *Madaba Map*), argued that the location of Gerizim in the vicinity of Shechem is a Samaritan falsification, since, according to Deut. 11:30, these mountains (Gerizim and Ebal) are close to Gilgal and Josh. 4:19 situates Gilgal near Jericho.
[2] James A. Montgomery, *The Samaritans: The Earliest Jewish Sect. Their History, Theology and Literature*, Philadelphia, Winston, 1907, is still the classic study on the Samaritans. With the exception of the Gerizim excavations, it is updated in the collection of Alan D. Crown (ed.), *The Samaritans*, Tübingen, Mohr-Siebeck, 1989.
[3] After having been perhaps more than a million a century or two earlier, cf. Michael Avi-Yonah, "The Samaritans in Romano-Byzantine Times," in: Joseph Aviram (ed.), *Eretz Shomron*, Jerusalem, Israel Exploration Society, 1973, pp. 34–47.

Emperor Theodosius I made Christianity, as defined at the Council of Nicaea (325), the state's only official religion.

In the West, these Samaritans, mentioned in the Bible and in several patristic texts, were considered to be a modest remnant of the past; that was until the sixteenth century, when they were rediscovered by the humanists.[4] So, their library became accessible, and hence it was possible to obtain certain knowledge of the interior, at least regarding the religious aspect, because they never had any political ambition. Here, we will limit ourselves to a brief consideration of the "historical" works or, more precisely, the narrative ones:[5]

- *Tolida*, a "genealogy" based on a composition by Eleazar b. Amram, which is dated to the twelfth century. It begins with a discussion, in Aramaic, about the meridian of Gerizim; it is followed by a table of the patriarchs from Adam to Moses and then a combined list of the high priests from Aaron to this Eleazar. The whole has been expanded in the form of a chronicle that goes as far as Napoleon, then recopied in 1859.
- *Book of Joshua*, a compilation translated into Arabic, known from a thirteenth-century ms. The original narrative goes from the death of Moses to the time of Alexander, but other texts were later added.
- *Kitab al-Ta'rikh*, or "Annals," is a collection composed in 1355 by Abu 'l-Fath, who indicates his sources and puts them into Arabic. The period covered reaches from Adam to the time of Muhammad and tells about many aspects of the Samaritans as they saw themselves: history, theology, chronology, and relations with Jewish, Christian, and Muslim neighbors.
- *Shalshela*, a "Chain" in Hebrew, which includes genealogies from Adam to the copyist's time, in 1909.
- *New Chronicle*, an ms. in Hebrew dating from about 1900; this text depends largely on the *Tolida* and the *Ta'rikh*.
- *Chronicle II*, a Hebrew ms. composed of a collection of biblical texts taken from Josh through 2 Chronicles and also from Psalm, augmented by passages borrowed from the *Ta'rikh* or its sources. In 1909, the ms., made in 1909, reproduces a copy that probably dates from the fourteenth century. The part parallel to Josh is very similar to the Arabic *Book of Joshua*.
- *Asatir*, improperly known as "Secrets of Moses," is a kind of midrash, written in Aramaic mixed with Arabic, that covers the entire Pentateuch; the extant ms.

---

[4] Cf. Matthias Delcor, "La Correspondance des savants européens, en quête de manuscrits, avec les Samaritains du xvie au xixe siècles," in: Jean-Pierre Rothschild and Guy Dominique Sixdenier (dir.), *Études samaritaines, Pentateuque et Targum, exégèse et philologie, chroniques* (Collection de la REJ, 6), Louvain/Paris, Peeters, 1988, pp. 27–43.

[5] A full presentation with historical discussion is given by Paul Stenhouse, "Samaritan Chronicles," in: Crown, *The Samaritans*, pp. 218–65; the following works are also noteworthy: Alan D. Crown, Reihard Pummer, and Abraham Tal (eds.), *A Companion to Samaritan Studies*, Tübingen, Mohr-Siebeck, 1993; Reihard Pummer, *Early Christian Authors on Samaritans and Samaritanism: Texts, Translations and Commentary* (TSAJ, 92), Tübingen, Mohr-Siebeck, 2002. For a more recent evaluation of the Samaritan sources, cf. Ingrid Hjelm, *The Samaritans and Early Judaism: A Literary Analysis* (JSOTSup, 303), Sheffield Academic Press, 2000, who deems the Pentateuch to be of Samaritan origin.

probably dates from the twelfth century, but the original may have been written much earlier, give the contacts with the Sibylline Oracles, Josephus and a *Targum*.

This collection makes it possible to reconstruct the history of the Samaritans from Roman times to the Crusades.[6] After the Arab conquest of the Near East in 636, the Samaritans were disadvantaged in comparison to Christians and Jews, because the conquerors were not sure whether they should be included in the Muslim definition of "People of the Book." The community, already reduced by conversions to Islam for economic, social, or religious reasons, was further diminished by the persecutions of the Fanatic caliphs.[7] This documentation would really not be of use for biblical history if it were not for the curious contacts with Josephus, as we shall see in Section 1.2.3.

Yet, one aspect of the Samaritans stands out: unlike rabbinic Judaism, there was always a high priest at the head of their community, even after the disappearance of the temple at Gerizim.[8]

1.2 Flavius Josephus

Josephus son of Mattathias, priest of Jerusalem (37–95), is the only Jewish historian of the period whose works have been preserved. Having gone over to the side of the Romans during the war of 66–70, he was emancipated by the emperor Flavius Vespasian, whose name he adopted, and he became a writer, taking his place in a long line of Greco-Latin historians. He first published, around 79, the *Jewish War* (*W*); in the first edition in Aramaic (now lost), for the barbarian Eastern world and addressed in particular to the many Jews outside the empire, he intended to show how it was futile to try to fight against Rome. Then, in 93/94, *Jewish Antiquities* (*Ant.*) was published; in this work, the author, wanting to present the whole history of his nation in Greek, paraphrases the Hebrew Bible from Adam onward, supplementing it up to his time by other documents. A little later, he published an *Autobiography* (*Life*), in which he sets forth his brilliant genealogy; however, the main part is a lengthy retelling of the *War* narrative that relates the seven months in 66/67 during which he was a notable actor in Galilee. Alongside these rather laborious works, one must add a very lively apologetic treatise, entitled *Against Apion* (*CAp*), in which the author has two aims that he considers complementary, that is, to refute the attacks on Judaism and to prove the great antiquity of his nation and its legislator, by assembling all the literary testimonies in Greek that he could find, since the Bible could not serve as an independent witness.

---

[6] The Samaritans, who have always refused to sell ancient texts, because of their sacred character, did however agree to make more or less neat "modern" copies on demand, and to sell them, cf. Philippe De Robert, "La naissance des études samaritaines," in: Rothschild and Sixdenier, *Études samaritaines*, pp. 15–26.

[7] Cf. Paul Stenhouse, "The Reliability of the Chronicle of Abu 'l-Fath, with Special Reference to the Dating of Baba Rabba," in: Rothschild and Sixdenier, *Études samaritaines*, pp. 235–57.

[8] Cf. Moses Gaster, *The Samaritans: Their History, Doctrines and Literature*, London, Oxford University Press, 1925, pp. 55–8; Reinhard Pummer, "An Update on Moses Gaster's 'Chain of Samaritan High Priests'," in: Magnar Kartveit and Gary N. Knoppers (eds.), *The Bible, Qumran, and the Samaritans*, Berlin/Boston, De Gruyter, 2018, pp. 149–72.

1.1.1 War

From the very first sentence of the exordium of *War*, Josephus does not fear to say that this was perhaps the greatest conflict of all times. He, thus, places himself in the line of Thucydides, who in the fifth century declared that the *Peloponnesian War*, which he had followed step by step as an eyewitness, was the greatest event in Greek history and in fact the only really important one. Like him, Josephus largely rejects supernatural explanations, considering that history is made by princes and generals.

Yet, the comparison is imperfect, for he began his account with the Maccabean crisis, that is, more than two centuries earlier. Indeed, for him, history is prophecy. Now, the present crisis is exemplary: the king of Syria, Antiochus IV, took advantage of dissensions among Jewish notables to persecute Judaism and to plunder the temple of Jerusalem; but then, the armed resistance of Judas Maccabaeus and his brothers led to a victory, and even to a restoration, under the Syrian umbrella, which was to become the regime of the Hasmonean high priests. These brothers took advantage of the rivalry between Syria and Egypt to get control over the intermediary region, Coele-Syria. In a parallel manner, Josephus sees in his time, after the war of 70, a future for Judaism under the Roman umbrella, beyond the ruin of Jerusalem; and he provides some clues which are mixed with obvious Flavian propaganda.

Now, let us look at the facts. In 66, the Zealots routed the army of Cestius, governor of Syria, who had come to calm the unrest in Jerusalem. They began minting money—which was a way of proclaiming the beginning of a state. Rome could not tolerate this movement of independence in the Mediterranean Basin, for it represented more than just another one of the ordinary Jewish public disturbances that the Romans periodically came to suppress. Jerusalem's leaders realized that they had to prepare for war, and so Josephus was sent to Galilee as a general or administrator. Barely thirty years old, he was not afraid to say that, despite a complete lack of military experience, he was able to raise an army of 100,000 men and train it in the Roman manner. This force does not appear in the military action that followed; it was probably fictitious but, by contrast, highlights Vespasian's victory. In the prologue he asserted that Rome is great not because it dominates the weak but because it knew how to conquer powerful peoples.

Facing them was the most experienced Roman general in the Eastern affairs, Corbulon, but Nero feared his notoriety and forced him to commit suicide. Vespasian, another general who was then in disgrace for having fallen asleep in front of Nero while he was singing, was sent to a post that nobody wanted, says Suetonius: he was made legate of Syria in Antioch, with the express mission of reconquering Judea.

Vespasian arrived at Akko-Ptolemais, on the border of Galilee, in 67 and then besieged the main nearby fortress, Jotapata, and conquered it. Now, Josephus, who had come to lead its defense, thus became an important prisoner. After conquering Galilee, Vespasian moved on to Judea, gradually occupying the area around Jerusalem. In 68, when Nero died the operations were stopped, because everything legally depended on his successor. Finally, Vespasian became emperor in 69, at the end of a curious "year of the four emperors" marked by civil wars. Consequently, it was his son Titus who finished conquering Judea in 70: Jerusalem was stormed and the temple was burned, but it did not disappear.[9]

Nero's death, which marked the end of the Julio-Claudian dynasty, and then the elevation of Vespasian could hardly have been foreseen. The new dynasty lacked a glorious narrative for its installation, especially since all this action against the Jews was ultimately very partial, for two reasons: on the one hand, they formed an important minority spread throughout the empire, and seen from Rome, a victory in Judea did not in any way change the reality of the situation. This is proven by the fact that neither Vespasian nor Titus ever took the title *Judaicus*, but other victorious generals had become *Africanus* or *Germanicus*.

The second reason is that the Romans were superstitious; so, after subduing a nation, they did not abandon its gods: they invited them, by an appropriate rite (*evocatio*), to separate themselves from their people and to come to Rome, where shrines would be built for them. Josephus thought he could say that God, weary of the turmoil in Jerusalem, was henceforth residing in Italy (*W* 5:367). However, unlike the other conquered nations, it was certainly out of the question for the Romans to create a Jewish sanctuary in Rome. Vespasian understood this, and in 75 he inaugurated a "Temple of Peace"[10] there, which was in fact not a sanctuary as such but a sort of museum containing the remains of Jerusalem and Judea, that is, all that had been paraded in the triumph of Vespasian and Titus in 71 (*W* 7:150, 162). One notable item from the triumph did not make it into this museum: a Hebrew Bible from the Temple archives. Vespasian kept it in his palace, and later, after Titus became emperor, he gave it to Josephus. This was the source of the biblical paraphrase of *Antiquities* (*Life* § 418).

Now, it is the same Josephus who finally provided the glorious founding account of the dynasty by writing *War*. In *W* 6:288-315, he expressly states that the victories of Vespasian and Titus in the East gave them legitimacy. Later, he asserted that Titus had ordered the publication of his work as the only acceptable account of the hostilities (*Life* § 363). Eusebius of Caesarea, generally well informed, indicates that a statue of Josephus was erected in a square in Rome, and that his works were deposited in the public libraries (*Eccl. Hist.* 3.9). *War* was certainly published at the state's expense, but his other works were probably not since they were not focused on Flavian propaganda.

The Samaritans appeared in these circumstances. Shortly after the fall of Jotapata, there was a gathering at Mount Gerizim that aroused suspicions of revolt, and Vespasian sent a tribune who ended up making a massacre (*W* 3:307-315). Mount Gerizim had no defense other than a very steep slope after the destruction of the temple by John Hyrcanus (cf. Section 3.1), and it must be assumed that Vespasian first considered the Samaritans as a variety of Jews but later perceived a difference: when, after Galilee, he launched the conquest of Judea, he passed through Samaria on the way to the Jordan

---

[9] Cf. Étienne Nodet, "On the Destruction of the Jerusalem Temple," in: Anthony Giambrone (ed.), *Rethinking the Jewish War. Archeology, Society, Traditions* (EB 84), Leuven/Paris, Peeters, 2020, pp. 232–44.

[10] The site has had a long archaeological history, up to modern times, cf. Pier Luigi Tucci, *The Temple of Peace in Rome*, Cambridge, Cambridge University Press, 2018; critical review: John E. Packer, "Investigating Imperial Grandeur: A New Approach to Rome's Temple of Peace," *Journal of Roman Archaeology* 31 (2018), pp. 722–9.

Valley and Jericho. In particular, he went through the city of *Neapolis* (Nablus), which he left untouched, unlike the Jewish settlements. Josephus even gives it an Aramaic name "Passage" (*W* 4:449), which corresponds to the topography of Shechem, situated in a steep east-west valley between Mount Ebal and Mount Gerizim. Yet, he commits a small anachronism, for it was only after the war that Vespasian formally created the *Colonia Flavia Neapolis* next to ancient Shechem, a city traditionally associated with the Gerizim sanctuary.[11]

This new colony was attached to the province of Syria, and the local coins collected indicate an era beginning in 72/73. Seen from Rome, this was a normal operation, since, unlike the Jews, the Samaritans were a purely local entity with a very small and easily controlled diaspora.

1.2.2 *Antiquities* and *Life*

Josephus' main work, *Jewish Antiquities*, has two successive conclusions, indicating two editions. The first ended with some biographical information, in which the author wanted to show his double competence, as both a priest of good lineage and a well-trained teacher, who studied the various schools of thought (Pharisees, Sadducees, Essenes). For the second edition, dated the thirteenth year of Domitian (93/94), Josephus detached the biographical elements and combined them with a new first-person account of his action in Galilee, thus forming a new book: *Life*. This work is very unbalanced, since 90 percent of the narrative deals with the seven months he spent in Galilee.[12] The reworking is rather disjointed and difficult to reconcile with the first version. Josephus gives himself a much more religious profile and, above all, speaks only about the disputes between Jews, that is to say, with purely local affairs; then, he stops as soon as Vespasian arrives and refers back to his first version of *War*.

Such a strictly provincial perspective, some twenty-five years after the fact, could hardly be of interest to the Roman public at large. Conversely, for the Jews, the events in Galilee were crucial, because it had long been a hotbed of Babylonian immigration. Indeed, the charter that the King Antiochus III of Syria granted to the Jews around 200 BCE gave rights to Jerusalem and to all the Jews in his empire, which then included Babylonia. After defeating the Egyptians at the sources of the Jordan (Panion, Banias), Antiochus "took Batanea, Samaria, Abila and Gadara, and soon afterwards gave him the Jews who were living around the sanctuary called Jerusalem." This is what the historian Polybius says in a fragment preserved by Josephus, who quotes in full the status granted by Antiochus to the "city of the Jews" (*Ant.* 12:136-144).

Archaeological surveys in Galilee have indeed shown, for the Hellenistic period, a very small population before the second century and then a significant rural settlement[13] that was, however, diffuse and without important cities, except for

---

[11] Cf. Pliny, NH 5.69, uses the ancient name *Marmortha*, a deformation of Josephus' *Mabartha* (מעברתא "passage, strait").
[12] Cf. Étienne Nodet, *Les Romains, les Juifs et Josèphe*, Paris, Cerf, 2019, pp. 34–44.
[13] Cf. Eric Meyers, James F. Strange, and Dennis E. Groh, "The Meiron Excavation Project: Archaeological Survey in Galilee and the Golan, 1976," *BASOR* 230 (1978), pp. 1–24; Eric Meyers, "Galilean Regionalism: A Reappraisal," in: W. Scott Green (ed.), *Approaches to Ancient Judaism. Vol.*

Scythopolis (Beth-Shan). It should be noted that, from this time onward and thanks to the rule of Antiochus III, a certain flow of Jewish immigrants settled in Galilee, which was very fertile (cf. *W* 3:35-43).

Much later, after the intervention of Pompey in 63 BCE and the organization of the governor Gabinius, who created the Sanhedrin, a certain Eleazar launched, from Sephoris in Galilee, movement of Zealots,[14] which was suppressed by the young Herod (*Ant.* 14:163-184). Once Herod became king, he proceeded skillfully: he settled a colony of Babylonian Jews east of the Lake, with their leader Zamaris, who established fortresses and the capital city, Bathyra (*Ant.* 17:23-28); it was there that Hillel the Babylonian, the recognized ancestor of the rabbinic tradition, arrived (*j.Pesahim* 6:1). One of the villages even took the name of Ecbatan, the ancient capital of Media; this was the inhabitants' region of origin (*Life* § 54). So, on both sides of the lake, there were Jews of the same Babylonian culture but of opposite political attitudes: some were quick to become zealots, accepting neither the Romans nor Herod, while others were indifferent and only preoccupied with sanctification.

In short, only Jews could be interested in Galilean events, and this conclusion must be extended to the whole of *Antiquities*. In the prologue, Josephus states that he translated his people's history and institutions from the Hebrew scriptures for the use of all Greeks. One must believe what he says with regard to his sources, because he never saw the LXX.[15] He in fact was often satisfied with approximate and always somewhat cumbersome paraphrasing. In *CAp* 2:39-41, he shows that these Hebrew writings, which he does not call sacred as a whole, were composed of two blocks of unequal authority: for the first, he gives a list of twenty-two books, subdivided into five of Moses, thirteen of the Prophets, and four of other writings, in which one fairly well recognizes the composition of the later Masoretic Bible, which only separates Ruth from Judges and Lamentations from Jeremiah. As for the content of these books, in several cases involving the Samaritans, his version has important differences that will be examined later (Sections 1.2.3-6): the high priest Jeshua son of Jozadak; the books of Ezra and Nehemiah, which must be considered distinct; one must add 1 Maccabees, which does not appear in the Hebrew Bible. The book of Ezra has a parallel version, 1 Ezra, known only in Greek and very similar to the Josephus source, which includes additional details, in particular Samaritan attacks and, at the end, a vegetal Feast of

---

5: *Studies in Judaism and its Greco-Roman Context* (Brown Judaic Series, 32), Atlanta, SBL Press, 1985, pp. 115-31; Mordechai Aviam, "The Transformation from Gelil ha-Goyim to Jewish Galilee: The Archaeological Testimony of an Ethnic Change," in: David A. Fiensy and James Riley Strange (eds.), *Galilee in the Late Second Temple and Mishnaic Periods*, Minneapolis, Fortress Press, 2015, II:9-21.

[14] Or "robbers," because they seized by force the tithes and other benefits due to the Levites or to the sanctuary; in Jerusalem, this was considered theft, cf. Étienne Nodet, "Barabbas, un 'brigand religieux' (Jn 18,40)," *RB* 119 (2012), pp. 288-99.

[15] This is contrary to a routine opinion. Here are three indications: (1) for Gen. 1:1 he puts "created," not "made" as the LXX does; (2) according to Gen. 4:4 Abel offers fat (בלח) from his flock, well understood by the LXX, but Josephus, who wants to concentrate all the violence on Cain, understands on the basis of the homonym "milk"; (3) the transcription of proper names follows different systems: for example, for Queen Athaliah (והילתע), the LXX puts Γοθολια and Josephus Ὀθλία (*Ant.* 9:96); cf. Étienne Nodet, *The Hebrew Bible of Josephus* (CRB 92), Leuven/Paris, Peeters, 2018, pp. 1-14, 260-3.

Tabernacles (*Ant.* 11:97-98, 114-115, 157). As for Nehemiah, the book bearing his name shows him in three roles: wall builder, governor, and reformer. Josephus has only a short form of this, in which he is only a builder (as in Sir. 49:13); but he makes three points clear: the lamentable situation of the walls of Jerusalem in Neh. 1:1-3 is probably due to Edomite incursions; the repairs made by Nehemiah in fifty-two days, despite his opponents, concerned only a modest district on the Ophel South of the temple (Neh. 6:15), the wall of which indicated a sacred perimeter (7:1); on the contrary, the great works of the high priest Eliashib, carried out without Nehemiah, concerned all the walls of Jerusalem and were completed in two years and four months (Neh. 3:1 and *Ant.* 11:179).

The second set of books follows. Josephus explains that since the Persian king Artaxerxes, corresponding to the books of Ezra-Nehemiah and Esther, "the entire history was written, but it was not deemed worthy of the same authority as the preceding accounts, because it did not contain a precise succession of the prophets." These are Hebrew sources concerning the Hellenistic and Roman periods, and in particular the Maccabean crisis, which will be examined later (Section 1.2.6). For Josephus, the prophet is a historian and the historian a prophet, and this obliged him to be somewhat prudent. For example, when he comments on Nebuchadnezzar's great inaugural vision, he sees that the enormous statue's feet of iron mixed with clay indicate the fragility of Rome and its inevitable downfall (Dan. 2:33-34), but he carefully avoids making this clear and simply refers the curious reader back to the Aramaic original (*Ant.* 10:210). Even if there is no way to escape Rome's power at present, Josephus has nothing but contempt for its paganism.

Another point must be made. From the time of the Maccabean crisis onward, *Antiquities* parallels *War* but with more documentation that sometimes contradicts the former account. Yet, the most notable fact is that Josephus stops his second account in 66, with the misdeeds of the procurator Florus, who—as he explains—forced the Jews to go into war against the Romans. After this brief allusion, he refers back to *War* for more details. At this point, for him, the war is nothing more than ancient history, and there is no need to repeat it. In *Life* § 422, he limits himself to recalling the general turmoil: "When Titus had suppressed the unrest in Judea" Josephus was then addressing the Jews, and insisting on Jerusalem's fall was no longer necessary for celebrating the glory of Vespasian and Titus. Moreover, in *CAp* 1:34, he notes that the priestly genealogical registers were reestablished in Jerusalem after each war: the persecution of Antiochus IV (170–164), the invasion of Pompey (63 BCE), the unrest under Varus after Herod's death (4 BCE), "and in our time"; the war of Titus is thus only the last of a long series of wars whose damage has been repaired. In *CAp* 2:77, he mentions, in the present tense, the sacrifices offered twice a day in honor of the emperor; in 2:193-195, he speaks, again in the present tense, of a temple for the one God and indicates the sacrifices offered by the priests. Therefore, in 95, Jerusalem is already to some extent reestablished but with no connection to rabbinical circles; and this situation will last until the so-called Bar-Kokhba war[16] (132–135).

---

[16] Cf. É. Nodet, "On the Destruction of the Jerusalem Temple," pp. 232–44.

As for the progress of Judaism, Josephus declares, as did Philo before him, that this ethical monotheism was very attractive, especially to women, who enjoy a status. Although there was no declared proselytizing as such, efforts were made to reach the Greek-speaking world. It is reported that around 100 the proselyte Aquila translated the Torah before the masters Eliezer and Yehoshua, who "praised" him, quoting Ps. 45:3 ("You are the most beautiful of the children of men"), with a pun on Japheth, son of Noah and ancestor of the Greeks[17] (*j.Megila* 1:11, 71c). Later, nonrabbinic proselytism continued for several centuries.[18] This is what could be called "synagogal Judaism," and it ended up being absorbed by the rabbinic system.[19]

In 68, when Vespasian arrived in Judea after conquering Galilee, he encouraged opening Jewish schools there that accepted Rome's authority. The most famous one was the academy of Yabneh-Iamnia, South of Jaffa, founded by Johanan ben Zakkai. It was the very first notable rabbinical institution;[20] Josephus did not identify, although he certainly wanted to have an influence on Judaism. Thus, on the subject of Passover, writing in Rome, he states that the rite of the lamb is maintained by "us" (*Ant.* 2:213, 3:248). This has not gone unnoticed, for a rabbinic saying indicates that in Rome a certain Theodosius (or Theodorus) wanted to establish (or restore) the Passover lamb, and from Yabneh he was told that if he were not such a prominent figure, he would be banished; regarding his prominence, some say that he was erudite and others that he had great power (*b.Pesahim* 53a-b). Both definitions correspond well to Josephus, but his name, carefully put in Greek, seems to be concealed: however, Theodosius is the equivalent of Matthias or Mattityahu, the name of his father and of several of his ancestors (*Life* § 4–5), whereas there are only easily recognizable transcriptions of "Joseph." Josephus himself, like the rabbinic tradition, ignores Joshua's Passover at Gilgal, which represents the entry into Canaan (Josh. 5:10-12); he keeps to the commemoration of the exit from Egypt. However, the Essene custom required celebrating Passover in the land of Israel to commemorate this entry.[21] Similarly, when Hillel the Elder, the ancestor of the rabbinic tradition, came from Babylonia he knew nothing about the Passover rite (*j.Pesahim* 6:1, p. 33a).

1.2.3 Joshua

There is no doubt that for this book Josephus reworks his source for the sake of coherence, for Joshua's conquest of Canaan was largely incomplete, despite various

---

[17] With puns: וסלק for "praised" is from κάλος; "the most beautiful" תיפיפי is similar to Japhet (תפי), cf. Saul Lieberman, *Greek in Jewish Palestine*, New York, Jewish Theological Seminary, 1942, pp. 17–26.
[18] Cf. the dossier established by Marcel Simon, *Verus Israël*, Paris, De Boccard, 1948, pp. 316-55.
[19] Cf. Ernest S. Frerichs et al., *Goodenough on the History of Religion and on Judaism* Atlanta, Scholars Press, 1986; José Costa, "Qu'est-ce que le 'judaïsme synagogal'?" *Judaïsme ancien, Ancient Judaism* 3 (2015), pp. 63–218; a good example is provided by the "God-fearers" of the synagogue of Aphrodisias in Asia Minor (third century), cf. Jerome Murphy-O'Connor, "Lots of God-Fearers: *Theosebeis* in the Aphrodisias Inscription," *RB* 99 (1992), pp. 418–24.
[20] Cf. Jacob Neusner, *A Life of Yohanan ben Zakkai, ca. 1–80 C.E.* (Studia Post-Biblica, 6), Leiden, Brill, ²1970, pp. 152–60.
[21] Cf. Dominique Barthélemy, "Notes en marge de publications récentes sur les manuscrits de Qumrân," *RB* 59 (1952), pp. 199–203, quoting the Persian sage al-Biruni (twelfth century), who dealt with calendars.

optimistic summaries suggesting the contrary. He glosses passages that seem too short or confused.

Apart from these inaccuracies, it has long been observed that the division of Canaan among the tribes, as described by Josephus (*Ant.* 5:81-87), is very brief, and that it has clear analogies with the parallel account of the "Samaritan Joshua" (hereafter SJ), that is, the first part of *Chronicle II* (cf. Section 1.1), which recorded traditions after Moses' death.[22] It is highly unlikely that Josephus stuck to a Samaritan text as such, or that Samaritans borrowed anything from Josephus' Greek; yet this similarity has hardly been exploited, for two reasons: on the one hand, Josephus' rather loose biblical paraphrase is most often considered a rewriting of a poorly known form of the LXX and thus without much authority;[23] on the other hand, it has sometimes been thought that this *Chronicle* was only a retroversion of an Arabic original, more or less inspired by the Masoretic Joshua and largely corrupted.[24] Finding obvious anomalies in the text of SJ has been easy: the presence of Tiberias, Caesarea, Nain in the lists of cities; the addition of verses from the Pentateuch; blessings of a Muslim style, and so on.

There are, however, some significant small details. One of the signs indicating the cantillation of the traditional Masoretic text (MT), the *paseq*—formed by a vertical line between two words—is atypical, since it does not follow the rigor of the general system of conjunctive and disjunctive signs. M. Gaster has observed that when the MT includes a *paseq*, SJ parallel, if it exists, presents a different text, often close to the LXX for small variants;[25] he concludes that this is a pre-Masoretic text control sign,[26] for this kind of device presupposes a Jewish collation on an ancestor of the present

---

[22] The first to make the connection was Mose Gaster, "Das Buch Josua in hebräisch-samaritanischer Rezension," *ZDMG* 62 (1908), pp. 209–79 (text), 494–549, where he responded to detailed objections (cf. next note). It is in fact a parallel version to the first part of the *Chronicle No. II*, published by John Macdonald, *The Samaritan Chronicle No. II (or: Sepher Ha-Yamim) from Joshua to Nebuchadnezzar*, Berlin, Walter de Gruyter, 1969.

[23] This is the implicit opinion that emerges from the careful inventory of Kristin de Troyer, *The Ultimate and the Penultimate Texts of the Book of Joshua*, Leuven/Paris/Bristol, Peeters, 2018; she concludes that the MT of Josh is not prior to the high priest John Hyrcan.

[24] Cf. Paul Kahle, "Zum hebräischen Buch Josua der Samaritaner," *ZDMG* 62 (1908), pp. 550–1; Abraham S. Yahuda, "Über die Unechtheit des samaritanischen Josuabuches," *Sitzungsberichte der königl. preuss. Akad. der Wissenschaften* 39 (1908), pp. 887–913; that same year, other critics expressed themselves.

[25] Cf. Gaster, *The Samaritans*, pp. 136–7.

[26] This completes the study of James Kennedy, *The Note-Line in the Hebrew Scriptures, Commonly Called paseq or pᵉsîq*, Edinburgh, Clark, 1903, pp. 19–20, which shows that this sign is ancient (and misnamed by the Massoretes): (1) it is simple and very apparent, almost cumbersome; (2) it always corresponds to a difficulty in the text, but, conversely, many difficulties are not indicated: they may be later; (3) it often coincides with the presence of a *qeré*; (4) it is posterior to the introduction of the final letters in the usual Aramaic alphabet. On the contrary, Israel Yeivin, *Introduction to the Tiberian Masorah*, trans. and ed. by E. J. Revell (Masoretic Studies, 5), Missoula (Mont.), 1980, p. 216 s. (§ 283 s.), notes that *paseq*, although marking a slight pause (as its name indicates) after a word with a conjunctive accent, has a use that does not follow simple and clear rules; he deduces that its introduction is not contemporary with the general (and coherent) system of conjunctive and disjunctive Masoretic accents. He then concludes that this introduction is later, but he does not provide any arguments, and it may be objected to him: (1) that this additional sign was not necessary to the Masoretic system; (2) that it affects the letters *bgdkpt* at the beginning of the following word (*dagesh*), whereas it is hardly probable that the Masoretic pronunciation was modified after its establishment.

Samaritan text. Likewise, in the parallel passages, Gaster compared[27] the divisions of SJ manuscripts into pericopes (*qiççot*) and the Masoretic divisions of Josh (*petuhot* and *setumot* combined). The result is significant: of the thirty-seven divisions in SJ, thirty appear exactly in the MT, four correspond imprecisely because of textual differences, and only three differ. These observations stand out only because other indications show that SJ *is not derived* from MT. This is the conclusion to be drawn from the similarities between SJ and Josephus, of which the following is a significant sample:

1. According to Josh. 2:1, Joshua sends the spies from Shittim, beyond the Jordan, to Jericho. Josephus says that they are sent to the Canaanites (*Ant.* 5:2), but he immediately adds that they come to report on Jericho (§ 5), that is, precisely the Rahab narrative (§ 6–14). Then, he concludes the episode with the report of the spies and the decision of Joshua, who sits with the high priest Eleazar and the council of elders, to confirm the oath made to Rahab (§ 15). The wording is clumsy, since the same report is given twice. SJ also says that the spies were sent to Canaan and then to Jericho, concluding "and they reported facts to him"; this is apparently what Josephus understood, for he introduces a first report. At the end of the account, SJ also says that the spies reported to Joshua, Eleazar, and all the chiefs of the tribes, whereas the conclusion in Josh. 2:24 is based on just one report of the spies to Joshua, and also on the panic of the inhabitants, which Josephus and SJ omit.

2. The scene of the circumcision before the Gilgal Passover (Josh. 5:2-8) is left out by both Josephus and SJ; and then comes a conclusion (v. 9): "The LORD said to Joshua, 'Today I have rolled away from you the disgrace of Egypt.' And so that place is called Gilgal to this day." SJ has different wording: "Then YHWH . . . 'I have removed from above you . . . all disaster,' and he called that place Gilgal." So, this is about the crossing of the Jordan, not the circumcision. Josephus (§ 34) explains that the name Gilgal means "freedom" because they were "freed from the Egyptians and the desert." This translation is more than imprecise if Josephus read "I rolled," and one cannot suspect him of not knowing Hebrew well. On the other hand, his explanation holds if he was reading something like the SJ. However, there is a seemingly accidental oddity, for he inserts this explanation after the capture of Jericho and the Achan's crime (Josh. 7:1).

3. Josh. 7:2-3 indicates that a reconnaissance mission preceded the first attack on 'Ai, but SJ and Josephus omit this (§ 35). After the defeat, Joshua summons Israel to find the thief by casting lots (Josh. 7:16); SJ and Josephus (§ 43) add that the high priest Eleazar and the magistrates are present. At the end of the episode, Achan is buried under a heap of stones; and unlike SJ and Josephus (§ 44), Josh. 7:26b adds the name of the place, Valley of Achor. There is, however, an unexplained discrepancy: SJ names the thief "Ilan," but this is probably just a misreading.[28]

---

[27] Cf. Gaster, "Das Buch Josua," p. 219.
[28] עכן partially obliterated may have been read (or guessed) as עילן.

4. The deceit of the inhabitants of Gibeon, who claim to be strangers from afar, leads Joshua to make an oath guaranteeing their protection, which is kept when they are unmasked (Josh. 9:3-27). According to SJ and Josephus (§ 55–57), Eleazar and the elders surround Joshua and validate the oath.
5. When a coalition of kings attacks the Gibeonites, Joshua helps the latter (Josh. 10:1-11); after the victory, without any clear connection with the context, sun and moon stop; this phenomenon is also mentioned in the *Book of the Righteous* (vv. 12-14). While SJ ignores this addition, Josephus mentions it, claiming that it comes from writings preserved in the temple (§ 61), as if it were an extrabiblical appendix of his source; for elsewhere he reports miracles by referring expressively to the "holy books" (e.g., *Ant.* 2:347, the crossing of the Red Sea; 10:210, the prophecy of Daniel 2). Likewise, 2 Sam. 1:18-27 speaks of David's lament after the death of Saul and his sons, which is also contained in the *Book of the Righteous*, but Josephus only says that David "composed lamentations, which have remained until me" (*Ant.* 7:6). This suggests that elements of this *Book* were not yet incorporated into the official biblical text.
6. Joshua's conquest of the North (Josh. 11:1-14) is followed by a first recapitulation (11:15-23) and then a second one (Josh. 12), omitted conjointly by SJ and Josephus (§ 68). SJ then adds the erection of a temple at Gerizim as well as elements of theocratic government. At the same time, this is where Josephus mentions the episode on Mount Gerizim recounted in Josh. 8:30-35 as foretold in Deut. 27–28, which is indeed its logical place, at the end of a supposedly completed conquest of the North.
7. The distribution of the western territory among the tribes occupies a long section (Joshua 13–21): after a reminder of the tribes that settled in Transjordan, those of Canaan are Judah, Caleb (in the midst of Judah), Ephraim, Manasseh, Benjamin, Simeon, Zebulun, Issachar, Asher, Naphtali, Dan (in that order after the migration of Dan to the North); then the Levitical cities are indicated and among them the cities of refuge. The list of the tribes of Transjordan in SJ is practically identical to that of MT; however, for Canaan, he gives a shorter and independent account, with a different order of the tribes: Judah, Dan (without migration), Simeon, Benjamin, Ephraim, Manasseh, Issachar, Zebulun, Asher, Naphtali. Josephus also has brief notices, with the same order of tribes, except for Dan, which is put at the end (§ 81–87). This similarity cannot be accidental, but the description of the tribes differs. Josephus briefly mentions the Levitical cities according to Num. 35:6 (§ 91), which implies that his source did not specify them, and SJ likewise ignores them. Conversely, the cities of refuge in Josh. 20:7 are indicated as such by SJ and Josephus (§ 91): Kedesh for Naphtali, Shechem for Ephraim, and Hebron (Kiriat-arba) for Judah.
8. According to Josh. 18:1-10 Joshua had a survey made so that the lots of the tribes would all have the same value; this refers to the seven tribes remaining after the allotment of the portions of Judah, Ephraim, and Manasseh. SJ ignores this passage, but Josephus paraphrases it by extending the operation to all the tribes so that all the shares have the same value (§ 76–79). Then he underscores that the lands of the inhabitants of Jerusalem and Jericho are exceptionally

fertile. Therefore, despite the appearances, the territories of Judah and Benjamin have the same value as the larger plots of other tribes, although they are indeed smaller. Now, this is what we find in the SJ: Judah is North of Simeon, whose southern border although imprecise but is in fact Edom-Idumah. On the contrary, the Judah of Josh. 15 is an immense stretch of land that extends toward the South, going as far as absorbing Simeon; consequently, for the Canonic text, Edom is confined east of the Jordan River and detached from Hellenistic Idumea (Figure 2).

The definition of the borders and the list of cities of each tribe only partially overlap, but it is certain that Josephus was following a source analogous to that of SJ: spontaneously, he would have put Jerusalem in Judah and would not have attributed to Judah such a small territory but in fact an area similar to the primitive Judah of Judas Maccabaeus (from Jericho to Emmaus-Nicopolis, Figure 3).

9. In the end, Josh. 23:1–24:28 presents two testaments-speeches of Joshua, but SJ and Josephus only put a shortened version of the second one, held in Shechem[29] (§§ 115–16). Joshua in fact has two profiles: first, as Moses' heir, he launches the conquest of Canaan, which culminates in the rite on Mount Ebal and Mount Gerizim, predicted by Moses in Deuteronomy 11 and 27–28 (cf. point 6). Second, the present passage shows him as an independent lawgiver in Shechem (the LXX puts "Silo"). This position is reinforced by an addition in the LXX that, after Joshua's death, recalls that he was the one who brought the Israelites out of Egypt according to the Lord's instructions[30] (24:31a); Moses' monopoly is thus contested.[31] Except for a small allusion to Mount Gerizim in SJ (v. 25), no connection is made between the two competing episodes. In any case, the spotlight is on the Samaritans or their ancestors (figure 4 below).

SJ contains some obvious "Samaritanisms" (in italics, vv. 1 and 25-26), but its characteristic feature is its brevity: the history of Israel, from Abraham to Moses, is entirely absent; there is only a mention of ancestral gods from beyond the Euphrates. In this respect, the insertion of the verse Deut. 4:34 has the effect of filling a glaring gap, by recalling the greatness of the exit from Egypt, but without Moses, as later in 2 Kgs. 17:34-36 (Figure 9, Section 2.1). Another detail shows the successive efforts to make the narrative more acceptable: in v. 5, instead of the sending of Moses and Aaron as in the MT, the LXX puts "the Egyptians did them harm."

Apart from an initial mention of the "tribes of Israel," which appears in a similar turn of phrase in the introduction to the first conclusion in 23:1, the narrative seems to involve new immigrants from the east, who are firmly called to worship the LORD. The

---

[29] The problems related to Joshua 24 are presented by William T. Koopmans, *Joshua 24 as Poetic Narrative* (JSOTSup, 93), Sheffield, Sheffield Academic Press, 1990.

[30] Cf. Thomas Römer, "The Problem of the Hexateuch," in: Ian C. Gertz et al. (eds.), *The Formation of the Pentateuch*, Tübingen, Mohr-Siebeck, 2016, pp. 813–27.

[31] Cf. Olivier Artus, "Gouverner et parler au nom de Dieu: la question du pouvoir en Nb 11-12," *RB* 124 (2017), pp. 26–37.

Figure 2 The Tribes' territories according to SJ and Josephus.

result is a kind of contract, with provisions stipulated in a new book that is not based on Moses' writings.

Such a short narrative has a certain coherence if one ignores the history of Israel. Conversely, the long canonical form has troubled commentators: it could be seen as a

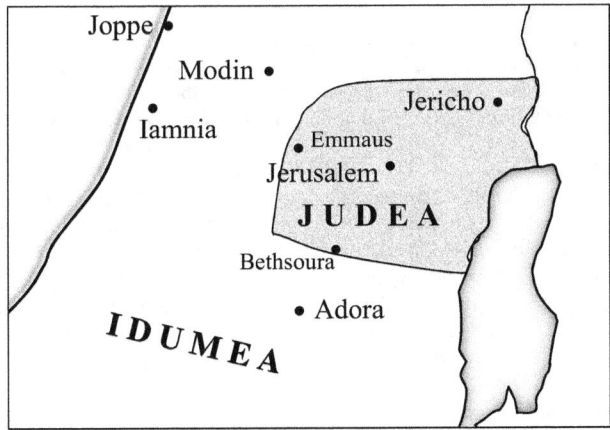

Figure 3 Judas' Judea.

conclusion of the Hexateuch,[32] but essential parts are missing,[33] such as the absence of the Law and the ignorance of the benefits since Egypt; thus, the typical elements that underlie the obligation to worship Yhwh are missing. The question is then dissolved by the hypothesis of a very late reworking, even later than Numbers 25–36, which offers an alternative account of conquest.[34]

However, we can keep the idea of a reworking. It is enough to consider SJ, without Samaritanisms, as primitive. In these conditions, the additions of Joshua 24 draw from all the books of the Hexateuch and so connect with Israel's history. There is no interference with the Law of Moses, for they are merely narratives. On the other hand, the SJ narrative is not in any way Israelite, and it strongly resembles the passage in 2 Kings 17 about the arrival of the Assyrian settlers, who know nothing of the worship of Yhwh, the local deity. This episode, which is considered to present the Samaritans' origin, will be examined later (Section 2.1); but there is already an underlying thesis that is properly Jewish, that is, that everything connected with Shechem is foreign to the Law of Moses (see Figure 4).

1.2.4 Ezra

It has long been noted that Josephus does not use the canonical form of Ezra and Nehemiah (or Ezra-Nehemiah, a single book for Jewish tradition and the LXX) in his biblical paraphrase. For Ezra, he had a version of content very close to 1 Ezra (or

---

[32] Cf., after others, Moshé Anbar, *Josué et l'alliance de Sichem: Josué 24:1-28*, Frankfurt a-M./Wien/Paris, Peter Lang, 1992, pp. 69–100.
[33] Cf. Thomas Römer, "Extra-Pentateuchal Biblical Evidence for the Existence of a Pentateuch? The Case of the 'Historical Summaries', Especially in the Psalms," in: Thomas B. Dozeman, Konrad Schmid, and Baruch J. Schwartz (eds.), *The Pentateuch: International Perspectives on Current Research*, Tübingen, Mohr-Siebeck, 2011, pp. 471–88.
[34] Cf. Rainer Albertz, "The Formative Impact of the Hexateuch Redaction: An Interim Result," in: Federico Giuntoli and Konrad Schmid (eds.), *The Post-Priestly Pentateuch: New Perspectives on Its Redactional Development and Theological Profiles*, Tübingen, Mohr-Siebeck, 2015, pp. 53–74.

Joshua 24	SJ (*Chronicle II*)
[1] Then Joshua gathered all the tribes of Israel to Shechem, and summoned the elders, the heads, the judges, and the officers of Israel; and they presented themselves before God.	[1] Joshua gathered all the tribes of Israel at Shechem; then, he summoned Israel's elders, heads, judges, and scribes who *ascended on Mount Gerizim and* lined up in the presence of God *at the entrance of the Tent of Encounter.*
[2] *And Joshua said to all the people, "Thus says the Lord, the God of Israel: Long ago your ancestors—Terah and his sons Abraham and Nahor—lived beyond the Euphrates and served other gods.*[3] *Then . . .*[4] *Jacob and his children went down to Egypt.*[5] *Then I sent Moses and Aaron. . .*[13] *I gave you a land on which you had not labored, and towns that you had not built, and you lived in them; you eat the fruit of vineyards and oliveyards that you did not plant.*	**Deuteronomy 4**[34] Has any god ever attempted to go and take a nation for himself from the midst of another nation, by trials, by signs and wonders, by war, by a mighty hand and an outstretched arm, and by terrifying displays of power, as the Lord your God did for you in Egypt?
[14] "Now therefore revere the Lord, and serve him in sincerity and in faithfulness; put away the gods that your ancestors served beyond the River and in Egypt, and serve the Lord. [15] Now if	[14] And now, fear the Lord and serve him in perfection and faithfulness; remove the *foreign* gods from your midst And serve *only* the Lord.[15] If

you are unwilling to serve the Lord, choose this day whom you will serve, whether the gods your ancestors served in the region beyond the River or the gods of the Amorites in whose land you are living; but as for me and my household, we shall serve the Lord."[16] Then the people answered, "Far be it from us that we should forsake the Lord to serve other gods;

[17] *for it is the Lord our God who brought us and our ancestors up from the land of Egypt, out of the house of slavery, and who did those great signs in our sight. He protected is along all the way that we went, and among all the peoples through whom we passed . . ."*[21] *And the people said to Joshua, "No, we will serve the Lord!"*

[22] The Joshua said to the people, "You are witnesses against yourselves that you have chosen the Lord, to serve him." And they said, "We are witnesses."

[23] *He said, "Then put away the foreign gods that are among you, and incline your hearts to the Lord, the God of Israel."* [24] *The people said to Joshua, "The Lord our God we will serve, and him we will obey."*

[25] So Joshua made a covenant with the people that day, and made statutes and ordinances for them at Shechem.	[25] That day Joshua made covenant for the people; he made statutes and ordinances for at Shechem which is at the foot of Mount Gerizim *and he*
[26] Joshua wrote these words in a book; He took a large stone	*made it the seat of justice.* [26] Joshua wrote these words in a book *that he gave to the priest sons of Levi.* He, then, took a large stone

And set it up under the oak in the sanctuary of the Lord. [27] Joshua said to all the people, "See, this stone shall be a witness against us; for it has heard all the words of the Lord that he spoke to us; therefore it shall be a witness against you, if you deal falsely with your God."

Figure 4 Joshua's final speech.

Rahlfs' Ezra A), which is an analogous account known only in Greek.[35] The first chapter of 1 Ezra is a translation of 2 Chronicles 35–36, which is clearly not linked to the LXX since it ignores the additional verses proper to the Greek (2 Chron. 35:19a-d; 36:2a-c; 5a-d Rahlfs). The decree of Cyrus (2 Chron. 36:22-23 // Ezra 1:1-3a) is not repeated; but this fact implies nothing.[36] Moreover, Josephus' source differs from 1 Ezra at both the beginning and the end:

- According to 2 Chron. 35:22, Josiah "did not listen to the words of Neco from the mouth of God," but the parallel 1 Ezra 1:25 puts "the prophet Jeremiah" instead of "Neco." Josephus, who, in *Ant.* 10:76, reported Josiah's death in his own time, was following the long version of 2 Chronicles 35; in this passage he merely says that Josias "ignored the request of Neco" and so avoids making this pagan king a prophet, whereas he would not have failed to mention "Jeremiah" if he had seen him mentioned in his source, especially since, following 2 Chron. 35:25 (// 1 Ezra 1:30), he indicates that "Jeremiah composed a lamentation for Josiah's funeral." In short, Josephus did not read the source of 1 Ezra 1.
- After Ezra's proclamation of the Law and its interpretation, the book ends with "and they gathered together" (1 Ezra 9:55). The parallel account in Neh. 8:1-18 places a very rural feast of Tabernacles after this gathering. Now, Josephus ends the story of Ezra precisely with this same feast (*Ant.* 11:157). It must therefore be concluded that 1 Ezra (or its exact Hebrew original) cannot have been Josephus' source, for it is too short. Moreover, he artificially develops Cyrus' action at the beginning, then introduces additional elements about the Samaritans (in **bold** in the detailed comparison later) and adds some comments (in *italics*).

The order of the Persian kings in the Book of Ezra is: Cyrus, Xerxes, Artaxerxes, Darius, another Artaxerxes (see Figure 1). 1 Ezra has the same sequence but omits Xerxes. Josephus, who read the Greek historians, understood that this succession made it impossible to honor Jeremiah's prophecy announcing a restoration at the end of the 70s, that is, in 515 BCE under Darius I (2 Chron. 36:21). He has therefore put a more likely succession: Cyrus, Cambyses, Darius I son of Hystaspes, Xerxes (§ 120, with the arrival of Ezra). An additional consequence of this arrangement is that Josephus lacked material to describe the rest of the Persian period: he puts Nehemiah under Xerxes, then Esther under an Artaxerxes, and finally a few anecdotes under another Artaxerxes and another Darius, to come to Alexander's time (see Figure 5). Consequently, he repeated the account of the difficulties between Cyrus and Darius, taking advantage of the reminder of Cyrus' decree under Darius; in the same way, he then extends as far as possible the story of Esther (§ 184–296).

---

[35] Cf. Alfred Rahlfs, *Septuaginta*, Stuttgart, Deutsche Bibelgesellschaft, 2006, pp. 873–903; Michael F. Bird, *1 Esdras: Introduction and Commentary on the Greek Text in Codex Vaticanus*, Leiden/Boston, Brill, 2012. For the textual traditions, cf. Dieter Böhler, *1 Esdras*, Stuttgart, Kohlhammer, 2016, pp. 13–14.

[36] In 1 Ezra 1:47-52; 2:11; and 8:5-6, the name "Jerusalem" is rendered Ἱεροσόλυμα, the normal Greek form used by Josephus, in contrast to the transcription Ιερουσαλημ used elsewhere in the book (and in all biblical books translated from Hebrew). This indicates that 1 Ezra is a composite translation.

Antiquities 11	1 Ezra	Ezra
Last kings of Judah; exile; Jeremiah's prophecy	1	2 Chronicles 35–36
1–4 Cyrus' decree to rebuild the temple in Jerusalem	2:1-3	1:1-3
5 Fulfillment of the prophecy of Isa. 44:28 about Cyrus		
6 Cyrus summons the Jewish leaders	2:4-5	1:4-5
7–8 Cyrus writes to the satraps; first departure of Jews		
9a friends help, perhaps also neighbors	2:6	1:6
9b they make the appropriate sacrifices (// § 75–77)		
10–11 return of the cult utensils to Sheshbazzar	2:7-8	1:7-8
12–14a Cyrus' letter to the satraps of Syria (// § 99–103)		
14b Zerubbabel, chief of the repatriates (// § 69)		
15 inventory of the cult utensils	2:9-11	1:9-11
16–17 decree of Cyrus (in the letter of Darius, // § 98–103)		
18 enumeration of the repatriates (// § 68)		
19 beginning of the work on the temple (// § 78–79)		
20 the enemies (Samaritans) block the work (// § 88)		
21–29 letter to *Cambyses* on the dangers of Jerusalem; reply	2:12-25	4:7-23
30 work interrupted until the second year of Darius	2:26	4:24
31–57 competition of Darius' pages; victory of Zerubbabel	3:1–4:46	
reminder of the misdeeds of the Edomites-Idumeans	4:45b.50	
58–67 Darius sends Zerubbabel, grants privileges to Jews	4:47–5:6	
68–74 census of the repatriates (summary)	5:7-45	2:1-70
75–77 Zerubbabel and Joshua reestablish altar, feast of Tabernacles	5:46-52	3:1-6
78–83 beginning of the work on the temple; festive music	5:53-62	3:7-13
84–86 refusal of collaboration offered by the Samaritans	5:63-68	4:1-3
87 *the temple will be accessible to everyone*		
88 the enemies (**Samaritans**) interrupt the work	5:69-70	4:4-5
89–95 Tattenai and Shetar-Boznai write to King Darius	6:3-21	5:3-17
96 fear of the Jews, Haggai and Zechariah encourage them	6:1-2	5:1-2
97–98 the Samaritans write to Darius against Jerusalem	?	?
99–105 Darius finds the decree of Cyrus and confirms it	6:22–7:1	6:1-13
106–110 Temple completed; inauguration; first Passover	7:2-15	6:14-22
111–113 on the transition from monarchy to aristocracy		
114–119 Samaritans attack Jews; Darius responds	?	?
120–132 Ezra, with the help of *Xerxes*, summons the exiles	8:1-40	7:1–8:14
133 most of them remain in exile; the repatriated are Israel		
134–138 the caravan of Ezra prepares, leaves, arrives	8:41-64	8:15-36
139–152 crisis of foreign wives; their expulsion	8:65–9:36	9:1–10:44 fin
153 Ezra's reform will last forever		
154–156 Ezra proclaims the Law; penance and rejoicing	9:37-55 end	Neh. 8:1-13a
157 feast of Tabernacles		8:13b-18
158 deaths of Ezra and the high priest Jehoiakim		

Figure 5 Josephus largely follows the source of 1 Ezra.

The question of the relative anteriority of Ezra and 1 Ezra has long been debated, and it is related to narrative and/or historical coherence, since it has to do with the laborious reconstruction of the sanctuary, the city, and the walls; but it is globally distorted,[37] because the discussions ignore Josephus' testimony, which proves that the

---

[37] Cf. Adrian Schenker, "La Relation d'Esdras A' au texte massorétique d'Esdras-Néhémie," in: Gerard J. Norton (ed.), *Tradition of the Text*, Fribourg, Éditions universitaires, 1991, pp. 218–48, with a

original 1 Ezra included a final Feast of Tabernacles. The result is a doublet: in 1 Ezra 5:47-48 (//Ezra 3:2-3), Jeshua son of Jozadak and Zerubbabel restored the holocaust altar and, with the returnees from exile, inaugurated the sacrificial cult according to the law of Moses, beginning with the Feast of Tabernacles in the seventh month. Then, in 1 Ezra 9:38-39 (//Neh 8:1-2), Ezra proclaims the law of Moses to the returnees who are already there, then they study it and enthusiastically make an entirely vegetable Feast of Tabernacles, without contact with the sanctuary; it is even said that "from the days of Joshua the son of Nun to that day the people of Israel had not done so" (Neh. 8:17).

However, the problem is not closed, for two quite separate parts must be distinguished in the Book of Ezra: first one without Ezra that goes from Cyrus' decree regarding the reconstruction of the Temple of YHWH in Jerusalem to its solemn inauguration, with a clergy in conformity with the law of Moses (Ezra 1–6 // 1 Ezra 2–7); then, the story of Ezra, a priest with a prestigious genealogy, sent by Artaxerxes, and who arrived as a reformer. Between these two parts Josephus intervenes regarding two aspects, without any identifiable source: on the one hand, after describing the splendor of the inaugural Passover, he slips in considerations about the new aristocratic constitution that was thus established, with the government of high priests. On the other hand, the Samaritans, who were supposed to finance the Jerusalem cult from the taxes of the province of Samaria and had already written to King Darius, were exerting increasing pressure against the Jews.

This break between the two parts suggests that they were two separate sources which were later put together. In these circumstances, Ezra's canonical account becomes difficult: after Cyrus' decree, a column of returnees is led by Sheshbazzar; a long list of returnees led by twelve notables, including Jeshua son of Jozadak, Zerubbabel, and Nehemiah, immediately follows; then, the first two rebuild the holocaust altar, and the cultic cycle is reestablished. Next comes a long series of setbacks until the inauguration of the Temple under King Darius, who rediscovered Cyrus' decree. The undertaking was accomplished thanks to the help of the prophets Haggai and Zechariah; in fact, according to Hag. 1:12-14, the work would not even have begun without Haggai's intervention.

Conversely, 1 Ezra organizes the same elements differently: after the arrival of Sheshbazzar, the authorities of Transeuphrates get Artaxerxes to stop the work until "the second year of Darius" and the latter then arbitrates a contest between his pages or bodyguards, and among them Zerubbabel, on the question of what reality is most powerful: wine, the king, women, or the truth. Zerubbabel, who has dealt with the last two, is declared the winner and sent to Judea to work with Joshua on the reconstruction of Jerusalem, both the city and the Temple together. The sequence on the Persian kings is more natural, but as in the canonical account, it cannot end with Darius I, since the first Artaxerxes is posterior to him. A significant detail then appears: wanting to

---

discussion of the twentieth-century commentators; Dieter Böhler, "On the Relationship between Textual and Literary Criticism. The Two Recensions of the Book of Ezra: Ezra-Neh (MT) and 1 Esdras (LXX)," in: Adrian Schenker (ed.), *The Earliest Text of the Hebrew Bible*, Atlanta, SBL, 2003, pp. 35–50; Lisbeth S. Fried (ed.), *Was 1 Esdras First? An Investigation into the Priority and Nature of 1 Esdras*, Atlanta, SBL, 2011.

prove the power of women, Zerubbabel cites before the king the case of his concubine Apame, daughter of Artabaze, who struck him in public or took off his diadem to put it on her own head. Now, historians report that, at the court of Darius III, there was a certain Apama daughter of Artabaze who was captured by Alexander and given to one of his generals.[38] Hence, the restoration of the Temple would have taken place at this time, and not under Darius I; but this seriously compromises the chronologies. Commentators are therefore quick to conclude that the contest between the pages is a late fiction added to the narrative, and they tend to prefer the canonical Ezra presentation. However, if the contest is excluded as too legendary (1 Ezra 4:1–5:6), one obtains a very different and somewhat incoherent sequence: interruption of the work under Artaxerxes until the second year of Darius (cf. Ezra 4:24); then, the list of returnees with Zerubbabel, Joshua, and Nehemiah; and, finally, the beginning of the work (cf. Ezra 2–3), which is interrupted again until the second year of Darius.

At the end of its gallery of biblical portraits, Sir. 49:7-10 mentions Jeremiah, Ezekiel, and the Twelve Prophets. Then, according to vv. 11-12, Zerubbabel and Joshua rebuilt the Temple. Finally, v. 13 briefly reports that Nehemiah reconstructed the ruined walls, restored the doors and locks, and rebuilt the houses. No foreign king is mentioned, but we can see that the author, who ignores any idea of reform, did not know the second part of Ezra. As for the first part, a distinction can be made: according to canonical Ezra, the initial role of Zerubbabel and Joshua is remote, and gradually fades away, for they are practically supplanted by Haggai and Zechariah (cf. Hag. 2:9; Zech. 4:9); on the contrary, in 1 Ezra, everything is more compact, because Zerubbabel is sent and then that Cyrus' decree is confirmed under the same Darius. So, it is appropriate to suppose that Sirach knew only the first part of Ezra, in a form similar to 1 Ezra 2–7; in any case, the figure of Ezra does not appear there.

1.2.5 Nehemiah

In the book that bears his name, the figure of Nehemiah, a Babylonian Jew who is not a priest, appears under three profiles: as the restorer of the walls of Jerusalem; the local governor in the service of the Persian king but whose only indicated action is to correct a social injustice; and, thirdly, a reformer attentive to the observance of the Sabbath and unhappy about the intrusion of foreign wives. Josephus, like Sir. 49:13, knows only the builder and credits him with all the work (see Figure 6).

The starting point of the story is poorly explained: Jewish visitors from Judea inform Nehemiah, cupbearer to King Artaxerxes, that Jerusalem's walls have been broken and the gates burned. It is not known why Nehemiah has a peaceful carrier in exile, nor do we know what exactly happened,[39] but Josephus amplifies the account and concludes that Nehemiah is upset to learn that the walls are being razed and that the Jews are constantly being harassed by the surrounding nations; there are even people dying

---

[38] According to Arrien, *Anabase* 7.4.6, she was given to Ptolemy Lagos, first king of Egypt; Strabon, *Géog.* 12.8.15, thinks that she was given to Seleucus, first king of Syria.

[39] Perhaps an Edomite attack (cf. 1 Ezra 4:45; Abd. 18; Ps. 137:7), cf. Nissim Amzallag, *Esau in Jerusalem: The Rise of a Seirite Religious Elite in Zion at the Persian Period* (CRB 85), Leuven/Paris, Peeters, 2015, pp. 43–61.

Antiquities 11	Nehemiah
159–161a Nehemiah, cupbearer to Xerxes, questioned the people of Jerusalem	1:1-3
161b the misdeeds of the neighboring nations are multiplied; walls broken down	
162 Nehemiah laments over Jerusalem (brief)	1:4-11end
163–168a in Susa, Xerxes allows him to leave; he gives him letters and escort	2:1-9
168b–172 in Jerusalem, Nehemiah urges the people to rebuild the walls	2:17-18
173 on the meaning of "Jews," designating the repatriates as true Israelites	
174a beginning of the work, *directed by Nehemiah* (Neh: *by Eliashib*)	3:1-32
174b–175 conspiracies of the Ammonites, Moabites, Samaritans	4:1-17
177–178 Nehemiah organizes the defenses against the enemies	6:1-11
179 completion of the work in two years and four months	6:15 (*52 days*)
180a dedication of the wall; sacrifices, eight-day festival (very brief account)	12:27-43
180b *anger* of neighboring nations (Neh puts: *admiration* of nations)	6:16
181a Nehemiah sees that the well-fortified city has few inhabitants	7:4
181b he urges the priests and the Levites to settle there	11:1
182 he demands that the people maintain them	12:44-47end
183 Nehemiah dies at an old age	

Figure 6 For Josephus, Nehemiah was neither a governor nor a reformer.

every day. The king agrees to send him to Jerusalem as an official, but Josephus does not make him a governor like Neh. 5.

Instead, he makes him the foreman of restoration of the walls, substituting him for the high priest Eliashib. The neighboring nations unsuccessfully plot to interrupt the work, and Josephus carefully omits that Nehemiah also has opponents in Jerusalem (Neh. 6:12-14). Then, Josephus omits the list of returnees and Ezra's proclamation of the Law to them, with the ceremonies that follow (7:5–9:37). He also omits the communal commitment of Nehemiah's companions to follow the Law (Neh. 10), which is signed by eighty-seven individuals; this is a very limited group that corresponds to the *Men of the Great Assembly* of the rabbinic tradition.[40] Finally, Josephus ignores the second journey of Nehemiah (Neh. 13) who, expressly camped as a reformer, acts with authority, though without an apparent mandate. It is unlikely that these major omissions are due to Josephus, since Sir. 49 already confirms them.

1.2.6 Maccabeans

The Maccabean crisis (167–164) led, in 135 BCE, to the founding of the heresy-based Hasmonean regime, which was a dynasty first of high priests and then of kings. This was an entirely new reality, which lasted until Herod the Great (37 BCE) but whose setup remains hard to grasp because the accounts that tell about it are jumbled and cannot be reduced to a simple narrative. Josephus has two versions, and the two canonical books of the Maccabees recount more or less the same crisis but in entirely different ways.

Josephus' first account presents itself as a kind of frontispiece to his entire account of the *War* and will be repeated as a kind of refrain (*W* 1:31-53): the misfortunes of the Jews have always come from rivalries between nobles. Syria and Egypt had long

---

[40] Cf. Élie Bikerman, "Viri magnae congregationis," *RB* 55 (1948), pp. 397–402.

competed for control of Coele-Syria, the southern extension of Phoenicia. After many wars since the succession of Alexander, Antiochus III of Syria had pushed back the Egyptian domination toward 200 BCE, but there was still rivalry between two large families, that of Onias (Oniades) and that of Tobias (Tobiades). The latter, driven out during a quarrel, took refuge in Antioch, the capital of Syria, and convinced King Antiochus IV Epiphanes to reconquer Judea, and he did this brutally; moreover, it is known that he was spendthrift and constantly in need of money.[41] He besieged Jerusalem, plundered the Temple, and interrupted the sacrifices for three and a half years, also prohibiting the practice of Judaism; this duration corresponds to the period of "a time, two times, and half a time" (Dan. 7:25, 9:27). Two reactions arose: on the one hand, the high priest Onias took refuge with Ptolemy VI in Egypt, where he obtained the right to build a miniature Jerusalem with a similar temple at Heliopolis (cf. Section 3.2). On the other hand, a priest of Modin, Mattathias son of Hasmonaeus, launched a very lively rebellion, and so the generals of Antiochus were driven out. Thanks to his success, his compatriots recognized him as their leader. Then his son Judas succeeded him, continuing the fight and taking care to make an alliance with Rome. He reconquered Jerusalem, purified the Temple, and personally restored the sacrifices. There is no mention of a commemoration.

At this time, Antiochus died, and his son, who bore the same name, continued the hostilities. Finally, Judas was killed in battle, and his brother Jonathan succeeded him. He took "various measures to protect himself from his countrymen"; in particular, he strengthened the alliance with the Romans. After a series of actions, he was put to death by the tyrant Tryphon, who coveted the throne of Syria, and his brother Simon succeeded him. Simon, the first to be called a high priest, was a brilliant general and "liberated" the Jews from the Macedonian domination that had lasted 170 years. Since Seleucus I, the founder of the Hellenistic Syrian dynasty, had reconquered Babylon in 312 BCE, the "liberation" must be placed in 142 BCE and hence under the high priest Simon.

Compared to his more extensive narration in *Antiquities* (*Ant.* 12–13), this one contains many inaccuracies, but it does already highlight a major problem concerning this new dynasty of high priests. We can formulate it in two ways: Why was there no junction between the dynasty of the high priest Onias and Mattathias or his sons after the defeat of the pro-Syrian part? One even has the impression that Judas acted as high priest. Another aspect is to question the relationship between an alliance with Rome and the protection against fellow countrymen.

---

[41] Polybe, 31.9 indicates that having wanted to find money, Antiochus had left on an expedition against the sanctuary of Artémis in Élymaïde, toward Suse, but that the "barbarian" tribes of the vicinity pushed him back, although without a real war. While withdrawing, he died in Tabai, not far from Ispahan, "struck by insanity, as some say, because of the manifestation of a divine displeasure in front of this outrage"; cf. Otto Mørkholm, *Antiochus IV of Syria* (Classica et Mediaevalia, Diss. 8), København, Gyldendalske, 1966. The money shortage may have been less than previously thought; cf. Georges le Rider, "Un essai de réforme monétaire sous Antiochus IV en 173/172? Remarques sur l'idée d'une pénurie d'argent dans les États hellénistiques au IIe siècle," in: Regula Frei-Stolba and Kristine Gex (dir.), *Recherches récentes sur le monde hellénistique*, Bern, Peter Lang, 2001, pp. 269–80.

In the parallel account in *Antiquities*, Josephus had more detailed documentation in Hebrew from the second block indicated in *CAp* 2:39-41 (and described in Section 1.2.2). The Maccabean crisis was only one of its aspects: at the death of the high priest Onias, his son Onias, who later built a temple in Egypt, was too young, and Antiochus IV gave the office first to his brother Jesus-Jason and then to his other brother Onias-Menelaus. This led to rivalry between Jason's party—the majority—and that of Menelaus, which included the Tobiades. The latter, being mistreated, fled to Antiochus and declared that they were abandoning the ancestral customs and wanted to live in the Greek manner; they built a gymnasium in Jerusalem and masked their circumcision. Later, in 170 BCE, Antiochus, in need of money, was prevented by the Romans from conquering Egypt and, while withdrawing, he came to plunder the Temple; his followers and Menelaus had opened Jerusalem's gates to him. Two years later, on the 25th of Kislev, Antiochus seized Jerusalem by trickery, plundered the Temple's treasures, and desecrated it; he built a citadel for a Macedonian garrison, forbade circumcision and the practice of Judaism, and ostensibly made pig sacrifices. Many Jews complied with the king's orders to escape torture.

This second expedition, in the presence of the high priest Menelaus, is not explained and seems to be exaggerated: the king himself moved, he pulled off a ploy about which nothing is known,[42] and he did many things in one day; the systematic persecution seems gratuitous and pointless, since the treasures of the Temple had already been plundered. We must suspect that this second action is only a duplication of the first, amplifying the Hellenization. This is probable, because we also know that Antiochus made two failed expeditions to Egypt,[43] and it is sufficient to assume that the second served as a framework to amplify the first.

The rebellion of Mattathias and then of his sons is reported. After a Sabbath on which the Syrians massacred Jews who had taken refuge in the desert, Mattathias decided to allow armed defense on that day. Seeing the situation in Judea, the Samaritans succeeded in being recognized as distinct from the Jews and regaining the good graces of Antiochus IV. In and around Judea, the rebels' action was quite complex, and after several incidents, Josephus magnifies the feat of Judas Maccabaeus, who managed to retake the Temple on 25 Kislev 164 BCE. This event is commemorated by a festival, and Josephus explains (*Ant.* 12:325): "Until now we celebrate this feast (of 8 days), which we call 'the Lights'—we give it this name, I think, because this freedom appeared in the midst of our despair." Although its duration places it among the principal biblical feasts, Josephus was unaware of this commemoration when he wrote *War* and hesitated over the origin of the name. There is reason to believe that, being in Rome, he identified the

---

[42] 2 Macc. 5:24-26 indicates a ploy: the officer Apollonius took up arms on a Sabbath outside the walls; the gates remained open, and those who had come out to see the spectacle were slaughtered, unable to defend themselves. According to *Ant.* 12:4, Ptolemy I took Jerusalem by a similar ruse, but no other evidence exists. It is possible and even probable that these two traditions refer to the same event, which in fact concerned at best only the district of the city where the absolute Sabbath of Nehemiah was practiced.

[43] Cf. 2 Macc. 5:1; Dan. 11:27-30; Polybius 29.27; Titus 45.12; Jerome, *In Dan.* § 29–30. Cf. Dov Gera, *Judaea and Mediterranean Politics 219 to 161 B.C.E.*, Leiden/New York/Köln, Brill, 1998, pp. 153–74.

festival with the solstice of December 25th on the Julian calendar,[44] when the sunlight starts increasing again—a fact that can explain an accompanying rite; starting from an equivalence Kislev-December suffices.

In reality, this high achievement was at best a symbolic action when the news of the death of Antiochus IV arrived. At the time, there was indeed a high priest in office, Menelaus, who is absent from the narrative; moreover, according to the documents quoted in 2 Macc. 11:16-37, the persecution itself had ceased in the preceding spring.[45] Now, according to 1 Macc. 1:59, Antiochus IV had instituted a sacrifice to be offered in his honor on the holocaust altar on the 25th of each month, and 2 Macc. 6:9 even specifies that it was the date of his birth.[46] Moreover, a Babylonian tablet made of unbaked clay[47] has provided a list of Seleucid kings from Alexander the Great to Antiochus IV, whose death is known to have occurred "in 148, the 9th month (Kislev)." The chronology is based on the Babylonian lunar calendar, where the year begins in Nissan (April), with an inception in 312 BCE.[48] There is reason to believe that the official date of his disappearance was fixed at the arrival of the information in Babylon, so as not to invalidate the last administrative acts issued in his absence. One can thus conclude that the announcement of the death of Antiochus IV arrived shortly before the monthly sacrifice of the 25th, which was then becoming insignificant, and that he had been pushed aside by rebels led by Judas Maccabees.

The book 1 Maccabees, which is known only in Greek translation, gives the same account as Josephus, so much so that one could believe that he was the source.[49] Yet, this is impossible for two reasons: on the one hand, small differences are well explained if we suppose a common source[50] taken from the Hebrew writings of lesser authority that Josephus mentions in *CAp* 2:39-41 (cf. Section 1.2.2); on the other hand, the narrative gaps are too large, especially at the two ends (see Figure 7). In *Ant.* 12:265, with the appearance of Mattathias, Josephus and 1 Macc. 2:1 clearly meet, but Mattathias is no longer the son of Hasmoneus: he becomes a priest of the class of Yoyarib of Jerusalem,

---

[44] Cf. Étienne Nodet, "Calendriers bibliques: Salomon, Éléphantine, *Jubilés*, Dédicace," *Trans* 39 (2010), pp. 119–48.

[45] Their authenticity is admitted since Christian Habicht, *2. Makkabäerbuch* (Jüdische Schriftungen, 3. Lieferung), Gütersloh, Gerd Mohn Vlg, 1976, pp. 179–84; Id., "Royal Documents in Maccabees II," in: *The Hellenistic Monarchies: Selected Papers*, Ann Arbor, University of Michigan, 2006, pp. 106–24, considers that these documents are authentic but badly classified, mixing Antiochus IV and his son Antiochus V.

[46] Such a monthly commemoration was not abnormal: there are other testimonies, from the third century (Egypt) to Hadrian, cf. Félix-Marie Abel, *Les Livres des Maccabées* (EB, 38), Paris, Gabalda, 1949, p. 362.

[47] Cf. Abraham J. Sachs and Donald Wiseman, "A Babylonian King List of the Hellenistic Period," *Iraq* 16 (1954), pp. 202–17. This tablet, acquired by the British Museum in 1880, was identified by the authors only in 1953.

[48] Useful conversion tables are provided by Richard A. Parker and Waldo H. Dubberstein, *Babylonian Chronology, 626 B.C.–A.D. 45*, Chicago, University of Chicago, 1946, p. 23.

[49] This is the common opinion; cf. typically Bezalel-Bar Kochva, *Judas Maccabaeus: The Jewish Struggle Against the Seleucids*, Cambridge, Cambridge University Press, ²2002, pp. 151–93.

[50] The detailed examination by Étienne Nodet, "Josèphe et 1 Maccabées," *RB* 122 (2015), pp. 507–39. A simple example: 1 Macc. 12:26 "(Jonathan) sent spies into their camp, and they returned (καὶ ἐπέστρεψαν)"; the return assumes a Heb. וישבו understood from וישבו. Josephus explains that the spies "made prisoners at night (τινας συλλαβόντων)," so he understood שוב from שבה "capture" (*Ant.* 13:175).

Antiquities 13	1 Maccabees
~	13:52a *commemoration of the reconquest of the Citadel (2ⁿᵈ month, 23ʳᵈ day).*
215-217 Simon *demolishes the Citadel and razes its hill in three years.*	13.52b Simon *reinforces the Temple Hill and resides in the Citadel.*
218-222 Tryphon attacks Demetrios II.	14:1-4 Tryphon attacks Demetrios II.
~	14:4-15 *Simon's panegyric.*
~	14:16-24 *diplomacy: Rome et Sparta.*
~	14:25-49 *official honors to Simon.*
223-224 Antiochus VII Sidetes with Simon against Tryphon the impostor.	15:1-14 Antiochus VII Sidetes with Simon against Tryphon the impostor.
227b *alliance* of Simon with Rome.	15:15-24 Rome *formally recognizes* Simon.
225-227a Antiochus VII sends Cendebeus to subdue Simon, but he is defeated.	15:25-16:10 Antiochus sends Cendebeus to subdue Simon, but he is defeated.
228-235 Simon is assassinated; his son John *Hyrcan* succeeds him.	16:11-24 Simon is assassinated; his son John succeeds him *brilliantly; details.*
236-244 Antiochus invades Judea, and so on.	~

Figure 7 Continuation and end of the reign of the Hasmonean high priest Simon.

and this fact confers on him a quite different dignity.[51] Earlier, Josephus spoke of the different Oniad high priests and the number of events that occurred on the 25th of Kislev, whereas 1 Macc. 1 limits itself to exposing the activities of the "rascals" who advocated Hellenization and unleashed a persecution against those who opposed it.

Toward the end of the account, in *Ant.* 13:215, Josephus says that after the final expulsion of the Syrians, the high priest Simon, brother of Judas, razed the citadel that the Syrian occupants had built in Jerusalem. On the contrary, 1 Macc. 13:52b states that Simon settled there with his family. So, from this point onward, there is a divergence that deserves examination.

The account of 1 Maccabees begins with the so-called Hellenistic crisis, at a time when in Jerusalem there was neither king nor high priest; and it stops as soon as Simon son of Mattathias has a son, John Hyrcanus, that is, as soon as a dynasty of high priests seems to have begun. This son is the subject of a short notice similar to those summarizing the lives of the kings of Israel and Judah in the books of Kings (and Chronicles). The commemoration of Judah Maccabeus' deed is called "Dedication of the Altar" (1 Macc. 4:59), which is also the inauguration of the dynasty. This perspective of a foundation narrative can be seen from another angle: while Josephus includes in his account various episodes relating to the Samaritans, the temple of Onias and the Jews in Egypt (which will be examined later, Section 3.1), 1 Maccabees does not explain the absence of a high priest in Jerusalem between Alkimus and Jonathan (159-152), when there was another temple in Egypt. More generally, the narrator is only interested

---

[51] The division of the priests into classes for the service of the Temple is attributed to David (1 Chron. 24:4, taken up in *Ant.* 7:365 but without eponyms), and that of Yoyarib is the first (Josephus himself claims that he is related to "the first" but without naming it, *Life* § 2). The term Ἀσαμωναῖος has the form of an adjective. The rabbinical tradition, which has little regard for the Asmoneans, ignores their attachment to the class of Yoyarib and always puts the adjective חשמונאי "of Hashmôn." In Judah, on the borders of Edom, there was a locality called חשמון (Josh. 15:27 MT, omitted by LXX). This is, therefore, at best a very lowly origin, with no connection to Aaron.

in the Hasmonean dynasty: it was born of the crisis—and not of a return to former arrangements of which we know nothing—and becomes the center of Israel's whole reality (cf. 1 Macc. 16:2). This is, therefore, a book with a message and not merely a chronicle.

Moreover, 1 Maccabees contains some elements that do not appear in Josephus' account but confirm the thesis of a *biblical* legitimacy; they concern especially the scriptural allusions and the relations with Rome. On the first point, we see that Mattathias' speech-testament (1 Macc. 2:51-64) is full of reminiscences of famous people, from Abraham to Daniel, and a particularly strong reference to the zealot Phinehas son of Aaron, who is recognized as "our father." On the contrary, the rise to power of his sons is never compared to the powers of the former high priests: the lyrical praises of Judas Maccabaeus (1 Macc. 3:3-9) and Simon (1 Macc. 14:4-15) do not allude to any biblical figures.[52] For Judas' preparation of the decisive battle at Emmaus (1 Macc. 3:47-49), there is mention of fasting, consulting the Law, priestly vestments, first-fruits, tithes, Nazirs having to fulfill their vow in the Temple, whereas despite some vague allusions to the holy war in Deut. 20, the parallel of *Ant.* 12:300 is limited to talking about prayers.

Later, under the high priest Alkimus, successor of Menelaus son of Onias, very pious people (scribes and/or Assidean)[53] were treacherously slaughtered by a Syrian officer (1 Macc. 7:16), and the author quotes Ps. 79:2-3:[54] "They scattered the flesh

---

[52] In fact, the expansion policy of the Asmoneans is never presented as a return to the conquests of Joshua, in spite of the obvious similarities, which are well demonstrated by Katell Berthelot, *In Search of the Promised Land? The Hasmonean Dynasty Between Biblical Models and Hellenistic Diplomacy*, Göttingen/Bristol, Vandenhoeck & Ruprecht, 2017, pp. 361–96. Jason A. Staples, *The Idea of Israel in Second Temple Judaism: A New Theory of People, Exile, and Israelite Identity*, Cambridge/New York, Cambridge University Press, 2021, pp. 142–79, shows by another approach that the term "Israel" represents an ideal never reached, even by the great Asmonean and then Herodian Judea.

[53] Cf. the survey of opinions in John Kampen, *The Hasideans and the Origin of Pharisaism: A Study in 1 and 2 Maccabees*, Atlanta, Scholars Press, 1988. The Hebrew original of "Hasidean" is an adjective meaning "pious, faithful," which is not at all surprising; cf. Étienne Nodet, "Assidéens introuvables," *RB* forthcoming.

[54] Which was probably composed in the wake of these events. The ancients considered it a prophecy: Eusebius, *Demonst. evang.* 10.1.12, easily shows that the oracle (which he assumes to have been pronounced in the time of David) was fulfilled at the time of the Maccabean crisis and Alkime; likewise, Theodore of Mopsuestia in his commentary on the Psalms (ed. R. Devreesse, 1939); Charles A. Briggs and Emilie G. Briggs, *A Critical and Exegetical Commentary on the Book of Psalms*, Edinburgh, T&T Clark, 1906–1907, II:197, consider that the psalm was originally a lament for the destruction of Jerusalem, since it was reworked in the Maccabean period. According to Marina Mannati, *Les Psaumes*, Paris, DDB, 1967, III:79, it is an anthology that draws together all the lamentations since 587 BCE. Most modern commentators prefer to assume that the psalm refers to the events of 587 BCE (586), although important details do not fit well (invasion of many nations, the forgetting of the burning of the Temple and the deportation, etc.); cf. Marvin E. Tate, *Psalms 51-100* (Word Biblical Commentary, 20), Dallas, Word Books, 1990, p. 299, which concludes that this psalm (like Ps. 74, also included in the preexilic "Asaph" collection) comes from the community that remained in Judea after the exile; but this conclusion leads to other difficulties, for it is precisely this "Israelite" community that remained outside the Babylonian Jewish revival led by Ezra and Nehemiah; also cf. Beat Weber, "Zur Datierung der Asaph-Psalmen 74 und 79," *Biblica* 81 (2000), pp. 521–32; Johannes Schnocks, "'Gott, es kamen Völker in dein Erbe': Ps 79 und seine Rezeption in 1 Makk," in: Ulrich Dahmen and Johannes Schnocks (Hg.), *Juda und Jerusalem in der Seleukidenzeit*, Göttingen, Bonn University Press, 2010, pp. 147–60 (paper by Jean-Marie Auwers).

of your saints and pours out their blood all around Jerusalem, and there was no one to bury them." Finally, a correspondence between Jonathan and the Spartans offers curious details: a letter from their king Arius to a former high priest Onias states that Jews and Spartans are brothers, as descendants of Abraham, and that it is advisable to renew this ancient alliance; it appears as an attachment to a letter addressed to them by Jonathan, in which he declares (1 Macc. 12:9): "We have no need of these things (alliance and friendship), since we have as encouragement the holy books that are in our hands." Josephus, who placed this correspondence well before the crisis, in Onias' time, makes him say somewhat strangely (*Ant.* 13:167): "We had no need of such proof (of kinship) since we are convinced of it by our holy writings." The nature of these writings, which are ancient, is difficult to grasp: for 1 Macc. 12, the "holy books" are a novelty known Jonathan but that the high priest Onias ignored; now, this strange fact reinforces Jonathan's biblical legitimacy and perhaps also his reluctance with regard to a Greek kinship of the Hasmoneans.[55]

As for relations with Rome, which began with Judas Maccabaeus, Josephus' first account in *War* already shows that he was very sensitive to them. One observes a paradox: 1 Macc. 8:2-11 highly praises the Roman institutions, with their political and military efficiency, which avoid the defects of monarchy, but in the parallel (*Ant.* 12:414), Josephus limits himself to succinctly noting the victories of the Roman army, without evoking the institutions. Then, in order to flesh out the profile of Judas in quest of an alliance with Rome, he goes as far as making him a high priest, successor of Alkimus—which is absurd.[56] More seriously, 1 Macc. 15:15-24 gives in full a Roman senatus-consult of 142 BCE, naming expressly the consul Lucius and the high priest Simon, who is officially considered as the ethnarch of all the Jews scattered around the Mediterranean.[57] Josephus limits himself to a minute allusion to this treaty (*Ant.* 13:227). Yet, he is so concerned about a good understanding with Rome that it is hard to imagine that he would not have quoted such a document in full if he had known about it, as he does in many other cases[58] (cf. *Ant.* 16:174).

These observations allow us to conclude that 1 Maccabees is later than Josephus' source, which has some complementary elements; but we must also conjecture that this elaboration is prior to the invasion, in 63 BCE, led by Pompey, who had come to arbitrate a civil war between Hyrcan and Aristobulus, the rival sons of Alexander Jannaeus; conversely, one could suppose a redaction linked to weariness in face of the civil war, caused by the deficiencies of the Hasmonean system of government. After this, royal supervision never slackened, and it was perhaps no longer really appropriate,

---

[55] Cf. François Villeneuve et al., *Les Antiquités juives de Josèphe. Vol. VI: livres XII-XIII*, Paris, Cerf, 2021, pp. xxx–xxxiii.
[56] Cf. Michael O. Wise, "4Q245 (PsDan'ar) and the High Priesthood of Judas Maccabeus," *Dead Sea Discoveries* 12.3 (2005), pp. 313–62; on the contrary, Vasile Babota, *The Institution of the Hasmonean High Priesthood*, Leiden/Boston, Brill, 2014, pp. 89–118, continues the trend inaugurated by Josephus.
[57] Cf. Joseph Sievers, *The Hasmoneans and Their Supporters*, Atlanta, Scholars Press, 1990, pp. 116–19; Linda T. Zollschan, "The Earliest Jewish Embassy to the Romans: 2 Macc. 4:11?" *JJS* 55 (2004), pp. 37–44.
[58] Cf. The detailed study by Miriam Pucci Ben Zeev, *Jewish Rights in the Roman World: The Greek and Roman Documents Quoted by Josephus Flavius*, Tübingen, Mohr-Siebeck, 1998.

even for Josephus, to celebrate its universal benefits. The fact remains that Josephus paraphrases, according to his biblical custom, while 1 Maccabees is a rather careful translation, which in many cases preserves details that Josephus neglects.[59]

The crisis is presented in a very different way in 2 Maccabees. After a prelude that includes two letters, which will be mentioned later (Section 3.1), the author declares, in the preface, that he has laboriously summarized a work written by a certain Jason of Cyrene, who is not otherwise known. In any case, he wrote in Greek, because nothing in his style lets suspect a Semitic original. A long prologue begins with the Syrian king Seleucus IV, who financed the Jewish cult presided over by Onias, the best of the high priests. After a denunciation, this king sent a notable named Heliodorus to take the Temple's treasure, which included important private deposits; but he miraculously failed, recognizing the presence of God in the sanctuary. After Seleucus was murdered, his brother Antiochus IV succeeded him, but lacking money, he sold to Jason, Onias' brother, both the office of high priest and the right to introduce Hellenism. Jason built a gymnasium and an ephebia, thus introducing the Greek cult of the body, and created a citizen entity of Antiochians of Jerusalem, while Onias had gone to take refuge at the sanctuary of Daphne close to Antioch, where he was later assassinated despite the right of asylum there.

Three years later Menelaus, whose origin is uncertain according to this version, in his turn bought the office by paying more. Antiochus was on his second unsuccessful campaign[60] in Egypt, when a rumor of his death reached Jason, who then tried to take back the power; but his attempt led to a civil war, and he had to flee. Antiochus, on the back from Egypt, thought that there was a rebellion; upon his arrival in Jerusalem, he began a strong repression and plundered the temple. When he left, he sent a general to take up arms on a Sabbath before the walls of Jerusalem; this was a ploy, for the people, curious and unarmed, came out, and he was able to slaughter them and enter the city, for they did not defend themselves. Then, Judas Maccabaeus went into hiding with some companions, while both Mattathias and his decision to allow armed defense on the Sabbath were ignored. The king then forbade Judaism on pain of death and rededicated the temples of Jerusalem and Gerizim to Zeus; there were martyrs, who were later venerated.[61] Judas led a war that led to the temple's purification on the 25th of Kislev, dated at the time of Antiochus' death in 164 BCE, after only two years of interruption. However, the situation was unstable, and the fighting continued; the high priest Menelaus was executed in 163 BCE by Antiochus V for having badly managed

---

[59] Francis Borchardt, *The Torah in 1 Maccabees: A Literary Critical Approach to the Text*, Berlin/Boston, De Gruyter, 2014, offers a fine analysis of the book's literary strata, which correspond to parties, but it ignores Josephus.

[60] Dan. 11:27-30 also mentions two campaigns of Antiochus IV (according to Polybius).

[61] The account of their martyrdom is developed in 4 Maccabees, dated in the middle of the first century; the event is set in Antioch, where King Antiochus personally acts and where Judea is ignored; cf. Jan W. van Henten, "Datierung und Herkunft des vierten Makkabäerbuches," in: Jan W. van Henten et al. (eds.) *Tradition and Re-interpretation in Jewish and Early Christian Literature* (Studia Postbiblica, 36), Leiden, Brill, 1986, pp. 136–49: it clarifies the findings of Elias J. Bickerman, "The Date of the Fourth Maccabees," in his *Studies in Jewish and Christian History. Part One* (AGAJU, 9), Leiden, Brill, 1976, pp. 275–81; Tessa Rajak, "Paideia in the Fourth Book of Maccabees," in: George J. Brooke and Renate Smithuis (eds.), *Jewish Education from Antiquity to the Middle Ages*, Leiden/Boston, Brill, 2017, pp. 63–84.

the crisis. Judas finally defeated the Syrian general Nikanor, and a commemoration of this victory was held in Jerusalem on 13 Adar 161 BCE, which happened to fall on the eve of the "Day of Mordecai" celebrated on 14 Adar in memory of Esther and the feast of *Purim*, a commemoration linked to Babylonia. The story then abruptly ends, even before the death of Judas Maccabaeus (2 Macc. 15:37): "From that time the city has been in the possession of the Hebrews. So, I will here end my story."

The perspective is thus the opposite of an account of the founding of a dynasty of kings or high priests. The fact that the city is "in the possession of the Hebrews" cannot mean political independence, since the citadel of the Syrians and their supporters was there until Simon's action in 141 BCE, some twenty years later (1 Macc. 13:51). However, various episodes show that the emphasis is on the Temple, with the presence of God.[62] The conclusion, therefore, says that it will be accessible to pilgrims. Consequently, the use of the name "Hebrews" is relevant, because unlike "Jews, Judeans," it has no geographical connotation.

A difficulty concerning the religious persecution remains. In his first account, Josephus presents plausible political-financial circumstances, but he does not explain the persecution or the hatred of Antiochus IV toward the Jews, inherited by his son. Secondly, 1-2 Maccabees and Josephus' second account have in common the emphasis on a matter of Hellenism that is, in fact, hardly intelligible. 1 Macc. 1:10-15 briefly reports that a "generation of renegades" wanted to make an alliance with the nations and obtained permission from Antiochus IV to make Jerusalem into a Greek city; no one responsible is named. This party built a gymnasium in Jerusalem and removed the marks of circumcision. It is not explained why this permission was necessary. Until then, the status granted by Antiochus III around 200 BCE (cf. Section 1.2.2) governed the whole of the large Jewish minority in his kingdom, even if the Oniad party remained attracted to Egypt. In accordance with these provisions, Seleucus IV, predecessor of Antiochus IV, financed the cult of Jerusalem's temple (2 Macc. 3:1-4).

Everything changed with the enthronement of Jason, who bought the office of high priest from Antiochus IV as soon as he was enthroned and paid a supplement to establish a gymnasium and an ephebia, a college of Greek education; he also wanted to draw up a list of Jerusalem's "Antiochians" (2 Macc. 4:9)—all things that Josephus avoids saying clearly. Thus, the status of Antiochus III was reversed since the monopoly of Judaism was broken in Jerusalem and the high priest had become a Seleucid royal agent. This did not transform Jerusalem into a Greek *polis* but created an "Antiochian" demesne, by reference to the king and not to the capital. Such was the Citadel, where Jews and Greeks were to mingle. A clue to this is provided by a case of a competition in Tyre (2 Macc. 4:19-20): the delegation from Jerusalem brought money for pagan worship (to Heracles), but in the end it was diverted and used to build triremes. Moreover, under Antiochus IV, the multiplication of the "Antiochian"

---

[62] Cf. Robert Doran, *Temple Propaganda: The Purpose and Character of 2 Maccabees*, Washington, The Catholic Biblical Association, 1981; Michael W. Duggan, "Epiphanies: Cosmic Transcendence in 2 Maccabees," in: Michael W. Duggan, Renate Egger-Wenzel, and Stefan C. Reif (eds.), *Cosmos and Creation: Second Temple Perspectives*, Berlin/Boston, De Gruyter, 2020, pp. 111-28.

entities, cities (*polis*) or organized groups[63] (*demos, politeuma*), was so important that even the citizens of the capital Antioch had to specify on their coins "Antiochians near Daphne,"[64] the great sanctuary dedicated to Apollo.

Despite of the scandalized expressions[65] in 2 Macc. 4:13-15 about the Jerusalemites' infatuation with Hellenism and the slackening of the priests in the altar service, there is reason to believe that these new arrangements were well accepted at the beginning, since shortly after Jason's enthronement, around 174 BCE, the king came to Jerusalem and was sumptuously welcomed there by the latter and by the people (4:22). Three years later, Menelaus succeeded in ousting Jason by paying more for the office, and he continued the same policy, endeavoring to broaden the "Antiochian" reality. However, there was growing tension, since we read in 2 Macc. 5:15-16 that Antiochus IV, having arrived from Egypt and guided by Menelaus, entered the Temple and plundered it: the high priest in office had become an enemy, and along with him all his supporters, who were probably the majority. Thus, everything is seen from the viewpoint of the intransigent party which cannot accept the change of status and managed to grow to the point of creating a new dynasty of high priests. The conclusion is then that such an upheaval in the Jewish world can obviously only be due to Antiochus' hatred.[66] However, this is only a literary effect, as other details show. Thus, the symmetrical treatment of the temples of Jerusalem and on Mount Gerizim (2 Macc. 5:22–6:2) shows, at least for the latter, that it was by no means a question of abandoning Yahwism (cf. Section 3.3). Or again, as 1 Macc. 1:41-42 states, the Antiochus IV plan to unify the cults of the whole kingdom[67] represents a seriously inept policy for a vast empire. Indeed, it is contradicted by the examination of local coinage of the time: the same portrait of the king appears on the obverse of all the bronze coins, thus implying the unity of the kingdom; but the reverse shows a great diversity of types:[68] only three

---

[63] Cf. Moyna Mcglynn, "The Politeuma: Guardian of Civil Rights or Heavenly Commonwealth in Ptolemaic and Roman Egypt," *Biblische Notizen* 161 (2014), pp. 77–98. Likewise, a politeuma of Ptolemais-Akko, created in 174 BCE, issued bronzes bearing "Antiochians in Ptolemais"; cf. Elias Bickermann, *Der Gott des Makkabäer. Untersuchung über Sinn und Ursprung der makkabäischen Erhebung*, Berlin, Schocken, 1937, pp. 61–2 notes.

[64] Cf. Jonathan A. Goldstein, *I Maccabees. A New Translation with Introduction and Commentary* (Anchor Bible, 41), Doubleday, Garden City, 1976, pp. 115–16.

[65] The same contrast is seen elsewhere: the illness and end of Antiochus IV is recounted in venomous terms, as the providential consequence of his hatred toward the Jews (2 Macc. 9:1-17); then he quotes a letter from Antiochus "to the excellent Jews," in which the latter mentions the benefits he had granted them; he speaks of his illness and for all practical purposes names his son Antiochus V as his successor. There is no allusion to Jerusalem or Judea, and the tone of the letter is in conformity with the spirit of Antiochus III's statutes.

[66] He was looking for money and did not care about the large number of Jews in his kingdom (outside Judea); cf. Erich S. Gruen, "Hellenism and Persecution: Antiochus and the Jews," in: Peter Green (ed.), *Hellenistic History and Culture*, Berkeley, University of California Press, 1993, pp. 238–74.

[67] This claim is repeated in the otherwise well-documented study by Gera, *Judaea and Mediterranean Politics*, who curiously concludes at the same time that Antiochus Epiphanes was a wise politician and that his persecutions attested a godless madness.

[68] Cf. Elias J. Bickerman, *Institutions des Séleucides* (BAH 26), Paris, Geuthner, 1938, p. 232; Christian Augé, "La monnaie en Syrie hellénistique et romaine," in: Jean-Marie Dentzer and Winfried Orthmann, *Archéologie et histoire de la Syrie. II. La Syrie de l'époque achéménide à l'avènement de l'Islam*, Saarbrücken, Saarbrücker Druckerei und Verlag, 1989, pp. 149–90.

autonomous cities reproduce the idol appearing on the royal issues (Zeus naked and standing), whereas all the others represent the local tutelary god.

1.3 The New Testament

The Samaritans are never mentioned by Paul, but they appear in various ways in the Gospels and in Acts. In the Synoptics, the Samaritans, who are rarely evoked, represent an unclassifiable category.[69] Indeed, Jesus sends his disciples on a mission telling them (Mt. 10:5-6): "Go nowhere among the Gentiles, and enter no town of the Samaritans, but go rather to the lost sheep of the house of Israel." Only the Jews constitute Israel; so, there is an entity that is neither Jewish nor Gentile, and it certainly has nothing to do with the refined monotheism of the philosophers.

Even James and John, the two brothers who were to become heavenly apostles, were ready to call down fire from heaven on the Samaritans who refused to welcome them when Jesus and his disciples passed through Samaria on their way up to Jerusalem (Lk 9:52). Yet, Jesus is keen to show that a benevolent Samaritan can be better than a cult official who is well established among the chosen people[70] (Lk 10:33). Finally, in Lk 17:11-12, we read an interesting episode: somewhere on the border between Samaria and Galilee, a group of ten lepers come to beg Jesus to have mercy on them. He briefly tells them to go and show themselves to the priest, as Lev 13:43-46 requires. After their healing, only one returns to give glory to God; he is a Samaritan, and Jesus recognizes the faith of this stranger. It is worth noting that in the face of the misery of leprosy, the barrier separating the Samaritans from the Jews was broken down to the point that they formed a single group: they were subject to the same legal constraints (Lev. 14:1-32), and we do not know to which priests they were sent.

The elements provided by the fourth gospel and by Acts are more significant; there, the Samaritans are not merely strangers to be avoided.[71]

1.3.1 The Acts of the Apostles

This book represents a journey that culminates when Paul arrives in Rome with "us." The work has two parts, and the turning point is Peter's visit to Cornelius, a Roman centurion from Caesarea Maritima (Acts 10:1-2). The episode, recounted at length, is framed by visions, and we see that Peter was far from imagining that he would go to meet a pagan: the scene inaugurates the mission to the nations (cf. Acts 15:7), of which Paul will be the undisputed champion. Around 200, Clement of Alexandria offered a

---

[69] Cf. John P. Meier, "The Historical Jesus and the Historical Samaritans," *Biblica* 81 (2000), pp. 202–32.
[70] Cf. Mark A. Proctor, "'Who Is My Neighbor?' Recontextualizing Luke's Good Samaritan (Luke 10:25-37)," *JBL* 138 (2019), pp. 203–19.
[71] The idea that the Letter to the Hebrews has a Samaritan substratum has now been abandoned; cf. Lincoln D. Hurst, *The Epistle to the Hebrew: Its Background of Thought*, Cambridge, Cambridge University Press, 1990, pp. 77–82.

significant summary: Jesus taught under Tiberius, then the apostles, "embracing the ministry of Paul," taught until Nero, and no heresies appeared until Hadrian.[72]

The first part of Acts, which takes place entirely in the Jewish world,[73] ends with a summary showing complete success throughout the entire region of Canaan that Joshua had conquered (Acts 9:31-32): "The church throughout Judea, Galilee, and Samaria had peace and was built up. Living in the fear of the Lord and in the comfort of the Holy Spirit." Behind this peace one discerns a sigh of relief, for Saul-Paul, having come to Jerusalem, was sent back to Tarsus. He had already made a name for himself in Damascus, where after his vision on the way, he had begun to preach. However, he had to flee, because the Jews wanted to destroy him, while Ananias, the disciple who had welcomed him, was not bothered. The same thing happened in Jerusalem, where Paul was first integrated into the group of the apostles thanks to the mediation of Barnabas. Yet, he was again in danger, even though the apostles were not threatened, and he had to be sent away. This rejection will become extreme during Paul's last journey to Jerusalem: when he is attacked by the Jewish and Roman authorities, James and his entourage do nothing to help him (Acts 21:28-29).

This first part of Acts began at the time of the Ascension when the apostles asked Jesus (1:6): "Lord, is this the time when you will restore the kingdom to Israel?" They were waiting for the Messiah son of David, king of Israel, not just of Judah, just like the two disciples who, disappointed, were on their way back to Emmaus (Lk 24:21). Jesus then announces the coming of the Holy Spirit and declares (Acts 1:8): "Then you will be my witnesses in Jerusalem, in all Judea and Samaria, and to the ends of the earth." Most commentators already see a universal mission,[74] in line with Isa. 45:14; but that does not make much sense before Peter's visit to Cornelius. In fact, the phrase concerns the Land of Israel and so represents the extension of David's messianic kingship over the whole country, from the Jordan River to the Mediterranean, that is, all the tribes that arrived with Joshua (forgetting a little about the Transjordan conquered by Moses). For this reason, the at least symbolic recovery of Samaria was essential. Similarly, in Mt. 19:28, Jesus announced to the apostles that, in the messianic era to come, they would govern the twelve tribes of Israel.

This era has indeed begun, and a mission to Samaria with Philip is reported, but it has some peculiarities. After the persecution of Stephen, Philip had gone there, although without a mandate (Acts 8:5-6). He preached and proclaimed the Messiah, which is a typically Jewish perspective and not a Samaritan one, since their only biblical reference is the new hoped-for Moses, announced in Deut. 18:18. Philip baptized, but Peter and John had to be sent to bring the Holy Spirit; now, this surprises the reader, since Philip was one of the Seven, who had been chosen precisely because they were "full of the

---

[72] Clement, *Strom.* 7,17, cf. 2 Pet. 3:15.
[73] The question of languages, settled at Pentecost, did not represent a notable turning point, even if it was the literary occasion for introducing the Seven; cf. the discussion in James D. G. Dunn, *Christianity in the Making. Vol. 2: Beginning from Jerusalem*, Grand Rapids/Cambridge, Eerdmans, 2009, pp. 241–54.
[74] Except Daniel R. Schwartz, "The End of the ΓH (Acts 1:8): Beginning or End of the Christian Vision?" *JBL* 105 (1986), pp. 669–76, who rightly sees in it an allusion to the Land of Israel, at least west of the Jordan.

Spirit and of holiness."[75] In fact, the approach of the two "columns" from Jerusalem may have been a way of neutralizing Philip, for they did not meet him, and when they returned to Jerusalem, they were the ones who evangelized the Samaritan villages, thus replacing him. Earlier, Philip had met Simon the Magician, who amazed the people with the signs he performed; he claimed to be great and was recognized as such. The narrative says that Simon was baptized by Philip and then wanted to buy from Peter and John the power to confer the Holy Spirit; he was, therefore, fundamentally deviant.

This Simon is known from other sources.[76] The earliest witness is Justin Martyr (ca. 100–165), who, as a native of the Roman colony of Nablus, was well placed.[77] His testimony is all the more interesting because he does not know Acts—or at least he never refers to it, although this book would have been useful to him in confronting both Marcion and the Judeo-Christians.[78] In *I Apol.* 26.1-8, he begins by saying that, after Christ's ascension, the demons raised up several figures who claimed to be gods. Then, he presents Simon as a Samaritan from Gitten, who was active under Claudius (41–54). He was a disciple of a certain Menander, whom he had met in Antioch, and had founded a movement with Helen, a former prostitute redeemed by him who became—according to his supporters—his "first intellectual emanation"—a theme that recalls the legend of Athena born from the forehead of Zeus. He practiced magic through the power of demons and baptized in his own name for resurrection and eternal life. His influence was so great in Samaria that a statue of him was erected in Rome, between two bridges over the Tiber, with a Latin inscription that Justin attests to in the following century: *Simoni deo sancto*.[79] In the rest of his exposition, Justin refuses to allow Menander, Simon, or Marcion to be called Christians, thus indicating that, in his time, a confusion was possible; the comparison of Simon with Marcion is certainly significant, because it suggests a common refusal of the Old Testament, as

---

[75] This deficiency remains poorly explained; cf. Michel Gourgues, "Esprit des commencements et esprit des prolongements dans les Actes: Note sur la 'Pentecôte des Samaritains' (Ac 8, 5-25)," *RB* 93 (1986), pp. 376–85; Sophie Reymond, "Paul sur le chemin de Damas (Ac 9,22 et 26): temps et espace d'une expérience," *NRT* 118 (1996), pp. 520–38; Pierre Haudebert, "Le Samaritain-étranger (Lc 17,18) dans l'œuvre de Luc," in: Jean Riaud (dir.), *L'étranger dans la Bible et ses lectures*, Paris, Cerf, 2007, pp. 185–94.

[76] Useful documents have been conveniently collected and discussed by Stephen Haar, *Simon Magus: The First Gnostic?* (BZNW,119), Berlin, W. de Gruyter, 2003, with a review of the modern commentaries.

[77] Cf. Andrew Hayes, "The Significance of Samaritanism for Justin Martyr," *Studia patristica* 93 (2017), pp. 141–53; Ingrid Hjelm, "Simon Magus in Patristic and Samaritan Sources: The Growth of a Tradition," in: Jörg Frey et al. (eds.), *The Samaritans and the Bible: Historical and Literary Interactions between Biblical and Samaritan Traditions*, Berlin, De Gruyter, 2012, pp. 263–84.

[78] Cf. Andrew Gregory, *The Reception of Luke and Acts in the Period before Irenaeus* (WUNT II/169), Tübingen, Mohr-Siebeck, 2003, pp. 310–21, who indicates small, inconsequential contacts. Since Henry J. Cadbury, *The Book of Acts in History*, New York, Harper & Brothers, 1955, pp. 136–64, it is admitted that Lk could have existed without Ac. Similarly, Justin did not know Jn; cf. Charles E. Hill, "Was John's Gospel Among Justin's *Apostolic Memoirs*," in: Sara Parvis and Paul Foster (eds.), *Justin Marty and His Worlds*, Minneapolis, Fortress Press, 2007, pp. 88–94.

[79] Which he gives in transliteration Σίμωνι δεωσάγκτῳ. The inscription was found in this place in the sixteenth century (CIL 6.567), but it is actually dedicated to SEMONI SANCO DEO, a Sabine deity who protected contracts; whether or not he himself saw the inscription, Justin's error is proof of the movement's importance as far as Rome in his time.

Irenaeus later noted. In *Dial.* § 120, Justin underlines that he refuses to listen to his Samaritan compatriots, who make Simon a god.[80]

After Justin, some authors add details, which are more or less true but indeed interesting. Irenaeus of Lyons, who succeeded Pothin in 177, refutes the heresies of his time, but he declares that they all proceed from this Simon (*Adv. Haer.* 1.30.15): by describing them, he shows that each one has borrowed some features from him. Earlier, he presented Simon as reinterpreting the Trinity: God appeared as Son to the Jews, as Father to the Samaritans, and then as Spirit descended upon the nations; Simon himself was the "great power" (cf. Acts 8:10) and Helen was his first thought; it was she who created the angels, who then created the world. As a victim of the angels' jealousy, she was then locked up in a body and passed from one woman to another, until she became a prostitute in Tyre. It was then that God became incarnate in Simon to redeem her and bring salvation to others (or the world). Her followers said that the Scriptures were no longer to be followed, because they had been inspired by the angel-demiurges. They led a licentious life and worshipped the images of Zeus and Athena (Jupiter and Minerva). Now, Irenaeus, who knew Justin, is the first author to mention Acts,[81] but he apparently also had other sources of a Gnostic nature, which must be considered as developments of traditions attributed, rightly or wrongly, to Simon.

The Pseudo-Clementine writings, linked to Clement of Rome, are known only from two distinct recensions, called *Homilies* (Hom.) and *Recognitions* (Rec.). These texts, which assume a lost "basic text," are dated to the third century and do not know Acts.[82] Among the various pieces gathered in these texts, we were able to isolate a second-century source.[83] The overall perspective is rather Judaizing or Gnostic, but above all strongly anti-Pauline, despite a somewhat atypical opening to the nations: because of the Jews' refusal, the number of descendants promised to Abraham had to be completed with pagans.

These texts give new details about Simon, which are more concerned with magic than with doctrines (*Rec.* 1.12; 2.7; *Hom.* 1.15; 2.14; 2.22-23): his parents were Antonius and Rachel; he was initiated into Hellenism and magic at Alexandria; he had been John the Baptist's first disciple and presented himself as the Christ, allowing people to call

---

[80] Cf. Paul Carbonaro, "Simon le magicien et la Bible grecque," *RB* 121 (2014), pp. 414–26.

[81] He knew the title and for him it was Scripture; cf. Andrew Gregory, "Irenaeus and the Reception of Acts in the Second Century," in: Thomas E. Phillips, *Contemporary Studies in Acts*, Macon, Mercer University Press, 2009, pp. 47–65.

[82] This is proven by a passage in which the twelve apostles successively refute various opponents (the high priest, a Sadducee, a Samaritan, etc.): after Simon the Canaanite comes "Barnabas also called Matthias, who as an apostle had taken the place of Judas" (*Rec.* 1.60.5), which is incompatible with the election of Matthias against Barsabbas according to Acts 1:23.

[83] *Rec.* 1.27-71, cf. F. Stanley Jones, "An Ancient Jewish Christian Rejoinder to Luke's Acts of the Apostles: Pseudo-Clementine Recognitions 1.27-71," in: Robert F. Stoops, Jr. (ed.), *The Apocryphal Acts of the Apostles in Intertextual Perspectives* (Semeia 80), Atlanta, Scholars Press, 1997, pp. 223–45, but there is no reason to suppose that the author knew Acts, because various details contradict it; cf. Étienne Nodet, "Les Douze, les Sept (Ac 6,2-3) et Ps.-Clément," *RB* 121 (2014), pp. 66–107. In French, see en français, on peut consulter Alain le Boulluec, "Les *Recognitiones* de Pseudo-Clément," in: Pierre Geoltrain et al., *Écrits apocryphes chrétiens II* (Bibl. de la Pléiade, 516), Paris, pp. 1649–81.

him "the one who stands,"[84] which is a divine attribute (cf. Exod. 17:6; Deut. 5:1); as such, he was superior to the creator-demiurge (corresponding to the rebellious angels in Irenaeus). He refuted the resurrection and refused to accept Jesus as the new Moses (*Rec.* 1:57.1). Thus, a contrast is drawn between Simon, the false Samaritan prophet with his deceptive magic that amazes, and Peter, the true Jewish prophet, whose "miracles of truth" promote conversion and salvation[85] (*Hom.* 2.33).

Two details are worth noting: Simon is thought to have been the first disciple of John the Baptist, but he baptized in his own name. The first point will be examined in the following section on the fourth gospel. The second point immediately recalls Paul, who in 1 Cor. 1:13 is pleased to note that he has not baptized anyone (or just a few!) so that no one could suspect him of doing so in his own name. We must conclude that the shadow of Simon or his ilk was not far away, since the risen Jesus had expressly sent the apostles among the nations to make disciples and baptize them (Mt. 28:19), and baptism plays an essential role in Paul's theology. This idea is reinforced by the fact that Peter does not baptize, as if he were sending people to the neighboring parish, which seems very incongruous: this is the case at Pentecost (Acts 2:38) and later at Cornelius' house in Caesarea[86] (10:48). Likewise, during Paul's travels, many are baptized, but it is not known by whom and how. The same is true of the strange group of twelve rather isolated disciples whom Paul finds in Ephesus: he has them baptized in the name of Jesus, but we do not know how or by whom, while immediately afterward Paul himself does not hesitate to lay his hands on them to confer the Holy Spirit (19:5-6).

However, one exception stands out: Philip baptizes. This is indicated in a general way in Samaria, then explicitly in the case of the Ethiopian eunuch when they come to a fountain on the road to Gaza (Acts 8:12.37). In consequence, Simon is thus presented as a disciple of Philip and not of John, which is perhaps a way of preserving the memory of the latter, since the Gospels insist on the closeness between John and Jesus. However, this Philip is rather poorly defined. He is introduced as one of the Seven, who were appointed by the Twelve to settle an unclear matter of serving the widows.[87]

The first two, Stephen and Philip, are the subject of narratives; but it appears that the apostles in fact did not know them. Indeed, the persecution against Stephen leads to his stoning, but he is buried by "pious men"; and, above all, the apostles were not bothered, even though they remained in Jerusalem (8:1-2). This suggests that Stephen was the leader of a particular group, which was more or less related to Jesus but not to the apostles. Similarly, Philip, after a series of episodes, finally arrives at Caesarea Maritima (8:39); there, he is followed by Peter, who comes to Cornelius' home at his request (10:27). Then, when he asks for the latter to be baptized, he is unaware that Philip is permanently in the area. In fact, during his last trip to Jerusalem, Paul, who

---

[84] Or *stans*, ἑστώς, cf. Patrick Fabien, *Philippe l'évangéliste* (Lectio Divina, 232), Paris, Cerf, 2010, p. 83, who notes that in Stephen's vision (Acts 7:55) Jesus is "standing (ἑστῶτα) at the right hand of God," whereas in the vision of the Son of Man (Mt. 26:64; Lk 22:69) he is seated (cf. Ps. 110:1; Dan. 7:13); this might be a way of countering Simon on his own ground.

[85] Cf. Charlotte Touati, "Pierre et Simon dans le roman pseudo-clémentin: notes critiques," *RHR* 225 (2008), pp. 53–74, who notes the opposition between prophets and false prophets.

[86] Les commentateurs se bornent à supposer un respect des églises locales, cf. Daniel Marguerat, *Les Actes des Apôtres (1-12)*, Genève, Labor et Fides, 2007, pp. 398–9.

[87] Cf. F. Scott Spencer, "Neglected Widows in Acts 6:1-7," *CBQ* 56 (1994), pp. 715–33.

knew him, stayed in his house, and we even learn that he had four virgin daughters and prophetesses (21:8-9).

Hence, we must assume that the Seven represented movements linked in different ways to Jesus but not to the apostles (or more exactly to the Twelve). Acts' redactor, who wanted everything to culminate with Paul's arrival in Rome, took care to situate them in this progression. Philip, who belonged to this group and was not afraid to baptize, represented a branch close to the Samaritans, who constituted a very important reality.[88]

1.3.2 The Gospel of John

Before Jesus' famous encounter with a Samaritan woman, we learn that he was baptizing in Judea, while John the Baptist was doing the same "at Aenon near Selim because water was abundant there" (Jn 3:22-23). This was a place in Samaria, near an important spring.[89] Then, there is a discussion on purity between Jews and John's disciples, who called their teacher "Rabbi." John may have had foreign disciples (cf. Lk 3:14), but these ones can only be Samaritans.

The question about purity is significant because we have reason to believe that John's "baptism" was a one-time, definitive cleansing, without daily repetition. With his baptism, John can be linked to the Essenes, as has long been proposed; he keeps his distance from the Temple, and his proclamation is based on the prophecy of Isa. 40:3 ("Voice cries out: 'In the wilderness'"), which is found in the *Rule of Community*.[90] There is, however, a major difference, highlighted by Josephus in his notes. For John "exhorted the Jews to practice righteousness toward one another and piety toward God, so that they might join in baptism. Thus, baptism would only be pleasing to him if it were not used for the forgiveness of certain sins, but for the cleansing of the body, after the soul had been thoroughly purified by righteousness" (*Ant.* 18:116-119). Therefore, baptism seals a journey.

---

[88] There was also the Dositheus movement, more or less related to Simon the Magician, according to Ps.-Clement, *Hom.* 2.23-24; *Rec.* 2.8-11, cf. Stanley J. Isser, *The Dositheans: A Samaritan Sect in Late Antiquity*, Leiden, Brill, 1976, pp. 22–6; Paul Carbonaro, "Les Samaritains et la naissance du Pentateuque," *RB* 120 (2013), pp. 42–71. Origen, *C. Cels.* 6.2, states that after Jesus Dositheus wanted to persuade the Samaritans that he was the Messiah announced by Moses; in 1.47 he mentioned him with John the Baptist, Theudas, and Judas the Galilean (cf. Acts 5:36-37), that is, with those whom the Jews wrongly believed to be the Messiah (Christ). As for Nathanael, the disciple of Jesus, his name is merely a Hebrew form of Dositheus. According to Jn 21:2, he was from Cana, but his characterization is remarkable: when Philip invites him (Jn 1:45), he speaks of Jesus with a clear allusion to the new Moses of Deut. 18:18; then on seeing him, Jesus says: "Here truly (ἀληθῶς) is an Israelite *(hapax)* in whom there is no guile," as if there had been some doubt as to his identity (neither Jew nor Gentile). One may wonder if there is not a discreet reference to Dositheus, duly transformed: the context places the scene in Galilee, but on the one hand, Philip's presentation of Jesus as "son of Joseph" (cf. Josh. 24:32: Joseph's bones in Shechem) and, on the other hand, Jesus' allusion to the dream of Jacob-Israel (Jn 1:51; cf. Gen. 28:10-17) discreetly suggest Samaritan ties, all the more so because Jacob was cunning.
[89] The name has an Aramaic form (עיינן "sources"); cf. Jerome Murphy-O'Connor, "Place-Names in the Fourth Gospel. I, Aenon near Salem (Jn 3,23)," *RB* 119 (2012), pp. 564–84.
[90] *1QS* 8:14.

In contrast, the Essenes' initiation process is more elaborate (*W* 2:137-140) and extends over several years: first, one year outside the community, but following the same kind of life; then, the candidate is partially integrated for two years, but he is not yet admitted to the common meal; more precisely, the *Rule* specifies, he is first admitted to dry foods, which are not susceptible to impurity, according to the biblical precept (cf. Lev. 11:38). If the test is conclusive, he is admitted to the moist foods, and he then commits himself by "dreadful oaths"; and the *Rule* specifies that it is a question of entering the Covenant by a return to the law of Moses.[91] The rule of life then imposes daily purifications.[92]

Thus, Jesus' indifference to questions of purity is not a personal fantasy: it results from his attachment to John's baptism. This is evident in various circumstances, and especially in the encounter with the Samaritan woman, where he shows no reservations. Jesus astonished her by approaching her and then speaking to her about her husbands; she thinks that he is a prophet (Jn 4:19). She considers Jacob as her ancestor, with the sign of a collective good represented by a well. This reference to Jacob, who was renamed Israel, indicates that the Samaritans have been introduced into the Israelite perimeter; the question of foreign settlers has entirely disappeared (cf. Section 2.1).

Next, Jesus speaks to her about knowledge: the Samaritans do not know what they worship, "but we worship what we know, for salvation is from the Jews." The Samaritan woman does not protest[93] and answers on the same theme of knowledge (v. 25): "I know that Messiah is coming [. . .] When he comes, he will proclaim all things to us." Obviously, the title Messiah is Jewish, since it relates to the hoped-for posterity of David[94] (cf. Dan. 9:25), whereas the Samaritans know only the Pentateuch. However, it is not necessary to conclude that the Samaritan woman puts a Jewish meaning under the term "Messiah": she is speaking about revelation, without any clear political connotation, and this is obviously an allusion to the "new Moses" announced in Deut. 18:18: "I will raise up for them a prophet like you[95] [. . .] who shall speak to them everything I command." Responding to the woman, Jesus reveals himself in a characteristic way that recurs elsewhere: "I am he." This is an allusion to the revelation at Mount Horeb (Exod. 3:14) and, so, intelligible to a Samaritan. He is therefore greater than Moses; yet, it is still surprising that he should accept the title of Messiah, even in a Samaritan sense.

As for salvation from the Jews,[96] it fits easily into the context. John's opening statement sets a general perspective (Jn 1:29): "Here is the Lamb of God who takes away the sin of the world." Then, John and Jesus are shown symmetrically baptizing

---

[91] *1QS* 1:16; 5:7-9.
[92] *War* 2:128 and *1QS* 6:7-8.
[93] Cf. Toan Do, "Revisiting the Woman of Samaria and the Ambiguity of Faith in John 4:4-42," *CBQ* 81 (2019), pp. 252–76.
[94] The "anointed priest" is mentioned in Lev. 4:3-16 and 6:15; these are rites to be performed by the high priest, but there is no allusion here to a restoration of the cult.
[95] Later tradition calls him *Taheb*; cf. John Macdonald, *The Theology of the Samaritans*, London, SCM Press, 1964, pp. 352–3.
[96] Rudolf Bultmann, *The Gospel of John: A Commentary*, Philadelphia, Westminster Press, 1971, pp. 189–90, deems that the whole phrase "salvation comes from the Jews" can only be a gloss. Others have followed him, without perceiving the significance of Caiaphas' prophecy in Jn 11:51-52.

Samaritans and Jews, thus pointing to "all Israel"; after this Jesus' renown grows while John's diminishes. There is thus a progression: before being seen as the savior of the world, Jesus must be recognized as the Messiah of all Israel and not just of the Jews. More precisely, Jesus declares (Jn 4:21): "You will worship the Father neither on this mountain (Gerizim) nor in Jerusalem." Jesus' "neither . . . nor" extends John's activity, for his baptism of repentance is a form of rejection of an official sanctuary (Jerusalem or Gerizim) and the rites surrounding repentance, which can be understood by both Samaritans and Jews. In this regard, there is no reason to suppose that some Samaritans could not be choosing to be Essenes, as Qumran manuscripts written in Paleo-Hebrew suggest.[97] Moreover, it is remarkable that Pliny the Elder's small note on an Essene gathering between Qumran and the Dead Sea in no way suggests that they were Jews (*Hist. Nat.* 5.15.73):

> This is a solitary tribe, which is remarkable beyond all the others in the whole world, because it lives without women, lives without sexual relations, without money, and only in the company of palm-trees. Each day their number is renewed by the throngs of newcomers who, weary of life and changing fortune, adopt their manners. Thus, it has been for thousands of centuries—it is incredible to say—an eternal race, in which no one is born. For, the difficulties others experience in their lives are to their advantage!

It should now be noted that the term "salvation," so frequent in the New Testament epistles with a Christian meaning, is atypical in John, no less than the final expression of the Samaritans recognizing Jesus as "savior of the world," even though he is a Jew (Jn 4:42). The title "savior" does not appear elsewhere during Jesus' public life; and, in classical Greek, a "savior" is someone who delivers people from hostile pressure. The possible interpretation oscillates between two poles: on the one hand, the Hellenistic kings attributed to themselves this title, which was later adopted by the emperors;

---

[97] Cf. Patrick W. Skehan, "Exodus in the Samaritan Recension from Qumran," *JBL* 74 (1955), pp. 182–7; other fragments followed, but it became customary to call them pro-Samaritan, without delving deeper into the question, because of the absolute incompatibility that is assumed between every Jew and every Samaritan. Yet, Eusebius, *Praep. euang.* 9.17.13, quotes a passage from Eupolemus according to which Hargarizim can be translated "Mountain of the Most High," which is appropriate for the Samaritan sanctuary; a papyrus fragment collected at Masada has only two identifiable words in Paleo-Hebrew, הנברל "in praise" and םיזירגרה "Mountgerizim" (in one word); cf. R. Pummer, "ΑΡΓΑΡΙΖΙΜ: A Criterion for Samaritan Provenance," *JSJ* 18 (1987), pp. 18–25. However, some have seen in this discovery not a Samaritan document but the trace of a Jewish hymn rejoicing over the destruction of Gerizim, parallel to the *Megilat Taanit* "Day of Gerizim" commemorating the destruction of the sanctuary by John Hyrcan; cf. Hanan Eshel, "The 'Prayer of Joseph' from Qumran, a Papyrus from Masada, and the Samaritan Temple on Mt. Gerizim," in: Shani Tzoref and Barnea Levi Selavan (eds.), *Exploring the Dead Sea Scrolls: Archaeology and Literature of the Qumran Caves*, Göttingen/Bristol, Vandenhoeck & Ruprecht, 2015, pp. 149–63. Furthermore, ancient Christian authors mention Essenes among the Samaritan sects: Hippolytus of Rome, *Refutatio* 9.18.2; Eusebius, *HE* 4.22.7; Epiphanius, *Panarion* 10.5.1; cf. John Bowman, "Contact Between Samaritan Sects and Qumran?" *VT* 7 (1957), pp. 184–9; Josephine Massyngbaerde Ford, "Can We Exclude Samaritan Influence from Qumran?," *RQ* 6/21 (1967), pp. 109–29; Epiphanius incidentally indicates that the Samaritan-Essenians continued following an old calendar, probably that of the Jubilees; cf. Sylvia Powels, *Der Kalender der Samaritaner anhand des Kitab Hisab As-Sinin und anderer Handschriften*, Berlin, Walter de Gruyter, 1977.

on the other hand, the term "savior," seen as a verb ("who saves"), is an attribute of God, with properly Jewish connotations related to the resurrection.[98] This is hardly satisfactory, either for the Samaritans as Israelites or for Jesus himself at this point.

One detail, however, allows us to continue. The exact phrase of the Samaritans is: "This is truly the Savior of the world." This phrase is hardly biblical, but it implies discussion about the identity of such a savior. Likewise, at the time of the upheaval after Jesus' death, a centurion, who knows nothing about the Bible, nevertheless says (Mt. 27:54), "This man was *truly* the God's Son." This represents a change in how the master of the world was considered, for likewise the title is not specifically biblical, since everyone is a son of God (Lk 3:38; Jn 10:34-35). However, for a centurion, subject to the imperial cult, the "son of god" *par excellence* is, first of all, Caesar,[99] just as for Pilate in Jn 19:7-8.

Traditionally, the first five "husbands" of the Samaritan woman are understood as the five pagan nations that the Assyrians sent with their gods to colonize the kingdom of Israel after its fall (2 Kgs 17:24, cf. Section 2.1); the Hebrew word for "husband" also means "idol" (*baal*). The explanation is only partial, for the Samaritan woman still has a "false husband"; but he is not present, which implies at least a distended relationship. By introducing the elements identified earlier, we can situate this Samaritan woman in relation to Helen, Simon's companion: she led a dissolute life, or else she abandoned the Pentateuch, the law of the Israelites. Her sixth "husband" would therefore be Simon. Yet she is reduced to laboriously drawing water; indeed, he is a false husband, and she has not entirely renounced the Israelite tradition, since she awaits the new Moses announced—and accepts him in the person of Jesus. It is also possible to admit that John has reshaped her profile in order to distance himself from a direct polemic, as he does elsewhere. Then, the Samaritans follow him, but in purely pagan terms, which perhaps suggests dissatisfaction or doubts; in any case, Simon would have paganized them.

As for John the Baptist, who was operating in Samaria, his disciples tell him there that everyone is going to Jesus (Jn 3:26). This would simply be a way of countering Simon on his own ground, for Ps.-Clement's assertion that Simon was a direct disciple of John the Baptist remains plausible, though difficult to assert firmly, because we lack evidence. Incidentally, it should be noted that in Jn 8:48, Jesus' opponents suspect him of being a Samaritan and of having a demon, that is, of being a magician. The shadow of Simon is still there.[100] This man obviously had considerable and threatening influence,[101] and it was necessary to affirm without unnecessary polemics that Jesus

---

[98] Cf. Raphael Loewe, "Salvation Is Not of the Jews," *JThS* NS 32 (1981), pp. 341-68.
[99] Who is even "god, son of god" in the case of Augustus; cf. Pliny, *NH* 2.94; Lily R. Taylor, *The Divinity of the Roman Emperor*, Atlanta, Scholars Press, 1931, p. 106.
[100] The only modern commentator who links Simon to Jn is Oscar Cullmann, *The Early Church*, Londres, SCM Press, 1956, pp. 185-92, seeing it as an independent testimony to the success of the "Hellenistic" mission in Samaria.
[101] Josephus, *Ant.* 18:85-86, reports, at the end of the reign of Tiberius (d. 37), the case of a Samaritan movement abusively crushed by Pilate: a man invited all the people to go to Gerizim to see the sacred vessels buried there by Moses. The information is imprecise, and there is little direct connection with Simon at the time of Claudius, but it is possible to imagine that Josephus is referring to one of Simon's predecessors.

was greater. The independent testimonies of Acts and Justin show this, no less than the traditions regarding the posterity of Simon's movement, which was linked to Gnosticism, at least according to his opponents. The story of the Samaritan woman in Jn 4 does not bear direct witness to this, since it fits easily into the Gospel's overall narrative, but it is put into a new light if the silhouettes of Simon and Helen are restored in the background.

After the departure of the Samaritan woman and before the encounter with the Samaritans, Jesus' speech to the disciples, who had returned with provisions, includes significant references (Jn 4:36): "Sower (John) and repear (Jesus) may rejoice together." Earlier, John had been told that Jesus was more successful than he was: "All are going to him." He rejoiced, recalling his position as a precursor (Jn 3:28-29); indeed, his own disciples were the first who followed Jesus (Jn 1:37). They were Jews, and then by baptizing in Aeneas, John "sowed" in Samaria. There is thus a certain symmetry displayed between Jews and Samaritans, and Jesus is going to take up an old question from another angle.

Indeed, he concludes his explanation to the disciples (4:38) by saying: "I sent you to reap that for which you did not labor. Others have labored, and you have entered into their labor." This seems contradictory or beside the point. In fact, it no longer refers to John but rather to a very old story, which has to do with Israel as a whole. In his final speech, precisely at Shechem, Joshua says, among other things, to the Israelites who have conquered the land (Josh. 24:13): "I gave you a land on which you have not labored, and towns that you had not built, etc." Combining the two successive sentences of Jesus, who bears the same name as Joshua, there is thus some hint of common rejoicing of the Israelites (represented by the Twelve) and the nations (Canaan), with the Samaritans forming a kind of intermediate link.

1.4 Conclusion

At the beginning of our era, the Samaritans represented a considerable reality, which was neither Jewish nor pagan; and their existence had a variable and often embarrassing significance. Around 95, twenty-five years after the war of 70 that he considered over, Josephus was astonished that there were Christian descendants. He foresaw a brilliant development of Judaism under the Roman umbrella, but he knew nothing of the rabbinic enterprise, which was still very marginal.[102] In his writings, he makes notable efforts to dismiss the Samaritans as parasites but without success.[103]

---

[102] A legitimate succession of the Jerusalem Sanhedrin emigrated to Galilee is confirmed in *b.Rosh ha-Shana* 31a-b; cf. Hugo D. Mantel, *Studies in the History of the Sanhedrin*, Cambridge, MA, Harvard University Press, 1965, pp. 54–101. On the difficulty of establishing the continuity of the Jerusalem authorities with rabbinic Judaism, cf. Moshe David Herr, "The Identity of the People of Israel during Second Temple Times and after Its Destruction: Continuity or Change?" *Cathedra* 137 (2010), pp. 27–62, who notes the absence of external (nonrabbinic) evidence of this movement in the second century.

[103] Cf. Matthew J. Chalmers, "Viewing Samaritains Jewishly: Josephus, the Samaritans, and the Identification of Israel," *JSJ* 51 (2020), pp. 339–66.

The Samaritan documentation is very modest, and the main writings preserved are medieval. In the absence of more precise information, one is obliged to assume that there was never a notable doctrinal evolution. Now, this is not true of Judaism, whose progression can be better followed. As far as the Bible is concerned, the Pentateuch, common to all, remained fairly stable; however, with regard to historical books that follow, Josephus' paraphrase shows that the Hebrew texts were not yet stabilized. This is the case especially for Joshua, Ezra, and Nehemiah, books which have an impact on the relations between Jews and Samaritans and, at the same time, make it possible for us to follow the evolution of Judaism. The case of 1 Maccabees is particularly interesting. The Hebrew original of the book was related to the source of Josephus' parallel account, but apart from notable differences, there is a very significant change: 1 Maccabees introduces biblical allusions which are entirely absent from Josephus' paraphrase.

This fact must be brought together with another, that is, the meaning of the expansion policy of the Hasmoneans: at the beginning, Judas Maccabees' Judea was very small, extending only from Jericho to Emmaus and from Bethel to Bethsoura (Figure 12, Section 3.4), and it had no interaction with Samaria; then, Jonathan, Simon, John Hyrcanus, and Alexander Jannaeus developed a policy of conquering the neighboring territories, aiming especially to absorb Samaria and to destroy the Gerizim temple. Thus, Judea became very large, comparable to the domain of the twelve tribes at the time of Moses and Joshua, on both sides of the Jordan; after various events, this ensemble became the heroic Judea. However, there was never any question of reconquering the Promised Land or reconstituting the ancient kingdom of Israel. The essential aim was more concrete: an enlarged territory provided more resources. This means that the Hasmonean regime had no clear biblical reference, despite the efforts of Alexander Jannaeus, son of John Hyrcanus, to get closer to the Sadducees, the champions of Scripture. It will be shown later that this regime had a Pharisaic-Babylonian origin and that it gradually acclimatized Scripture. In the Roman Empire, the majority of the Jews were Pharisees; and it is characteristic that Josephus, who wanted to be a Pharisee and was concerned for his people, took the trouble in his time to make a biblical paraphrase for the use of his coreligionists.

We can note in passing that there is no trace of a comparable political project on the Samaritan side. David and Solomon are entirely ignored or, more exactly, reprobated as dissidents. On a broader level, Deut. 17:14-20 expresses the greatest distrust of kingship.

2

The Royal Period

The harvest will be rather meager as far as the Samaritans are concerned. This is a paradox, because the Pentateuch clearly highlights the importance of Shechem since Abraham but does not mention Jerusalem.[1] The North should remain predominant. Yet, the Hebrew Bible contains only two allusions to the Samaritans: the first is a kind of foundation story, set at the time of the fall of the kingdom of Israel in 721 BCE; this is the subject of the present chapter. The second is a refusal of the Jewish returnees from exile to mix with them, which will be examined later with the books of Ezra and Nehemiah (Section 4.2.4).

2.1 Foreign Colonists?

The first step is to consider the account of the fall, in 721 BCE, of Samaria, the capital of the dissident kingdom of Israel, and its consequences: the Assyrians deported the population and replaced it with colonizers. This is the remote origin of the Samaritans according to 2 Kings 17, while the southern kingdom of Judah, around Jerusalem, lasted for over a century, until its destruction by Nebuchadnezzar in 587 BCE[2] and the exile of a large part of the population to Babylonia.

After Solomon's death, his kingdom was divided into two parts, with an unequal distribution of the tribes: in the South, Judah, sometimes increased by Benjamin, with Jerusalem as its permanent capital, and a royal dynasty descending founded by David and Solomon; in the North, Israel, formed by the other ten tribes, with various capitals and a succession of dynasties that began with Jeroboam, an officer of Solomon who had revolted. A phase of consolidation of the North as a kingdom is linked to King Omri (885–874), who is executed in a few sentences as a bad subject, although he was

---

[1] This observation is the basis of a useful inquiry; cf. Jean-Louis Ska, "Why Does the Pentateuch Speak so Much of Torah and so Little of Jerusalem?" in: Peter Dubovský, Dominik Markl, and Jean-Pierre Sonnet (eds.), *The Fall of Jerusalem and the Rise of the Torah*, Tübingen, Mohr-Siebeck, 2016, pp. 113–28.
[2] Or 586 BCE, cf. the conclusion of the detailed examination of Gershon Galil, "The Babylonian Calendar and the Chronology of the Last Kings of Judah," *Biblica* 72 (1991), pp. 367–78. On the contrary, 587 BCE is maintained by Henri Cazelles, "587 ou 586?" in: Carol L. Meyers et al. (eds.), *The Word of the Lord Shall Go Forth*, Winona Lake, Eisenbrauns, 1983, pp. 427–35.

recognized abroad:[3] we only learn that he bought a hill from a man named Shemer and there established a new capital that he called Samaria[4] inspired by this name (Shomeron, 1 Kgs 16:23-26). He thus founded a dynasty. Later, after some turbulent episodes, the king of Assyria invaded the country and besieged Samaria for three years. Having taken the city, he deported the Israelites to Mesopotamia in 721 BCE. This is the account in 2 Kgs 17:3-6 that calls the king Salmanasar, probably by mistake, instead of Sargon II, his brother and successor[5] (721–05).

Then, 2 Kgs 17:24-41 tells about the arrival and settlement of colonizers sent by Assyria's king;[6] they came from five regions: Babylon, Cuthah, Avva, Hamath, and Sepharvaim. They did not revere YHWH, the land's deity, and he sent lions against them that slaughtered them. Alerted, the king of Assyria sent one of the deported priests to instruct them; he settled in Bethel and apparently calmed the crisis. However, these colonizers did not abandon their former gods, which they reestablished in their place: they then practiced a hybrid cult "to this day," mixing YHWH with their original cults (vv. 29-34a), though without suffering punishment. Thus, the Samaritans' disgrace was twofold: they were heirs to the breakaway kingdom and guilty of polytheism.

This is the account in the MT, but there is a serious textual difficulty with the syncretism of these newcomers, for the next paragraph (vv. 34b-40) presents a very different view depending on whether one follows the Hebrew or the Greek (Figure 8):

According to the MT, the colonizers became entirely unfaithful to the commands given to the sons of Jacob, without arousing the animosity of the lions, whereas for the LXX, they are declared faithful to the point that one wonders whether the texts are really talking about the colonizers or rather about a remnant of the ancient Israelites of

---

[3] Cf. Ernst A. Knauf, "Was Omride Israel a Sovereign State?" in: Lester L. Grabbe, *Ahab Agonistes*, London, T&T Clark, 2007, pp. 100–3; Baruch Halpern, "Archaeology, the Bible and History: The Fall of the House of Omri, and the Origins of the Israelite State," in: Thomas E. Levy (ed.), *Historical Biblical Archaeology and the Future: The New Pragmatism*, London/Oakville, Equinox, 2010, pp. 262–84; Omer Sergi, "The Omride Dynasty and the Reshaping of the Judahite Historical Memory," *Biblica* 97 (2016), pp. 503–26.

[4] Then, the same name as in 1 Kgs 13:32 is given to the region, in anticipation of the land of the deportees. To avoid confusion, the inhabitants of the city and sometimes of the region are called "Samarians," whereas the term "Samaritans" is reserved for the followers of the Yahwism centered on Mount Gerizim. Regardless of the name Shemeer, the underlying Hebrew root means "to guard, guardians."

[5] The presentation of the facts is complex, and according to the literary analysis of Ernst Würthwein, *Die Bücher der Könige (1. Kön. 17-2. Kön. 25)* (Das Alte Testament Deutsch, 11/2), Göttingen, Vandenhoeck & Ruprecht, 1984, p. 394, there are two parallel relationships, one (vv. 1-4) centered on Hoshea and the other (vv. 5-6) on Samaria, the imprisonment of the king corresponding to the siege of the city; for Mordechai Cogan and Hayim Tadmor, *II Kings* (Anchor Bible, 11), New York, Doubleday, 1988, pp. 195, 216, the two notices ignore each other, because, according to their interpretation of the Assyrian chronicles, the siege of Samaria began at the end of the reign of Hosea; also cf. Timo Tekoniemi, "Between Two Differing Editions: Some Notable Text-Critical Variants in 2 Kings 17," in: Shuichi Hasegawa, Christoph Levin, and Karen Radner (eds.), *The Last Days of the Kingdom of Israel*, Berlin/Boston, De Gruyter, 2019, pp. 211–27; in the same book, Christian Frevel, "Wicked Usurpers and the Doom of Samaria: Further Views on the Angle of 2 Kings 15–17," pp. 303–34, concludes that these complicated chapters are not from the archives of Israel (or Samaria), but that they were more or less invented according to Jewish prejudices.

[6] In fact, he is not named, and for Ezra 4:2 it would be Essar-haddon (680–69), son of Sennacherib, that is, well after Sargon; cf. Section 4.2.1.

The Royal Period 51

MT	LXX
	17:34 To this day they continue
The practice of *their former customs*.	The practice of *their customs*.
They *do not* fear the LORD	They fear
And they *do not follow* their statutes	And they *follow* their statutes[a]
and the rites, the laws, and the commandments that the LORD commanded to the sons of Jacob, whom he named Israel. 17:35 The LORD made a covenant with them and commanded them, You shall not fear other gods or bow yourselves to them, [. . .] 17:36 You shall fear only the LORD who brought you out of the land of Egypt [. . .] you shall bow yourselves to him and to him you shall sacrifice.	
17:40 *They would* not *listen*, but *they continued* to practice their *former* custom.	And *you shall* not *listen* *to what concerns* the custom they practice.

[a] The Greek Lucian version is largely consistent with the MT; cf. Natalio Fernández Marcos et al., *El Texto Antioqueno de la Biblia Griega. 1-2 Reyes*, Madrid, Instituto de Filología del Consejo Superior de Investigaciones Científicas, 1992, a. l.

Figure 8 Colonists' loyalty or infidelity?

the northern kingdom. Both cases are difficult because they presuppose an exclusive fidelity to YHWH, which can be attributed neither to the colonizers nor to the ancient Israelites, since they are heirs of Jeroboam's dissidence.

The foundation of the required conduct toward YHWH is given by a double narrative: the commandments he gave to Jacob renamed Israel and a departure from Egypt without Moses. The whole can be unified, but there are apparently two quite distinct components: on the one hand, the local heirs of Jacob, with their customs that recall the Samaritan woman of Jn 4 (cf. Section 1.3.2) and on the other hand, immigrants from Egypt. It is implicitly a question of all the tribes; in the same way, on mount Carmel, Elijah had built an altar with twelve stones, according to the number of the tribes of the sons of Jacob-Israel (1 Kgs 18:31). In the present context, this means that Judah is a negligible quantity or dissident. Thus, it is understandable that in the matter of the lions there was a desire to recover the local traditions of the North (Israel) for the worship of YHWH, without addressing Jerusalem.

Josephus' paraphrase, based on biblical scrolls collected in the Temple archives by Titus, will provide a solution, because it provides a context for the dissident version of the LXX. In terms of secondary details, we observe that, with regard to the crisis threatening the newcomers, he speaks of a plague and not of lions, and he indicates that several priests—and not just one—had been dismissed since the captivity. Above all, he avoids making YHWH a purely local deity and prefers to speak of God Most High. However, it is improbable that he thus bears witness to real variants, especially since he is in the habit of reducing marvelous facts to a minimum.

The passage of the LXX in italics corresponds to the syncretism displayed in the MT, and it includes an anomaly, for the term "Samaritans" refers not to the colons but to the dissident Israelites who were deported but has, at best, a purely geographical meaning ("Samaritans"). This suggests that vv. 29-33 are an awkward addition, unknown to Josephus. He would certainly have denounced the idolatry of the Samaritans if

Antiquities 9	2 Kings 17 LXX
(290) And having been instructed in the precepts and religion of this God, they revered him with great zeal, and were at once delivered from the plague.	²⁸ (The priest) taught them how they should fear the LORD.
	²⁹⁻³³ *And every nation still made gods of its own and put them in the shrines of the high places that the people of Samaria*ᵃ *had made [. . .] So they worshiped the Lord but also served their own gods, after the manner of the nations from among whom they had been carried away.*
The same rites have remained in use to this day, among those who are called Kuthim in Hebrew and Samaritans in Greek.	³⁴ To this day they continue to practice their former customs. They fear the LORD [. . .],
(291) When they see the Jews prosper, they call them their parents as descendants of Joseph,	³⁵⁻³⁹ (the customs) that the LORD had commanded them the children of Jacob, whom he named Israel, and with whom he made a covenant, saying, "You shall not fear other gods [. . .]
	⁴⁰ And you will not listen to their custom, according to which they act."
but when they see the Jews in distress, they declare that they are foreigners, of another race.	

ᵃ This is the only biblical use of the term שמרנים "Samaritans," but the meaning is purely geographical, since it concerns the Israelites of the North.

Figure 9 Conversion of settlers?

he could have done so,⁷ for he has nothing but contempt for them; however, here as elsewhere, he is content to reproach them for their versatility or opportunism.

As for assessing the quality of these different witnesses, it must first be observed that at no time has any trace of a Samaritan cult, other than the biblical monotheism, ever been found. The rabbis developed Josephus' opinion of the Samaritans,⁸ but some divergent traditions attract attention. For example, in the middle of the second century, the ethnarch Simon son of Gamaliel II declares, in connection with a discussion on unleavened bread (*t. Pesahim* 1.15): "For all the commandments which the Samaritans observe, they are more meticulous than Israel," that is to say, "than the Jews." Clearly, he appreciates their *biblical* accuracy, whereas rabbinic Judaism is largely based on

---

7   The anti-Samaritan prejudice is such that some think that Josephus could not have written § 290; cf. for example, Rita Egger, *Josephus Flavius und die Samaritaner. Eine terminologische Untersuchung zur Identitätsklärung der Samaritaner*, Freiburg (CH), Universitätsverlag, 1986, pp. 48–50.
8   Typically in the small Talmudic treatise *Kuthim* ("Samaritans"), where we read that they are excluded from the assembly of Israel (cf. Deut. 23), because they mixed with the priests of the high places; R. Ishmael says that they were originally sincere converts (גרי צדק) and then degraded themselves by not observing the levirate (*Kuthim* 2:7). The initial sincerity (not just fear of lions) is analogous to Josephus' version.

an oral "Torah" of Mosaic authority but poorly related to Scripture.⁹ According to *b. Sanhedrin* 21b, Israel first received the Torah in Hebrew script, then in the time of Ezra, who came from Mesopotamia, it was given in Aramaic writing, but the ancient script was preserved by the inhabitants of Neapolis¹⁰ (Nablus), which remained the capital of the Samaritans, at the foot of Mount Gerizim.¹¹ It is, therefore, accepted that they had received the written Torah before the reforms of Ezra and Nehemiah, which correspond to the beginning of Judaism as such.¹²

In these circumstances, the MT version regarding the colonizers would have the status of a *lectio difficilior* to be preferred, but it would follow that the LXX is absurd, since it asserts first polytheism and then monotheism, and this leads to a *lectio difficillima*, without any real profit. It is more natural to see in the LXX a trace of the version partially harmonized with the MT and attested by Josephus that develops an anti-Samaritan polemic.¹³

It is also noteworthy that Moses' name does not appear in the account of the fall of Samaria and its consequences, contrary to what we read in 2 Kgs 18:9-12, which presents another version of the deportation: the catastrophe that took place in the sixth year of Hezekiah, king of Judah, is attributed to the transgression by Israel's inhabitants of "all that Moses the servant of the LORD had commanded."¹⁴ This parallel version does not mention the colonizers so that the origin of the Samaritans is erased, unless it is assumed that the deportation was not total and a remainder survived the fall of the kingdom of Israel; this could be similar to 2 Kgs 17:34-40 in the LXX, quoted earlier. Another possibility is that the colonizers were sent later, under Essar-haddon (cf. Section 4.2.1).

It also appears that YHWH is a strictly local deity, and even specifically attached to the kingdom of Israel, since at the time of the event of the lions no competent priest was sent to Jerusalem. One could argue that Judah's religion was then different from

---

⁹ According to *m.Abot* 1:1, Moses received it from Sinai, and a set of texts has been preserved, the Midreshé Halakha, which propose to put these ancestral traditions in the form of juxtaposed scriptural commentaries, not without developing rules of interpretation that are sometimes very subtle.

¹⁰ Or *Colonia Flavia Neapolis*, created by Vespasian in 73 near the ancient Shechem; cf. *War* 4:449 and Schürer-Vermes 1:520.

¹¹ This is the Hebrew or Paleo-Hebrew script (כתב עברי) from which the Samaritan alphabet derives, whereas the Jews have retained to this day the square Aramaic alphabet, said to be Assyrian (כתב אשורי). In fact, some coins prove that the use of Paleo-Hebrew continued under the Hasmoneans, and it is found in some Qumran fragments; cf. Schürer-Vermes 1:603-606.

¹² For an overview of Samaritan customs as seen by the ancient rabbis, cf. Lawrence H. Schiffman, "The Samaritans in Tannaitic Halakhah," *JQR* 75 (1985), pp. 323–50.

¹³ Cf. Jean-Daniel Macchi, "Les controverses théologiques dans le judaïsme de l'époque postexilique: L'exemple de 2 Rois 17,24-41," *Transeuphratène* 5 (1992), pp. 85–93; Magnar Kartveit, "Anti-Samaritan Polemics in the Hebrew Bible? The Case of 2 Kings 17:24–41," in: Jan Dušek (ed.), *The Samaritans in Historical, Cultural and Linguistic Perspectives*, Berlin/Boston, De Gruyter, 2018, pp. 3–18.

¹⁴ No consensus emerged from the discussions regarding the relative anteriority of the two narratives; cf. the review of Jean-Daniel Macchi, *Les Samaritains. Histoire d'une légende: Israël et la province de Samarie* (Le Monde de la Bible, 30), Genève, Labor et Fides, 1994, pp. 47–72; the absence of Moses in the first account is, however, a clear indication, since in the North Kingdom accounts after Solomon, the name of Moses is never mentioned, which suggests that the version of 2 Kings 18 is secondary.

that of Israel. Yet in 2 Kgs 17:7-23, before the colonizers were sent, we read a reflection, written in Deuteronomic style, on the ruin of the kingdom of Israel: in spite of the repeated injunctions of the prophets in Israel and Judah, the Israelites had adopted the cults of the nations of Canaan that Joshua had driven out; they had multiplied the high places in the land; they had made two golden calves; they had worshipped Baal and had practiced magic. In a kind of anticipation of the future fall of Jerusalem, it is even said that "Judah [. . .] walked in the customs that Israel had introduced" (v. 19).

As for the point of arrival of the deported priest, it is called "Bethel," and, quite surprisingly, he was not sent to Shechem, the old capital, or Samaria, the new one. Now, let us first observe that the meaning of the name Samaria, which designated the royal city at the time of the deportation, had changed and henceforth designates a whole region, with cities and high places; secondly, within this whole, there is a very clear distinction between Bethel, where a priest of YHWH, heir to the traditions of the North, has returned, and the clergy of the foreign cults in the high places. This distinction is found again at the time when Josiah's reform was extended to the North: according to 2 Kgs 23:15 and 19, he dealt first with "the altar at Bethel" and then with "the shrines of the high places that were in the towns of Samaria."

In the context of the royal era, Bethel appears to be a preexisting city, for at the time of Jeroboam's secession, Jeroboam made two golden calves, one in Dan and the other in Bethel (1 Kgs 12:29), after having declared to the people, as Aaron did in the desert (Exod. 32:4): "Here are your gods, O Israel, who brought you up out of the land of Egypt." The tribe of Dan, at first close to the Philistines near the coast, had emigrated to the North and had given its name to the ancient city of Laish, at the sources of the Jordan River, to make it a capital (Judg. 18:29). As for Bethel, it has been mentioned since Abraham's arrival in Canaan: having moved away from Shechem, he "pitched his tent, with Bethel on the west and Ai on the east" (Gen. 12:8). These two sites, which are found again at the time of Joshua's capture of Ai (Joshua 7–8), are in Benjamin (Josh. 18:22) and, so, quite close to Jerusalem.[15]

Dan and Bethel thus represent the whole extension of the kingdom of Israel, with a boundary marker at each end, by analogy with the earlier expression "from Dan to Beersheba," which appears ten times and in 1 Kgs 5:5 characterizes the peace established by Solomon throughout his kingdom. However, in the history of the northern kingdom, Dan will no longer play a role, while Bethel will remain, from Jeroboam to Josiah, the symbol of the dissident cult. It is, therefore, indeed surprising that this place should be so peripheral, especially since according to Amos 7:13 the priest Amaziah wanted to drive the prophet Amos out of Bethel, "for it is the king's sanctuary, and it is a temple of the kingdom." There would be no better way to say that it was the capital.[16]

---

[15] Bethel is identified with Beitîn, a small village that Eusebius, *Onomast.*, p. 4, situates near the twelfth milestone between Ælia (Jerusalem) and Neapolis (Nablus). Local excavations have shown that this is the only site in the region with significant Middle and Late Bronze Age occupation, ending with a layer of destruction around 1250 BCE, but nothing in the Iron Age; cf. James L. Kelso et al., *The Excavations at Bethel (1934–1960)* (AASOR, 39), Boston, American Schools, 1968.

[16] Cf. William Ross, "Is Beitin the Bethel of Jeroboam?" *PEQ* 73 (1941), pp. 22–7.

Now, we must note that in Hebrew Bethel or "house of El (god)" can designate any sanctuary. It is therefore not really a proper name. Long after Abraham, Jacob, who was fleeing from his brother Esau, had a dream while sleeping on a stone and when he woke up he said (Gen. 28:17): "How awesome is this place! This is none other than a house of God, and this is the gate of heaven." Then he put up the stone like a pillar and called the place Bethel.[17] Verse 19 adds that the city was previously called Luz; there is a superimposition of two realities, for Jacob's stone was in the wilderness, not in the city. Exiled to Laban's house, Jacob had a vision of the "God of Bethel" who told him to go back (Gen. 31:13).

When he returned, he came to Shechem, but his sons Simeon and Levi slaughtered the inhabitants after raping their sister Dinah. God then told him to go up to Bethel and settle there, and he came to Luz and built an altar there, calling the place El-bethel (35:1-7); this must be Mount Gerizim. Eusebius of Caesarea distinguishes Luz, the first name of Bethel (Gen. 28:19), from Luz, a substitute for Bethel "in the land of the Hittites" (Judg. 1:26). He places the latter "near Shechem, nine miles from Neapolis,"[18] and he indicates that the ruins on the summit of Mount Gerizim are still called Luza. This is not an isolated duplication: thus, according to Deut. 11:30, Gilgal is close to Shechem and the oak of Moreh in Gen. 12:6, and in Josh. 4:19, close to Jericho as well;[19] in fact, the term can designate any circular masoned or erected structure of stones.

In short, the confusion surrounding Bethel, as a stele or as a city, leads to the conclusion that the priest who came to teach the cult of YHWH came to the sanctuary on Mount Gerizim. Finally, the Assyrian chronicles of Sargon II, compiled in the palace of his capital Khorsabad (before Nineveh), provide a context for the fall of Samaria.[20] First, they indicate only a partial deportation: "I besieged and occupied the city of Samaria and led 27,280 of its inhabitants into captivity. I took 50 chariots from them but left them the rest of their belongings."[21] These documents indicate that when Sargon had conquered a region, he deported part of the population and sent colonizers to establish the local administration. There is no mention of such a dispatch for Samaria, but the bilateral account is ambiguous, because it is split, and the second version ignores the colonizers. We can only say that the deportation was not total and that an Israelite population remained: this would be the primitive core group of the Samaritans.[22]

---

[17] The first expression is בית אלהים and the second בית אל, which is hardly more specific. According to Exod. 23:24 and Lev. 26:1 steles are forbidden (*bétyles*).
[18] *Onomast.*, p. 120; Jerome's translation puts only three miles.
[19] And Jerome, *Onomast.*, p. 67 (on Deut. 11:30), indicates *aliam Galgalam* in his translation.
[20] Cf. Josette Elayi, *Sargon II, King of Assyria*, Atlanta, SBL Press, 2017.
[21] Cf. Jamie Novotny, "Contextualizing the Last Days of the Kingdom of Israel: What Can Assyrian Official Inscriptions Tell Us?," in: Hasegawa, Levin, and Radner, *The Last Days of the Kingdom of Israel*, pp. 35–53. There is uncertainty about "Samaria," which may have referred to either the city or the entire region.
[22] Cf. Macchi, *Les Samaritains*.

2.2 Two Kingdoms?

Judah and Israel are thus united in the same reprobation, and it is no longer clear what was to be a true cult to YHWH, in the North or in the South. We must, therefore, go back to the end of the supposedly unified kingdom, that is, to Solomon's succession. The most remarkable thing is that his son Rehoboam had come to Shechem to be proclaimed king (1 Kgs 12:1), as if Solomon's grandiose works in Jerusalem had become insignificant as soon as he disappeared. Rehoboam, ill-advised, planned a tougher policy than his father, and the people seceded, apart from Judah (12:19): "So Israel has been in rebellion against the house of David to this day." Consequently, the name "Israel" is immediately separated from David's descendants.

Then, when the people found out that Jeroboam had come back from exile,[23] they made him "king over all Israel." Solomon had put this Jeroboam, an Ephraimite, in charge of all the "forced labor of the house of Joseph," that is, over the contribution to the great works imposed on the tribes of Ephraim and Manasseh, which represented a territory similar to the future Samaria. According to 1 Kgs 11:27-39, Jeroboam had rebelled, but we do not know how because nothing is said about that. It is only said that a prophecy of a certain Ahijah of Shiloh, an important shrine[24] of Ephraim, told him that he would become king over ten tribes. Then, Jeroboam had to flee to Egypt to escape Solomon, but he returned after his death and was called to Shechem. The narrative is not very clear, but putting all these elements together, we can assume that Jeroboam's revolt was an uprising of the "house of Joseph" because of the severity of the forced labor or perhaps also because the dynasty of David's descendants was poorly accepted. In other words, the situation was ripe for him to take power in Shechem and for Rehoboam to be rejected, despite his brutal character.[25]

The rupture was eminently political, and Rehoboam was tempted to reconquer the dissident tribes by force. Jeroboam strengthened Shechem, his capital, and then wanted to consolidate the religious rupture, of which three aspects are presented (1 Kgs 12:28-32). First, he made the two golden calves mentioned earlier. Then, he established shrines with priests taken from the tribe of Levi.[26] Finally, in order to distance himself from the Jerusalem calendar, he instituted a feast on the fifteenth day of the eighth

---

[23] The account of Jeroboam's arrival in Shechem is confused, but Rehoboam was certainly there before him; cf. Adrian Schenker, "Jéroboam et la division du royaume dans la Septante ancienne: LXX 1 R 12,24 a-z, MT 11-12; 14 et l'histoire deutéronomiste," in: Albert de Pury (dir.), *Israël construit son histoire*, Genève, Labor et Fides, 1996, pp. 193–236.

[24] According to Josh. 18:1-2, Joshua set up the Tent of Meeting at Shiloh (Exod. 33:7-8), probably after camping at Gilgal, and there he divided up the seven remaining tribes and, according to the LXX, gave his last speech, Josh. 24:1 (the MT puts "Shechem"). At the time of the Judges, this is where the Ark was, 1 Sam. 1:3; 4:3-4. This sanctuary only disappeared at the time of the deportation of Teglat-Phalassar in 734 BCE; cf. Judg. 18:30; 2 Kgs 15:29.

[25] The situation was perhaps more complex, for 1 Kgs 9:20-21 explains that in order to carry out his great works, Solomon imposed servile duties on the remaining descendants of the seven nations of Canaan, which Joshua and the Israelites should have wiped out (Deut. 7:1; Josh. 3:10).

[26] Yet, of the forty-eight Levitical cities established by Joshua according to Josh. 21:41, most were in the northern kingdom, and this suggests that these Levites were anxious to remain faithful to Jerusalem, as 2 Chron. 11:14-15 expressly indicates (but the Chronist is not very objective, cf. later in the text).

month, that is, one month after the Feast of Tabernacles in the seventh month. This deviation is illogical, since the feasts are not mutually exclusive,[27] and Josephus corrects it by putting the seventh month (*Ant.* 8:230). Curiously, it is not explicitly said that Jeroboam, with all these initiatives, deviated from the law of Moses, unlike the behavior of which the kingdom of Israel is accused in the second account of the fall of Samaria (2 Kgs 18:9-11 quoted earlier).

Jerusalem's inferior position must be emphasized, for David had operated in strength: ancient Jebus was the capital he had created, outside the tribes (but very close to Benjamin, 1 Chron. 8:28). After having conquered it, he decided to build a royal palace there, but it was Hiram, king of the powerful city of Tyre, who sent cedar wood and the construction workers. When this Phoenician operation was completed, David drew a remarkable conclusion (2 Sam. 5:12): "David then perceived that the LORD had established him king over Israel." Later, after David's death, we learn that the same Hiram of Tyre sent servants to Jerusalem to anoint his son Solomon as king in his place (1 Kgs 5:15 LXX). Yet, Solomon had already been formally anointed (1:39), and various episodes indicate that, after a few years, his kingship had become well established (2:46). In other words, the rather late intervention of Hiram is an aberration, or more precisely it is the trace of another largely censored account,[28] according to which the king of Jerusalem was a simple Phoenician vassal[29]—or Canaanite vassal, since the two terms are equivalent. Then, Hiram provides materials for the construction of Solomon's temple and palace, and the dates are indicated according to the Phoenician calendar[30] (1 Kgs 6:37-38).

In addition to this Phoenician link, the origins of David and his descendants are worth noting. David himself was a descendant of Ruth the Moabite[31] (Ruth 4:17), and when he was pursued by Saul, he had the opportunity to put his parents under the protection of the king of Moab (1 Sam. 22:3-4). As for his son Solomon, he was born of Bathsheba, "daughter of Eliam, the wife of Uriah the Hittite" (2 Sam. 11:3). Eliam, son of Ahithophel of Gilo, is found among David's valiant men (2 Sam. 23:34); this Ahithophel was also one of David's counselors who joined the revolt of Absalom (2 Sam. 15:12-13). Uriah himself has a Yahwist name ("YHWH is my light"), but his

---

[27] In fact, the construction of the Temple was completed in the eighth month (cf. 1 Kgs 6:38), and then it was merged with the Feast of Tabernacles in the seventh month (cf. 8:2).

[28] Cf. the archaeological reflections of Israel Finkelstein and Neil A. Silberman, *Les rois sacrés de la Bible: à la recherche de David et Salomon*, Paris, Bayard, 2006 (Eng. Original, 2001).

[29] Subsequently, 1 Kgs 9:11-14 indicates that in addition to the delivery of building materials Hiram sent Solomon gold "as much as he wanted." Then Solomon offered him twenty cities in Galilee, but Hiram was not satisfied; yet he still sent large sums of gold. This incoherent account is explained by a supplement in the records of Tyre, quoted by Josephus (*Ant.* 8:141-142; *CAp* 1:106-107) and Eusebius (*Praep. evang.* 9.33): Hiram and Solomon exchanged riddles by correspondence, and the loser had to serve a fine. Solomon won, until a certain Abdemon of Tyre solved the riddles for Hiram, who then won—and looked down on the offers of Solomon, who had no more gold; cf. Nadav Na'aman, "Hiram of Tyre in the Book of Kings and the Tyrian Records," *JNES* 78 (2019), pp. 75–85.

[30] Cf. Étienne Nodet, "On the Biblical 'Hidden' Calendar," *ZAW* 124 (2012), pp. 583–97.

[31] And according to Ruth 4:18 Boaz, David's ancestor, was a descendant of Judah and Tamar (cf. Gen. 38:29), but this ending is secondary; in any case, it is ignored by Josephus, who describes David as a simple shepherd of common origin (*Ant.* 7:95).

Hittite status in principle places him among the heirs of the seven nations of Canaan[32] (cf. Gen. 10:15). As for Solomon, he reigned forty years (1 Kgs 11:42), and his son Rehoboam succeeded him at the age of forty-one (14:21);[33] so, he was born before David's death, and his mother was Naamah, an Ammonite.[34] Now, according to Deut. 23:4, Moabites and Ammonites, descendants of Lot, were permanently banished from the assembly of Israel, and it is noteworthy that Solomon, in his decline, built shrines in Jerusalem to the gods of Moab and Ammon (1 Kgs 11:7). So. there was reason enough to discredit David and his descendants.

The beginnings of monarchy in Israel are linked to Samuel, who grew up in Shiloh, where Joshua had distributed the land to the tribes and where the Ark of the Covenant had been since that time (cf. Josh. 18:1). Shiloh was not far from Shechem,[35] in the territory of the sons of Joseph, Ephraim, and Manasseh. Joshua, who was himself from Ephraim, had told them to clear the mountains and dispossess the Canaanites. There was therefore no organized conquest of the future Samaria. As for Samuel, according to 1 Sam. 3:20, "All Israel from Dan to Beersheba knew that Samuel was a trustworthy prophet of the Lord"; thus, he is introduced as the father of a politically unified Israel. With regard to the geography of the West Bank, this Israel thus largely coincided with Canaan.

The elders of Israel later came to Samuel to ask for a king "like other nations." He was displeased, but the divine response was to accept, explaining that a king would always be abusive and irresponsible because he would not be controlled by any law[36] (1 Sam. 8:1-18). Saul is then appointed and crowned king in three different ways,[37] one of which was a casting of lots among the people (10:20-21): "the tribe of Benjamin was taken by lot ... then the family of the Matrites was taken by lot ... and Saul the son of Kish was taken by lot." In the conclusion of the whole process (13:1), we read, "Saul was one year old when he became king, and he reigned over Israel for two years."[38]

This implausible chronology, which has confused translators and commentators, is a way of saying that this kingship over Israel, prior to David, was not real, since the three enthronement accounts do not coincide.[39] It is said that Saul fought against the enemies around him, Ammon, Moab, Edom, the Philistines, and even Amalek, and "wherever he turned, he did evil" (14:47-48); the versions have corrected or softened

---

[32] According to Josh. 1:4 MT, the "land of the Hittites" seems to coincide with the whole of Canaan, but in reality the Hittite Empire had its greatest extension in Anatolia in the second millennium, and it had no known extensions in Canaan; cf. Itamar Singer "The Hittites and the Bible Revisited," in: Aren M. Maeir and Pierre de Miroschedji (eds.), *I Will Speak the Riddles of Ancient Times*, Winona Lake, Eisenbrauns, 2006, II:723-56.

[33] However, according to 12:24a LXX, Rehoboam was then sixteen years old; the contradiction is not explained.

[34] And even the daughter of King Nahash, according to 1 Kgs 12:24a LXX; this one, who was very fierce, had been beaten by King Saul; cf. 1 Sam. 11:1-11.

[35] The LXX places Joshua's final assembly at Shechem in Shiloh, Josh. 24:1.

[36] This distrust vis-à-vis a king's arbitrariness is expressed in Deut. 17:14-20.

[37] Cf. Philippe Lefebvre, *Saül, le fils envoyé par son père: lecture de 1 Samuel 9*, Bruxelles, Lumen Vitae, 1999.

[38] The LXX omits the verse, but the Hexaples and the Lucianic Recension put that he was thirty years old at his advent; according to Acts 13:21, he reigned forty years.

[39] Cf. François Langlamet, "1 Samuel 13-2 Samuel 1: Fokkelman et le prêtre de Nob (1 Sam 21,2-7)," *RB* 99 (1992), pp. 631-75.

the facts,[40] but it is still a way of rejecting the king of Israel. Saul's capital, apparently identical to his hometown, was Gibeah of Benjamin, and there is no mention of Shechem.[41]

After Saul's death, "the people of Judah came [to Hebron], and there anointed David king over the house of Judah" (2 Sam. 2:4); this led to a long war with the house of Saul,[42] which was defeated. Then all the tribes (or elders) of Israel came to anoint David as king of Israel (5:3). Finally, David conquered Jebus-Jerusalem, and after a victory against the Philistines, he solemnly introduced the Ark of the Covenant (6:5) that King Saul had completely ignored. This was a major sign of legitimacy, the other being the anointment.[43] When David had to flee from Saul's attacks, he was always careful to respect him as "the LORD's anointed" (1 Sam. 24:7-8 and 26:11-12; 2 Sam. 1:14-15), thus protecting the dignity of the office.

The letters of El-Amarna mention two small kingdoms in the hills in the fourteenth century, that is, long before Saul and David:[44] one had Shechem as its center and the other, more modest, Jerusalem. The unity of the whole, even in the biblical accounts, is never entirely clear. If we omit Saul's kingdom, whose extension is in fact rather vague, it appears that David's rise to power, culminating in Solomon, is a kind of momentary intrusion. When it is dissolved, Israel remains the majority entity, centered on Shechem, while David's legacy is only Judah. The latter is valued, since the Davidic dynasty will continue and remain as the bearer of the hope of the Messiah. Finally, since, because of David, this reality must concern all Israel, it is projected into an indeterminate future.

2.3 Looking for Moses

In the account of the misdeeds of King Manasseh of Judah, we are reminded of what YHWH had said to David and his son Solomon (2 Kgs 21:7-8): "In this House, and in Jerusalem, which I have chosen out of all the tribes of Israel, I will put my name for ever [. . .] if only they will be careful to do according to all that I have commanded them, and according to the Law that my servant Moses commanded them." Such is indeed David's final recommendation to Solomon (1 Kgs 2:3), but in the texts we never see them practicing any observance: David waged multiple wars without ever being hindered by the Sabbath's cessation; much later, during the Maccabean crisis,

---

[40] MT ובכל אשר יפנה ירשיע, but the Greek puts ἐσῴζετο "he was saved (victorious)," derived from יושיע or יושע.
[41] Except indirectly by the fact that Saul, from his shoulder (from his shechem), was greater than the others (1 Sam. 9:2; 10:23). Similarly, before his actual will, Jacob gave Joseph "a shechem" (LXX "a shoulder") above his brothers (Gen. 48:22).
[42] David becoming the leader of a mafia-like gang; cf. Emanuel Pfoh, "A Hebrew Mafioso: Reading 1 Samuel 25 Anthropogically," *Semitica et Classica* 7 (2014), pp. 37–43.
[43] In the Law, anointing is only mentioned for Aaron and his sons (Exod. 28:41, etc.), and the title of Messiah is strictly reserved for the high priest (Lev. 4:3-4).
[44] Cf. Jean-Louis Ska, "Salomon et la naissance du royaume du Nord: Fact or Fiction ?," in: Claude Lichtert and Dany Nocquet (dir.), *Le Roi Salomon, un héritage en question: hommage à Jacques Vermeylen*, Bruxelles, Lessius, 2008, pp. 36–56; Emanuel Pfoh, "Prestige and Authority in the Southern Levant during the Amarna Age," in: Aren M. Maeir et al. (eds.), *The Late Bronze and Early Iron Ages of Southern Canaan*, Berlin, Boston, De Gruyter, 2019, pp. 247–61.

Mattathias and his companions authorized armed defense on the Sabbath, but they could not invoke any precedent (1 Macc. 2:41). As for Solomon, he built a temple that would be the residence of the name of YHWH, but he made himself the high priest of a cult that owed nothing to Moses.

The artificiality of the primacy of Judah and Jerusalem is carefully corrected by the Chronicler, who largely ignores the events related to the kingdom of Israel after the secession. The account begins with Saul, briefly mentioned as the fallen king of all Israel (1 Chron. 10:1). Then 1 Chron. 11:1 reports that David was immediately anointed king of Israel in Hebron, without the characteristic preliminary step of making him king of Judah. He then gathered all Israel to bring the Ark of the Covenant up to Jerusalem, in accordance with the Law of Moses (1 Chron. 13:6), whereas in 2 Sam. 6:2 there were only the nobles of Judah. Then the Chronicler omits the inglorious episodes of Bathsheba, Amnon, and Absalom (2 Samuel 11–20), but he adds that David prepared everything for the Temple, with materials, the organization of the cult, and even an admonition to the people (1 Samuel 22–29). As 2 Sam. 25:25 concludes the book rather abruptly with the altar built by David on the threshing floor of Araunah-Ornan the Jebusite, 1 Chron. 21:30 makes a point of specifying that the abode built by Moses was then at Gibeon, but that David could not go there; 2 Chron 1:3 adds that the Tent of Encounter built by Moses was also there. All this helps to normalize Salomon's visit to Gibeon, where he had a dream and his prayer was answered (1 Kgs 3:4-14).

Then the Chronicler omits Solomon's vengeance, his shrewdness of judgment, his greatness (1 Kings 2–5). It continues with other omissions: Salomon's faults; the secession of Jeroboam and his cult (1 Kgs 11; 12:25–14:23); all the kings of Israel; the prophets Elijah and Elisha. Only a few wars between Judah and Israel remain, but the end of the kingdom of Israel is not reported (2 Kings 17). Then, after the northern kingdom's political disappearance, two great reforming kings took charge of all Israel: first Hezekiah, who reformed the cult, organized a solemn Passover to which Israel and Judah (from Dan to Beersheba) were invited (2 Chron. 30:1-2). The second is Josiah, who hunts down idols in Judah, Manasseh, Ephraim, Simeon, Naphtali, and indeed in all Israel (34:3-7 and 33); at the end of the narrative, 35:27 indicates that Josiah's deeds are recorded "in the Book of the Kings of Israel and Judah," whereas 2 Kgs 23:28 mentions only the kings of Judah (the same applies to King Jehoiakim, 2 Chron. 36:8).

The final part is a partial quotation of Cyrus' decree reported in Ezra 1:104, which says (2 Chron. 36:23): "The Lord, the God of heaven, has charged him to build him a Temple in Jerusalem, in Judah," and "whoever is among you of all his people, let him go up!" Then, according to Ezra 1:5, the chiefs of Judah and Benjamin set out, as well as the priests and Levites—these are, therefore, indeed Nebuchadnezzar's exiles. However, in the condensed form of 2 Chron., the appeal is addressed to the totality of the exiles of both kingdoms, who are all invited to Jerusalem (Section 4.2).

In short, the Chronicler's reinterpretations highlight two points about the history of the royal period: on the one hand, the maintenance of the name Israel to designate the northern kingdom after the secession reflects a reality that predates David; on the other hand, the emergence of the Davidic dynasty is a kind of intrusion into Israel that will have a significant posterity, with the notion of the Messiah. It may be added that, despite some literary thrusts, the concept of the "Law of Moses" does not appear to be prevalent. Among the atypical details, 1 Kgs 3:1 reports that Solomon had married the daughter of the Pharaoh of Egypt, while the Chronicler carefully omits this, but it is not known whether she had children. Rehoboam, Salomon's successor, was the son of an Ammonite woman (1 Kgs 14:21).

From another perspective, it should be emphasized that in matters of religion there are still no real differences between the two kingdoms: we shall see that the genealogy of Judah's priests (Figure 13) is no firmer than that of the non-Levite priests installed by Jeroboam. As for the golden calves that Jeroboam had placed in Dan and Bethel, even Jehu, the violent reformer, did not remove them (2 Kgs 10:28-29). The fact that these statues were kept is not surprising, but it must be compared with the bronze serpent that Moses had made in the desert (Num. 21:8-9) and which remained in the temple of Jerusalem for a long time. According to 2 Kgs 18:4 King Hezekiah is the one who destroyed it but after the fall of Samaria.

2.4 Which Yahwism?

The theme of the antiquity of the law of Moses, which disappeared for a long period of time, is very biblical: when the *Book of the Covenant* was found in the Temple in the eighteenth year of Josiah's reign (640–609), it had been absent since the time of the Judges (2 Kgs 23:22) or the time of Samuel (according to the parallel in 2 Chron. 35:18) so that all the kings of Judah and Israel had been unaware of it, including Saul, David, and Solomon. Similarly, after Ezra proclaimed the Law in Jerusalem (cf. Section 1.2.4), those who had returned from exile studied it and celebrated a very lively feast of Booths (Tents), and it is stated (Neh. 8:17): "from the days of Joshua son of Nun to that day the people of Israel had not done so." In other words, since the time of his successor, the law of Moses had been lost.

Another explanation, again related to the troubled period of the Judges, is provided by the *Damascus Document*: not only the two tablets of the Law given to Moses (Deut. 10:5) but the entire written Torah had been hidden in the Ark of the Covenant since the death of the high priest Eleazar son of Aaron, and then Joshua, the elders, and all Israel had served the goddess Astarte (cf. Judg. 2:13). Finally, when David installed the Ark in Jerusalem, the priest Zadok, who was its custodian (cf. 2 Sam. 15:24), opened it and gave the Torah back to David and all Israel (CD 5:2-5). It follows that, if Zadok is the eponymous ancestor of those who advocate a return to the written Law, the later Sadducees are certainly among his heirs, though obviously without any genealogical link (cf. Figure 13, Section 4.2.1).

We need to go back for a moment to Josiah's *Book of the Covenant*. According to the account in 2 Kings 22–23, it was after this discovery that the king launched reforms throughout the country, burning the objects of worship made for Baal and Asherah, demolishing the high places, abolishing sacred prostitution; this, in particular, supposes that the ancient Israelites of the North and the colonizers who had become Yahwists are indistinguishable. The parallel account in 2 Chronicles 34 puts the *Book*'s discovery, followed by the renewal of the Covenant with the people, after the suppression of widespread idolatry. For the ancient commentators, the *Book* went back to Moses, author of the whole Pentateuch, and it had certainly disappeared, since it is written that it was found. Moreover, since Josiah's reform is clearly in conformity with Deuteronomy's prescriptions, the simplest deduction was that this was the book that had been lost in the Temple. In the fourth century, this conclusion was drawn by Jerome and John Chrysostom, who may have depended on Origen. However, the attribution of the Pentateuch to Moses, which had already been discreetly contested in the Middle Ages,[45] can no longer be maintained, and various theories have been developed to explain a literary genesis that is certainly very complex.[46]

Without entering directly into the debate here, it is necessary to start from a paradox: while the history of the Israelite monarchy (from 1 Samuel to 2 Kings) is clearly centered on Jerusalem and Judah, with the distortions indicated earlier, Deuteronomy foresees an arrival of the Israelites marked by a ritual of curses/blessings on Mount Ebal and Mount Gerizim surrounding Shechem, with the prophecy of the Law on pillars (Deut. 11:29 and 27–28). This ceremony, actually performed later by Joshua, is mentioned in Josh. 8:30-35 (MT),[47] but after 9:2 in the LXX, and by the Samaritan and Josephus (*Ant.* 5:69), who both omit the recapitulation of Joshua 12, after the entire conquest (11:23). It should also be added that the last reported gesture of Joshua is the final gathering at Shechem, where he is a legislator (Joshua 24, cf. Section 1.2.3).

Whereas, from Genesis to Numbers, the cult is dispersed without any central reference, outside the mobile structures of the desert, the Deuteronomic Code (Deuteronomy 12–26) imposes a centralization of the cult in a single unnamed "chosen place"[48]—an expression that occurs twenty-two times. The MT and the LXX put "the place which the LORD will choose to make his name dwell there," with the verb in the imperfect tense. The Samaritan systematically puts a perfect tense "which the LORD has chosen," and it was long thought that this was a "Samaritanism" identifying the place with Mount Gerizim (or the site of Shechem), but it is not isolated. Indeed, Nehemiah, who in a completely different context has just learned that the wall of Jerusalem is damaged, addresses a prayer to God in which he reminds him of his promise, with the verb in the perfect tense (Neh. 1:9 paraphrasing Deut. 30:4): "I will gather (the exiles) and bring them to the place at which *I have chosen* to establish my name." The passage cannot be suspected of undue Samaritan influence (cf. Section 4.2.2).

---

[45] Thus, Abraham Ibn Ezra (1092–1165) observed that various details could not have been written by Moses. For example, at the time of Abraham's arrival, Gen. 12:6b says that "the Canaanites were in the land then," which is necessarily after Joshua's conquest.

[46] See the detailed chapters on the Pentateuch in Thomas Römer, Jean-Daniel Macchi, and Christophe Nihan (dir.), *Introduction à l'Ancien Testament*, Genève, Labor et Fides, ²2011, pp. 63–113. There are some reasons to think that the whole Pentateuch was published at once; cf. Étienne Nodet, "Les Samaritains, Aristée et le Pentateuque," *RB* 127 (2020), pp. 161-95.

[47] The rabbinic tradition, unconcerned with such an emphasis on the Samaritans, observes that the expression ביום אשר תעברו את הירדן "the *day* you cross the Jordan" in Deut. 27:2 makes it possible to understand that everything was achieved in one day (by pure obedience) and that the people went back to spend the night in Gilgal (*m.Sota* 7:5). For the traditional Christian thesis of a Samaritan forgery, cf. ch. I, n. 1.

[48] Sandra L. Richter, "The Place of the Name in Deuteronomy," *VT* 57 (2007), pp. 342-66, concludes from inscriptions on Mesopotamian royal monuments that the biblical formula refers to inscribed monuments, which would fit well with the steles erected on Mount Ebal according to Josh. 8:30-32; it is enough to put "Gerizim" there to correct the Judean bias.

However, A. Schenker has shown that distant versions depending on the LXX (Sahidic, Bohairic, Guezic, etc.) also have the verb "have chosen" in the past tense. It is therefore not a Samaritan deformation but rather an adjustment of the LXX to the MT, which must have taken place before Origen.[49] This is indeed a Judean "rectification:" in his inaugural prayer in the Temple, Solomon reminds us that YHWH choose not any city among the tribes of Israel to build a temple where his name might be (1 Kgs 8:16) but David, and so on. The parallel 2 Chron. 6:6 takes care to add that he chose Jerusalem (repeated in 2 Chron. 12:33), thus resolving the question of the "chosen place:" it is no longer linked to Moses but only to David and Jerusalem.

These considerations indicate that if the *Book of the Law* discovered at Josiah's time was Deuteronomy,[50] it certainly did not originate in Jerusalem,[51] and it should be linked either to the Samaritans (Assyrian colonizers) or to their Israelite predecessors,[52] but given their two golden calves, they did not seem to desire a centralized cult. In fact, one would have to go back to Solomon and David, with the one Temple, and this is indeed what Solomon's prayer, quoted earlier, suggests, but it is difficult to see it as more than a literary effect. On the other hand, the extant version of Deuteronomy is suspicious of kingship (17:14-15) and clearly announces the exile (28:47-68); and this suggests that it was published after the complete disappearance of the monarchy during the exile of 587 BCE. It has also been suggested that Josiah's *Book*, which is not attributed to Moses, is a kind of "Urdeuteronomium" centered on the Deuteronomic Code and originated in the ancient kingdom of Israel and its prophetic circles: this party would have fled when Samaria fell in 721 BCE, while the only remaining hope was Jerusalem, through reforms; there would have been first a failure with Hezekiah (716–687), then a better result with Josiah; but the latter had to justify calling on the northerners and wanting to renew the Covenant with all Israel.[53] However, such hypotheses again give primacy to Judah and the Davidic dynasty and so are close to a petition of principle, especially since they do not fit in well with the history of the colonizers, who in order

---

[49] Cf. Adrian Schenker, "Le Seigneur choisira-t-il le lieu de son nom ou l'a-t-il choisi? L'apport de la Bible grecque ancienne à l'histoire du texte samaritain et massorétique," in: Anssi Voitila and Jutta M. Jokiranta (eds.), *Scripture in Transition* (JSJ Suppl., 126), Leiden, Brill, 2008, pp. 339–51.

[50] And it refers even less to the whole Pentateuch, as it is wrongly assumed; Israel Finkelstein and Neil A. Silberman, *La Bible dévoilée: les nouvelles révélations de l'archéologie*, Paris, Bayard Éditions, 2002.

[51] Unless it was a literary maneuver (unrelated to Moses) to justify the king's reforms; cf. Nadav Na'aman, "The 'Discovered Book' and the Legitimation of Josiah's Reform," *JBL* 130 (2011), pp. 47–62.

[52] This is suggested by Albrecht Alt, "Die Heimat des Deuteronomiums," in his *Kleine Schriften*, München, Beck, 1953, II:250–75.

[53] Cf. Norbert Lohfink, "Die Bundesurkunde des Königs Josias (Eine Frage an die Deuteronomiumsforschung)," *Biblica* 44 (1963), pp. 261–88, 461–98; Moshe Weinfeld, "The Emergence of the Deuteronomic Movement: The Historical Antecedents," in: Norbert Lohfink (ed.), *Das Deuteronomium*, Leuven, University Press, 1985, pp. 76–98; Kurt L. Noll, "Deuteronomistic History or Deuteronomic Debate? (A Thought Experiment)," *JSOT* 313 (2007), pp. 311–45; Bill T. Arnold, "Number Switching in Deuteronomy 12-26 and the Quest for the Urdeuteronomium," *Zeitschrift für Altorientalische und Biblische Rechtsgeschichte* 23 (2017), pp. 163–80; on the contrary, Nadav Na'aman, "Shechem and Jerusalem in the Exilic and Restauration Period," *Zion* 58 (1993), pp. 7–32, concludes that Deuteronomy 11 and 27, on Ebal and Gerizim (completed by Joshua 8 and 24), are to be situated between the exile and the restoration of Cyrus and Darius: the sanctuary of Shechem would have been promoted after the ruin of Jerusalem.

to learn about Yahwism turned neither to the Israelite survivors of the deportation nor to Jerusalem.

Independently of the Law, it is evident that, since David, many proper names are Yahwist, most often with the suffix -*yah*, sometimes with a prefix *yo-* or *yeho-*. The most notable is *Yedidyah*, Solomon's second name (2 Sam. 12:24). More generally, there is little doubt that YHWH can be identified as a deity of Israel prior to the exile, especially by epigraphic findings. The fortress of Kuntillet ʿAjrud, halfway between Gaza and the Red Sea, in the Negeb, has yielded inscriptions from the early eighth century.[54] In one of them, King Joash of Samaria invokes upon certain recipients the blessing "of YHWH of Samaria and of his Asherah." The king, who resides in Samaria, asks for the blessing from his own place of worship. Another inscription invokes the blessing of "YHWH of Teman and of his Ashera." At Khirbet el-Qom, in Judah not far from Hebron, a votive inscription from the same period was found in a tomb, which presents Asherah as YHWH's helper.[55] In Semitic mythology, Ashera is a mother goddess, associated with Baal or El.[56] Yet, Jerusalem was not in the dark, since amulets with a text similar to the priestly blessing of Num. 6:24-26 have been found there.[57]

Yahwist traces are found as early as Samaria's foundation: the name Omri, founder of the city in the ninth century, is likely an abbreviation of Omriyah "YHWH is my strength."[58] The Bible limits itself to judging him as very pagan (1 Kgs 16:23-26), but as a ruler he was noticed abroad: he and especially his dynasty, the "house of Omri," appear in Assyrian inscriptions[59] dating from 853 BCE (Salmanasar III) to 720 BCE (Sargon II). He, his successors, and his kingdom were of notable importance, and he can be considered as a true founder of the kingdom of Israel.[60] His son Ahab married Jezebel, daughter of Ittobaal, king of the Sidonians;[61] She was therefore Phoenician—or

---

[54] Cf. Émile Puech, "Les inscriptions hébraïques de Kuntillet ʿAjrud (Sinaï)," *RB* 121 (2014), pp. 161–94, who refuses the idea that Ashera designates a materialized divine presence, unlike various predecessors: P. Kyle Mccarter, "Aspects of the Religion of the Israelite Monarchy: Biblical and Epigraphic Data," in: Patrick D. Miller et al., *Ancient Israelite Religion*, Philadelphia, Fortress Press, 1987, pp. 137–55; Tilde Binger, *Asherah: Goddesses in Ugarit, Israel and the Old Testament* (JSOTSup, 232), Sheffield, JSOT Press, 1997; William G. Dever, *Did God Have a Wife? Archaeology and Folk Religion in Ancient Israël*, Grand Rapids, Eerdmans Publishing, 2005.

[55] Cf. André Lemaire, "Les inscriptions de Khirbet el-Qôm et l'*ashérah* de Yhwh," *RB* 84 (1977), pp. 595–608; Émile Puech, "L'inscription 3 de Khirbet el-Qôm revisitée et l'*ashérah*," *RB* 122 (2015), pp. 5–25.

[56] Cf. Stéphanie Anthonioz, "Astarte in the Bible and Her Relation to Asherah," in: David T. Sugimoto (ed.), *Transformation of a Goddess: Ishtar, Astarte, Aphrodite* (OBO 263), Fribourg, Academic Press/Göttingen, Vandenhoeck & Ruprecht, 2014, pp. 125–39.

[57] Cf. Gabriel Barkay, Andrew G. Vaughn et al., "The Amulets from Ketef Hinnom: A New Edition and Evaluation," *BASOR* 334 (2004), pp. 41–71.

[58] That is עמריה, cf. James B. Pritchard, *ANET*, Princeton, Princeton University Press, ³1969, p. 283: an Assyrian text mentions the Omrid dynasty calling it *Bit Hu-um-ri-a*, with the yahwist suffix.

[59] Brad E. Kelle, "What's in a Name? Neo-Assyrian Designations for the Northern Kingdom and Their Implications for Israelite History and Biblical Interpretation," *JBL* 121 (2002), pp. 639–66; André Lemaire, "The Mesha Stele and the Omri Dynasty," in: Grabbe, *Ahab Agonistes*, pp. 135–44.

[60] Cf. Sergi, "The Omride Dynasty and the Reshaping of the Judahite Historical Memory," pp. 503–26.

[61] Sidon is a Phoenician port North of Tyre, which metaphorically represented all of Phoenicia, the Sidonians thus becoming the Phoenicians. This is already the case in Homer (*Iliad* 6:290, 23:743; *Odyssey* 4:84). On coins minted at the time of Antiochus IV Epiphanes, Tyre is called the "metropolis of the Sidonians": the term was detached from the city of Sidon, when it was supplanted by Tyre, and applied to the Phoenician population; cf. Catherine Apicella, "Sidon à l'époque hellénistique:

"Canaanite," the equivalent term in the Phoenician language—and it was against her that Elijah fought (cf. 1 Kgs 19:2). His daughter Athaliah (Atalyahu) married Jehoram, king of Judah (2 Kgs 8:26), who was succeeded by his son Ahaziah (Ahazyahu).

Then Elisha, in accordance with the order received from Elijah (1 Kgs 19:16), had Jehu anointed king of Israel, and the latter put to death the followers of Baal, both in Israel and in Judah (2 Kgs 10:14). Having massacred the two royal families, he attacked the temple of Baal established in Samaria and its followers. He reigned for a long time as a very violent defender of YHWH (841–14), but an ambiguity remained (2 Kgs 10:29): "Thus Jehu wiped out Baal from Israel. But Jehu did not turn aside from the sins of Jeroboam son of Nebat, which he caused Israel to commit—the golden calves that were in Bethel and in Dan" (cf. 1 Kgs 12:28).

All this means that the attraction power of Baal, or more generally that of the Phoenician gods, constantly remained stronger than that of YHWH. This is easy to understand, because of their banality and lack of history: Baal, linked to the sun, represents the cyclic fecundity of nature, and his paredra Ashéra-Astarté, linked to the moon, governs feminine fecundity, which is no less cyclic; one can even add something about storms or telluric phenomena.[62] This differentiates them from YHWH, who was characterized by a narrative.[63] According to 1 Kgs 16:32-33, King Ahab built a temple to Baal in Samaria, with an altar, and he also made the "Asherah" (LXX "a sacred pole"), which could be a sacred statue indicating a presence, in the same way that Baal is present at the altar. Just shortly after that, Elijah summoned all Israel to Carmel, together with "the four hundred fifty prophets of Baal and the four hundred prophets of Asherah" (1 Kgs 18:19).

Now, this is the point on which the precise prohibition of identifying YHWH with Baal is formulated (Deut. 16:21): "You shall not plant any tree as a sacred pole—Asherah—beside the altar that you make for the Lord your God." Whether this Asherah is a statue or a simple sacred pole, it represents a power made present; in any case, it is not an abstraction but perhaps a statue, or a stone, that is to say a *baetylus*, according to the biblical model.[64] In fact, a prototype appears in Gen. 28:17-19: Jacob, sent to his uncle Laban the Aramean to find a wife, had a dream on the way, while he was sleeping on a stone: he saw a ladder on which angels were climbing and descending. When he woke up, "he was afraid, and said, 'How awesome is this place! This is none other than the house of God and this is the gate of heaven. [. . .] He called that place Bethel (house of God)." He set up the stone where he had slept as a pole, and this was indeed the "house of God."

---

quelques problèmes méconnus," in: Maurice Sartre (dir.), *La Syrie hellénistique* (Topoi, Suppl. 4), Paris, PUF, 2003, pp. 125–47; Ead., "Du roi phénicien au roi hellénistique: les sanctuaires et le pouvoir royal en Phénicie," *Topoi* 16 (2014), pp. 101–21.

[62] Cf. Brigitte Servais-Soyez, "La 'triade' phénicienne aux époques hellénistique et romaine," in: Charles Bonnet (dir.), *Religio Phoenicia*, Leuven, Peeters, 1986, pp. 347–60.

[63] Cf. John Day, *Yahweh and the Gods and Goddesses of Canaan* (JSOTSup 265), Sheffield, Sheffield Academic Press, 2000; Mark S. Smith, "Yhwh's Original Character: Questions about an Unknown God," in: Jürgen van Oorschot and Markus Witte (eds.), *The Origins of Yahwism*, Berlin/Boston, De Gruyter, 2017, pp. 23–43.

[64] Cf. Brigitte Servais-Soyez, "Le bétyle dans le culte de l'Astarté phénicienne" *Mélanges de l'Université Saint-Joseph* 47 (1972), pp. 147–69.

2.5 Israel and the Tribes

Long before the territorial definitions, Israel is first the name given to Jacob by a mysterious figure, at the end of a fight with him. Jacob comes out of it with a wounded hip, but the new name is explained in a positive sense (Gen. 32:28): "for you have striven with God and with humans, and have prevailed."[65] However, the original meaning of the name was probably "El showed himself strong"—El being another title of God.[66]

Then, the "sons of Israel" are firstly Jacob's immediate descendants, who are seventy or seventy-five when they arrive in Egypt and then become a numerous people (Exod. 1:7) by staying there 430 years.[67] However, it is not known where the women who allowed such an increase came from, since Abraham and Isaac had previously taken care to give their heirs wives from the family. Moses himself came from a consanguineous marriage, later forbidden by the Law (Lev. 18:12), since his father had married his own aunt (Exod. 6:20); but nothing is said for the others. Thus, the traditional link between the twelve tribes and the twelve sons of Jacob is considered artificial: except in Genesis 29–30 and in a psalm of David cited in 1 Chron. 16:13, Jacob never appears as the ancestor of the tribes or of all the people.[68] Moreover, if one omits the parenthesis formed by David and Solomon, the kinship of population between the two kingdoms (or entities) Israel and Judah is not evident. The various lists of tribes are composite, but three of them are worth examining because they provide specific details: the first comes from the Song of Deborah and Barak, which celebrates the unlikely victory of the Israelites against the army of Jabin, king of Canaan; the other two are the final blessings of Jacob and Moses.

In the Song of Deborah, which is often considered ancient,[69] the action mentioned took place in the North, near Mount Tabor, but the praise is addressed to YHWH, who "went out from Seir and Edom," that is, from the South[70] (Judg. 5:3-5). The situation is

---

[65] In Hos. 12:5 the expression has a negative meaning; cf. Karl W. Weyde, "The References to Jacob in Hos 12:4-5: Traditio-Historical Remarks," in: K. Arvid Tångberg (ed.), *Text and Theology*, Oslo, Verbum, 1994, pp. 336–58.

[66] Cf. Baruch Margalit, "The History of El (ca. 3500-500 BCE)," in: Christophe Nicolle (dir.), *Amurru 3: nomades et sédentaires dans le Proche-Orient ancient*, Paris, Éd. Recherche sur les civilisations, 2004, pp. 355–75; Aren M. Wilson-Wright, "Bethel and the Persistence of El: Evidence for the Survival of El as an Independent Deity in the Jacob Cycle and 1 Kings 12:25-30," *JBL* 138 (2019), pp. 705–20.

[67] Gen. 15:13-16 indicates 400 years or four generations; Eusebius, *Praep. euan.* 9.21, quoting the historian Demetrios and the ages of Moses' ancestors, comes up with 215 years, or half of the total.

[68] Cf. Robert R. Wilson, *Genealogy and History in the Biblical World*, New Haven, Yale University Press, 1977, pp. 183–4; Andrew Tobolowsky, *The Sons of Jacob and the Sons of Herakles: The History of the Tribal System and the Organization of Biblical Identity*, Tübingen, Mohr-Siebeck, 2017.

[69] Cf. Volkmar Fritz, "The Complex of Traditions in Judges 4 and 5 and the Religion of Pre-State Israel," in: Aren M. Maier and Pierre de Miroschedji, *I Will Speak the Riddles of Ancient Times*, Winona Lake, Eisenbrauns, 2006, pp. 689–98. However, there is now debate regarding the antiquity of the poem; cf. Jacob L. Wright, "War Commemoration and the Interpretation of Judges 5:15b-17," *VT* 61 (2011), pp. 505–21; Serge Frolov, "How Old Is the Song of Deborah?" *JSOT* 36 (2011), pp. 163–84; Israel Knohl, "The Original Version of Deborah's Song, and Its Numerical Structure," *VT* 66 (2016), pp. 45–65.

[70] Cf. Deut. 1:2 "By the way of Mount Seir it takes eleven days to reach Kadesh-barnea" (the entry into Canaan from the South); Deut. 33:2-3 "The LORD came from Sinai, and dawned from Seir upon them."

not very clear, for according to Josh. 11:8, Yabin and the kings of the North had already been defeated. Moreover, the victory celebrated seems to be against the Philistines, because it is indicated (Judg. 5:6) that there was oppression in the days of Shamgar son of Anat, but according to Judg. 3:31 it was due to the Philistines.[71] Then the list of the "people of the LORD" who did or did not fight is given: Machir and Gilead appear as separate tribes,[72] while elsewhere they are only parts of Manasseh son of Joseph, and four tribes are not mentioned: Judah, Simeon, Levi, and Gad.[73] It is not because they did nothing useful, for we learn that Gilead and Reuben remained inactive beyond the Jordan, that Dan stayed on its vessels, and that Asher, on the seaside, remained quietly in its ports.[74] The people are called Israel, but no patriarch is named.

At the time of the departure from Egypt, the sons of Israel were "six hundred thousand men on foot," not counting women and children, and a mixed crowd joined them (Exod. 12:37-38), which will later be referred to as "a rabble of people" (Num. 11:4). At this point, the identity of the tribes is not yet expressed, except perhaps for Levi, since there is a genealogy of Moses (Exod. 6:16-17); but the tribes reappear on the occasion of two military-style censuses that produce a double effect: the first, shortly after the departure from Egypt, counted 603,550 at least twenty-year-old males (Num. 1:46), to which must be added the Levites, that is, 22,273 males over one month old (3:43);[75] this was the repartitioning of the people around the Tabernacle, at rest or walking (9:12-28). The second census took place at the end of the journey, after Aaron's death, when the sons of Israel arrived near Jericho; there were 601,730 males at least twenty years old (Num. 26:51) as well as 23,000 Levites over one month old (26:62). These demographic details, which ignore foreigners, give the impression of a duplicate and are probably derived from much later censuses, when it was necessary to monitor military resources after a sedentary installation. Between the two censuses, there is the selection of the men sent to explore Canaan from Kadesh-Barnea. There was one from each tribe, but after returning, they discouraged the people; but there were two exceptions, men who had a special destiny: Caleb son of Yephunneh, from the tribe of Judah, and Joshua, from the tribe of Ephraim, who was to be Moses' heir.

---

[71] It is a largely poetic composition, without any factual precision. Comparisons with Greek epic poetry have been attempted; cf. Charles L. Echols, *"Tell Me, O Muse": The Song of Deborah (Judges 5) in the Light of Heroic Poetry* (JSOTSup 487), London, T&T Clark, 2008, pp. 22-5; Andrew Tobolowsky, "The Problem of Reubenite Primacy: New Paradigms, New Answers," *JBL* 139 (2020), pp. 27-45.

[72] Cf. André Lemaire, "Galaad et Makîr: Remarques sur la tribu de Manassé à l'est du Jourdain," *VT* 31 (1981), pp. 39-61.

[73] Cependant, Johannes C. de Moor, "The Twelve Tribes in the Song of Deborah," *VT* (1993), pp. 483-94, has endeavored to show, by restoring matres lectionis, that the twelve tribes are present in the poem. This would be a trace of the Israelite amphictyony conjectured by Martin Noth in 1930, but practically abandoned since, for such a structure is essentially an association around a traditional sanctuary, and there never was one in ancient Israel, cf. Cornelis H. J. de Geus, *The Tribes of Israel: An Investigation into Some of the Presuppositions of Martin Noth's Amphictyony Hypothesis*, Assen, Van Gorcum, 1976; Eben Scheffler, "Beyond the Judges and the Amphictyony: The Politics of Tribal Israel (1200-1020 BCE)," *Old Testament Essays* 14 (2001), pp. 494-509.

[74] Cf. Raymond de Hoop, "Judges 5 Reconsidered: Which Tribes? What Land? Whose Song?" in: Jacques van Ruiten and J. Cornelis de Vos (eds.), *The Land of Israel in Bible, History, and Theology*, Leiden/Boston, Brill, 2009, pp. 151-66.

[75] But only 8,580 between thirty and fifty years of age, that is, fit for demanding worship service; cf. Num. 4:48.

They represent rather well the two future kingdoms, and they are the only two of the entire people who entered Canaan; all the others were to die in the desert, leaving their children in their place.

In his blessing prophecy over his twelve sons (Gen. 49:1-27), Jacob follows the order of their birth.[76] For most of them, the future is either negative because of the past or insignificant. For example, Reuben, the elder, is dispossessed because of his sin (Gen. 35:22); then Simeon and Levi, mentioned together, are condemned to dispersion in Israel because of their violence against the Shechemites (Gen. 34). On the contrary, the prophecies regarding Judah and Joseph are flattering: Judah will overcome the enemies, praised by his brothers, and "the scepter shall not depart from Judah until Shiloh comes"[77] and the peoples obey him" (Gen. 49:8-18). As for Joseph, his blessing is both long and elliptical: he is a fruitful plant; he has suffered, but God has helped him; he is surrounded by blessings; he is consecrated, "a *Nazir* among his brothers."[78] This evokes the whole story of Joseph, seen in a providential way (cf. Gen. 50:20): he was sold by his brothers in order to be elevated above them—a permanent state which will end up being, because he received from Jacob "a shekem above his brothers"[79] (Gen. 48:22), with a probable pun on the city of "Shechem," for the term also means "slope," and the expression can indicate great size, as in King Saul's case in 1 Sam. 9:2.

Moses also gives a final blessing to the tribes just before his death; it is placed between two stanzas of a hymn of praise, in which Israel, called Yeshurun, enters its inheritance upon arriving from the desert (Deut. 33:1-5;26-29). The order of the tribes is jumbled: Simeon is not mentioned (and will be dissolved into the tribe of Judah, according to Josh. 19:1), but Levi is promoted for teaching and the cult. Regarding Judah, the note is brief and contains an intercession (33:7): "O Lord, give heed to Judah, and bring him to his people." Leaving aside the later singularity of David, this can only be an allusion to an episode in which Judah, separated from his brothers, married a Canaanite woman (Genesis 38). Joseph's blessing (vv. 13-18), which is long and very favorable, is like that of Genesis 50, with the same phrase calling him "a *Nazir* among his brothers"; but here Ephraim and Manasseh are named so that even without Simeon the total of the tribes remains twelve.

---

[76] A very complete study is presented by Raymond de Hoop, *Genesis 49 in Its Literary and Historical Context* (Oudtestamentische Studiën, 39), Leiden, Brill, 1999, which proposes a literary evolution of the blessings, where we see rivalries between Joseph and Judah, with phases of domination by one and then by the other.

[77] MT שילה (which cannot be confused with the sanctuary of Shiloh, Josh. 18:1) is obscure, with a variant שלה (mss. sam.), which was read or understood שלו by the Greek and Syriac "until the one comes to whom it belongs." After the disappearance of a legitimate Jewish kingship, the formula was understood as a messianic announcement by Justin, *Dial.* 120:3-4; and Irenaeus, *Haer.* 4:10. Similarly, the Targum (Onqelos) explicitly puts "until the Messiah comes."

[78] The condition of permanent nazir is not provided for by the Law, which knows only temporary vows (Num. 6:1-21); permanent consecration (with retroactive effect for Joseph) is attributed only to Samson (Judg. 13:5) and to Samuel (1 Sam. 1:22 according to 4 QSama), who is thus a precursor of John the Baptist (Lk 1:15).

[79] *Jubilees* 45:14 makes it explicit that Jacob gives two portions to Joseph; earlier there is an account of Jacob's victory over the seven Amorite kings at Shechem (34:2-8), a tradition recorded in the *Testament of Judah* 3-7 but unknown to Josephus. It is a kind of anticipation of Joshua's conquests.

If we consider the two blessings in the Pentateuch as the ends of a trajectory, we see globally Joseph's indisputable primacy.[80] For Judah, on the contrary, a sort of bifurcation appears: first an essential role of government until an interruption and then a frank divergence. This fact should be seen in the light of Judah's historical evolution: with Solomon, he is the master of all Israel, then in very different circumstances, with Ezra and Nehemiah, Israel is reduced to the exiles from Judah who return. It is this evolution that should be followed step by step.

2.6 Conclusions

The account of Samaria's fall and its consequences must be understood in accordance with the inscriptions of Sargon II and Josephus' version, which maintains that the Samaritans always remained strictly Yahwist: only part of the population of the kingdom of Israel was deported, then colonists came, perhaps later, and adopted Israel's religion, to the extent that the distinction between the tribes and the foreigners became imperceptible. However, there was already a divorce between Judah and Israel; this can be seen in the crisis with the lions, since the newcomers, although anxious to honor the local deity, did not turn to Jerusalem.

This religious divorce is in fact not very intelligible, for several reasons. First, even if some inscriptions attest that YHWH was a local deity, there is no precise distinguishable form of worship but only a recurrent struggle against the Phoenician deities. The rare allusions to the Law of Moses are only literary effects. Local Yahwism is apparently common. On the other hand, an ancient political divorce is very clear: the unity of the kingdom attributed to David and Solomon was at best only a momentary phase, especially since these kings, of feeble Israelite origin, were established as vassals of the Phoenician power of Tyre.

Despite Moses' infinitesimal presence during this royal period, the literary formation of the Pentateuch is largely related to it, at least according to the classical theory of the documents. The latter would have it that the Yahwist was born in Solomon's time, and that the Elohist came later, in the kingdom of Israel. Then, after the fall of Samaria in 721 BCE and the flight of the Israelites with their traditions to Judea, a fusion of the two would have taken place in Judea. The next step would have been the discovery of the *Book of the Law* in the Temple in the eighteenth year of King Josiah (622 BCE). Since the reformation of the latter is in conformity with the stipulations and style of Deuteronomy and extends to the ancient kingdom of the North, one has been led to suppose that this was indeed the *Book*.

There are, however, two difficulties: the first is that the book highly values Mount Gerizim and indicates that the place where YHWH's name resides is already chosen, while Jerusalem is ignored. In other words, the *Book* did not originate in Judea but somewhere in the ancient kingdom of Israel; then, despite the conversion of the

---

[80] Hans Ulrich Steymans, "The Blessings in Genesis 49 and Deuteronomy 33: Awareness of Intertextuality," in: Jurie H. le Roux (ed.), *South African Perspectives on the Pentateuch: Between Synchrony and Diachrony*, London, T&T Clark, 2007, pp. 71–89.

colonizers, it was forgotten, which seems strange, especially since it is said that Josiah's reforms represented a complete novelty, unknown to the kings before him. Yet at the time of Samaria's fall, King Hezekiah had accomplished a vast reform according to the Law of Moses (2 Kgs 18:6), abolishing the high places, destroying the idols, and defeating his enemies. The second difficulty is that after a series of curses, Deut. 28:47-68 announces war and exile (cf. Lev. 26:33-35), which implies that the calamity has already arrived when it was written.

The issue of the tribes is relatively clear on the territorial level, but the genealogy and the connection to Jacob remain difficult, especially if one has to consider a fusion of the Samaritans with the survivors of the North.[81] Joshua's final great assembly at Shechem suggests another story without Moses, where the Israelites from Mesopotamia form an undifferentiated people. Ready to welcome YHWH by entering Canaan, they are not really different from the later Assyrian colonizers (cf. Section 1.2.3).

The present form of the narratives of 1-2 Samuel and 1-2 Kings massively privileges Judah and the Davidic royal dynasty but leaves the term "Israel" attached to the northern kingdom, which 1-2 Chronicles has taken care to correct by integrating Judah with Israel; thus, Jerusalem unquestionably becomes the "chosen place" of the Deuteronomic Code.[82]

---

[81] Cf. Walter R. Wifall, "The Tribes of Yahweh: A Synchronic Study with a Diachronic Title," *ZATW* 95 (1983), pp. 197–209.

[82] John van Seters, *The Biblical Saga of King David*, Winona Lake, Eisenbrauns, 2009, defines the story of David as a post-Deuteronomistic "saga," added in the Persian period; cf. also Israel Finkelstein, "Saul, Benjamin and the Emergence of 'Biblical Israel': An Alternative View," *ZATW* 123 (2011), pp. 348–67. The difficulty is that this is hardly consistent with the Persian period according to Ezra and Nehemiah.

3

The Shock of the Maccabean Crisis

The investigation of the royal period in the previous chapter does not lead to firm conclusions, since it is not clear what made the Samaritans the heirs of the ancient kingdom of Israel. Moreover, the split from Judah and the Davidic dynasty seems more political than religious. If we move to a much later context, the separation between Jews and Samaritans was firm and long-standing at the time of the New Testament. Two episodes after the Maccabean crisis (167–4) lastingly established it: the destruction of the temple on Mount Gerizim by the Asmonean high priest John Hyrcan and a little earlier a litigation in Alexandria between Jews and Samaritans to determine which temple—Jerusalem or Gerizim—was the true one according to Scripture. However, before the crisis, there is evidence of the peaceful coexistence of these two temples.

3.1 Discord After the Crisis

Josephus reports a serious conflict between Jews and Samaritans in Alexandria, which occurred around 150 BCE (*Ant.* 13:74-79). The attack came from the Samaritans, who claimed that the true temple built according to the laws of Moses was that on Mount Gerizim, whereas the Jews held to Jerusalem. They brought their dispute before King Ptolemy, asking him to punish the forgers by putting them to death. The representatives of both sides swore by God and the king to provide only evidence from the Law. Their names are mentioned, and so there is a certain effect of reality: Sabbaios and Theodosios spoke for the Samaritans, and Andronikos son of Messalamos for the Hierosolymitans and the Jews. Josephus indicates that the latter were worried about this threat against their temple. Andronikos was allowed to plead first. As proof, he presented the succession of the high priests and explained that the kings of Asia had all honored the sanctuary with sumptuous offerings,[1] while the temple on Mount Gerizim was totally unknown. Given the enormous difference between the Jewish diaspora and that of the Samaritans, these arguments are plausible, but they are political and entirely unscriptural, whereas the Samaritans could simply say that Shechem and Gerizim are expressly mentioned in the Pentateuch but there is no mention of Jerusalem: according to Deut. 27:1-13, the ceremonies connected with the entry into Canaan were to

---

[1] The fame of the Temple is suggested by 2 Macc. 3:2-3 and Josephus quotes in this sense a passage of Polybius not attested elsewhere (*Ant.* 12:136).

begin on Mount Gerizim and Mount Ebal; and that was indeed done by Joshua (cf. Section 2.4). The kings ruled in favor of the Jews, but certainly for political reasons, since the Jews also formed an important minority in the rival kingdom of Syria, whereas the Samaritans had no notable diaspora.[2]

This narrative does not specify which Ptolemy it was. However, the affair immediately follows Ptolemy VI Philometor's approval of the temple of Onias at Heliopolis (to be discussed in Section 3.3), but there is no link between the two episodes. The whole is inserted as a double excursus between the death of Demetrios I (*Ant.* 13:61) and the marriage of Alexander Balas, the presumed son of Antiochus IV, with the daughter of the same Ptolemy VI at Ptolemais (13:80, cf. 1 Macc. 10:51-58). These two events took place in 150 BCE,[3] but such a dating is not assured for either of the two inserted events; we shall see in particular that the one concerning Onias' temple is clearly earlier (Section 3.2).

A circumstance must be found to explain the Samaritans' sudden and total rejection of Jerusalem, without any warning signs. We shall see later (Section 3.4) that at the time of the crisis itself they had kept their distance from the rebellion of Mattathias and his sons, under the high priest Menelaus (173–62). Alkimus, who died in office, had succeeded him, and then there was a seven-year gap (159–52) before Demetrios I appointed Jonathan as high priest of Jerusalem. His somewhat precipitated elevation was confirmed by Alexander Balas, but initially it was due to Demetrios' fear after the arrival, in 152 BCE, of Alexander, who came to regain the throne of his father Antiochus IV. Consequently, the event that provoked the Samaritans' rejection was none other than the promotion of Jonathan, for according to them he had no title to occupy the office. Moreover, they could not intervene with the Syrian authority, which since Antiochus III, around 200 BCE, appointed the high priests of Jerusalem. Indeed, the Samaritans had better chances in Egypt, as is shown by a letter quoted in the preface to 2 Maccabees: the Jews of Jerusalem wrote to their brethren in Egypt to ask them to celebrate the Dedication on the 25th of Kislev[4] (2 Macc. 1:1-10a). The

---

[2] Their *explicit* modest presence in Egypt has been shown by Pieter W. van der Horst, "The Samaritan Diaspora in Antiquity," in: ID., *Essays on the Jewish World of Early Christianity*. Göttingen, Vandenhoek & Ruprecht, 1990, pp. 136–48; Reinhard Pummer, "The Samaritans in Egypt," in: Christian-Bernard Amphoux et al. (dir.), *Études sémitiques et samaritaines offertes à Jean Margain* (Histoire du Texte Biblique, 4), Lausanne, Éd. du Zèbre, 1998, pp. 213–32. These studies rely heavily on personal names, but any Israelite name can be of Judean or Samaritan origin. There were traces of Samaritans in distant places; cf. Magnar Kartveit, "Samaritan Self-Consciousness in the First Half of the Second Century B.C.E. in Light of the Inscriptions from Mount Gerizim and Delos," *JSJ* 45 (2014), pp. 449–70. On the Samaritan "synagogue" of Delos, which has an inscription (dated around 200 BCE) recalling that the Israelites made offerings at the "holy Mount Gerizim" (Αργαρ ιζειν), cf. Philippe Bruneau, "Les Israélites de Délos et la juiverie délienne," *BCH* 106 (1982), pp. 465–504; Michael White, "The Delos Synagogue Revisited: Recent Fieldwork in the Graeco-Roman Diaspora," *HTR* 80 (1987), pp. 133–60.

[3] However, the affair of the temple of Onias is rather to be compared with the death of the high priest Menelaus in 163 BCE (cf. *Ant.* 12:387); but the renewed authority of Jerusalem came only with Simon in 142 BCE, and the first festive letter signaling a renewal to the Jews of Egypt is also dated in 142 BCE. In any case, the Alexandria quarrel necessarily predates the destruction of Gerizim by John Hyrcan.

[4] The authenticity of the letter was established by Elias J. Bickerman, "Ein jüdischer Festbrief vom Jahre 124 v. Chr.," in: Id., *Studies in Jewish and Christian History II* (AGAJU, 9), Leiden, Brill, 1980, pp. 136–58. Cf. Timo Nisula, "'Time Has Passed Since You Sent Your Letter'. Letter Phraseology

letter is dated 124 BCE, under John Hyrcanus, and it quotes another similar letter dated 142 BCE, that is, from the time when Rome recognized Simon as high priest of the Jews. This means that despite Roman approval, the "brothers" in Egypt refused to accept the Hasmonean restoration for a long time: more than forty years after Judas Maccabaeus' great deed, they still refused to accept what had become the foundation festival of the new regime.

Furthermore, the idea that there is no room for two temples built according to the law of Moses seems new, although it apparently conforms to Deuteronomy, which requires a single place but never mentions its name. Thus, there is indeterminacy, and the rabbinic tradition says that the place of worship may be changed "if a prophet so decides."[5] However, the Samaritan text, which puts "place which YHWH has chosen" with an accomplished form, must be taken as original, whereas the Jewish version has "will choose," which refers to Solomon's prayer later at the Temple's inauguration (cf. Section 2.4). Consequently, the coexistence of two sanctuaries is conceivable, each based on the appropriate lesson, but a crisis may arise. This is all the easier since, before the crisis, there was no connection between the domains associated with the two temples (cf. Figure 12, Section 3.4).

The Samaritans' adversity continued, and their visible presence was deemed unbearable in Jerusalem. The first Hasmonean high priests sought to enlarge the small Judea of Judas Maccabaeus, but theoretically they remained vassals of the Syrian king. However, internal rivalries gradually weakened this kingdom, and when John Hyrcanus saw himself strong enough, he pursued a policy of energetic expansion. In particular, he took care to take the city of Samaria and to destroy the temple on Mount Gerizim toward 111 BCE.[6] He did not seek to absorb the Samaritans into Judaism, as he did with Idumea, whose inhabitants he forced to convert or leave (*Ant.* 13:257). This means that the very existence of this Samaritan sanctuary was a threat.

In short, there is a symmetry between the Samaritans and the Jews of Egypt regarding the Hasmonean regime and its justifications. This rejection remains unexplained, and the low extraction of the Hasmoneans (cf. Section 1.2.6) is probably not a sufficient reason. Moreover, Judaism in Egypt had two poles: Alexandria, which will be examined in connection with the *Letter of Aristaeus* (Section 3.3), and the so-called Temple of Onias, which appeared at the time of the crisis.

---

in 1 and 2 Maccabees," *JSP* 14 (2005), pp. 201–22. In the letter, the Dedication is described as σκηνοπηγία, with the meaning "planting a sanctuary" and not "feast of tabernacles," as elsewhere in the LXX; the result was the misunderstanding of equating the commemoration of Judah's deed with a feast of tabernacles; cf. 2 M 10:6. However, some connection between this feast and the inauguration of the sanctuary is suggested in 1 Kgs 8:2.65: the dedication of Solomon's temple coincides with the Feast of Tabernacles (likewise in 1 Chron. 7:5), but it is the seventh month (Tishri).

[5] Cf. *Sifré Num.* § 70 on Deut. 12:13-14, in allusion to the altar erected by the prophet Elijah in Carmel, because YHWH was present there (1 Kgs 18:30); similarly Josephus, who paraphrases Deuteronomy (*Ant.* 4:203).

[6] Josephus (*Ant.* 13:256) puts this destruction right after the death of Antiochus VII Sidétès, that is to say toward -129 BCE, but coins collected recently show that it was later, at a time when its successors Antiochus VIII and Antiochus IX disputed the throne; cf. Reinhard Pummer, *The Samaritans in Flavius Josephus* (Texts and Studies in Ancient Judaism, 129), Tübingen, Mohr-Siebeck, 2009, pp. 250–5.

3.2 Around the Crisis: Onias' Temple

In his list of all the high priests since Aaron, Josephus offers a summary clearly indicating that the Hasmoneans filled a void (*Ant.* 20:235-238):

> The afore-mentioned Antiochus[7] and Lysias the general of his army, then deprived Onias, also called Menelaus,[8] of the high priesthood, and executed him at Berea.[9] They deprived his son of the inheritance and made Yacimus[10] high priest, for he was indeed a descendant of Aaron but not of the family of Onias. (236) Consequently, Onias, the nephew of Onias who had been put to death and bore the same name with his father, went to Egypt, where he became the friend of Ptolemy Philometor and his wife Cleopatra. He persuaded them to build, in the district of Heliopolis, a temple for God like the one in Jerusalem and to appoint him high priest.[11] (237) But we have already often spoken about the temple built in Egypt.[12] As to Jacimus, he died after three years as high priest. No one succeeded him, and the city remained without a high priest for seven years. (238) But then the Asamoneus, having been entrusted with power over the people and fought against the Macedonians, resumed the tradition and appointed Jonathan high priest.

Regarding the seven-year interruption, Josephus only says that there was no high priest in Jerusalem; but for the Jews there was one elsewhere.[13] As for the Hasmoneans, he avoids recalling that their authority comes from the kings of Syria, and he forgets their priestly origin: according to 1 Macc. 2:1 Mattathias was a descendant of Joarib, the ancestor of the first priestly class (1 Chron. 24:7), of the house of Eleazar son of Aaron.

In *War*, Josephus first said that the high priest Onias was sent into exile by Antiochus Epiphanes, who pillaged the city and desecrated the Temple. Fleeing to Egypt, Onias obtained from King Ptolemy a territory in the district of Heliopolis and there established "a small city resembling Jerusalem and a temple like ours" (*W* 1:32-33). At the end of the book, when this temple was dismantled on the orders of the emperor Vespasian, around 75—because it served as a rallying point for the Zealots and other Egyptian sicarios—Josephus gives a more detailed account (*W* 7:423-432). The high priest Onias, fleeing Antiochus who was fighting the Jews, took refuge in Alexandria with Ptolemy VI, explaining to him that if he allowed him to build a temple in Egypt,

---

[7] Antiochus V Eupator, son of Antiochus IV.
[8] Menelaus (172–62) was guilty to have pushed Antiochus IV to persecute the Jewish rebels, which had proved to be a costly political error (*Ant.* 12:285).
[9] In Syria (Aleppo).
[10] Or in Greek *Alkimos* "Valiant" (162–59); cf. 1 Macc. 7:5-6.; 2 Macc. 14:3-4 (which ignore Yaqim).
[11] Cf. *Ant.* 12:387-388; 13:62-73.
[12] High priest of all the Jews, in direct competition with Jerusalem under Syrian domination; for Ptolemy, the political interest was certain.
[13] It has been assumed that during these seven years a legitimate high priest "sadocide" would have been in office, and that after being exiled he would have become the Master of Justice of the Qumran documents; cf. after many others Heerak Christian Kim, *Zadokite Propaganda in the Late Second Temple Period: A Turning Point in Jewish History*, Toronto/Plymouth, University Press of America, 2014. However, there has never been a "Sadocite" dynasty. Cf. Étienne Nodet, "Sadducéens, Sadocides, Esséniens," *RB* 119 (2012), pp. 186–212; and Section 4.2.1, figure 12.

he would rally the whole Jewish nation around it. The king accepted, out of hatred for Antiochus who had twice tried to invade Egypt (in 169 and 168 BCE, cf. 2 Macc. 5:1-14). "Thus, the Jews would become even more hostile to Antiochus, who had ruined the temple in Jerusalem." The enterprise succeeded, and the king gave the sanctuary vast properties to provide it with income, "thus assuring the priests a comfortable life and God all that piety required." Josephus concludes with two contradicting indications: on the one hand, Onias was acting only out of ambition and resentment against the Jews of Jerusalem and wanted to draw the multitude away from the metropolis; on the other hand, a prophecy of Isaiah was thus fulfilled.

Later, just before the Samaritan dispute, Josephus gives a second account of Onias' foundation;[14] parallel to the first, it is both better documented and more legendary. The young Onias, son of the high priest Onias who was dismissed by Jason in 175 BCE, was already exiled in Egypt. When he learned that Judea was being ravaged by the Macedonians (Antiochus IV), he wrote to Ptolemy to obtain permission to build a temple like Jerusalem's in the district ("nome") of Leontopolis. He explained to him that there were many Jews in the region, but that they had a multitude of temples which were not in conformity with the Law,[15] and this caused conflicts between them and also with their Egyptian neighbors. It was, therefore, in the interest of Egypt to unite them around a single temple. Onias was motivated by a prophecy of Isaiah that he wanted to fulfill. The king, in his favorable response, relies on this prophecy and institutes Onias as high priest, that is, responsible for the good order of the whole ethnic group. Josephus then concludes: Onias built his temple[16] on the site of an ancient shrine in ruins, in a place called Bubastis-of-the-Field,[17] and installed priests and Levites there. The choice of this place is not well explained, but an examination of the prophecy will shed light on it.

Indeed, this prophecy of Isaiah (19:16-24) is atypical. It is situated between an oracle against Egypt and a curse against Babylon but concludes lyrically: "On that day Israel will be the third with Egypt and Assyria, a blessing in the midst of the earth." Reconciliation between Egypt and Syria, especially with the mediation of Israel, is a phenomenon unknown in the Bible and very unlikely, except perhaps in one largely postexilic case: Alexander Balas, who became king of Syria as the presumed son of

---

[14] Ant. 13:62-73.
[15] Apart from the Judaean temple at Elephantine in the fifth century, the oldest known traces of synagogues (places of study and/or prayer, προσευχή) are found in Egypt; cf. Lee I. Levine, *The Ancient Synagogue: The First Thousand Years*, New Haven, Yale University Press, 2000.
[16] Joan E. Taylor, "A Second Temple in Egypt. The Evidence for the Zadokite Temple of Egypt," *JSJ* 29 (1998), pp. 297–321, notes that the sanctuary described by the excavator is rather reminiscent of the Gerizim, that is, a traditional Israelite temple, but the reference to the sadocides is inadequate (cf. Section 3.3, figures 10–11 and Section 4.2.1, Figure 13).
[17] Neither Leontopolis nor Boubastis ("City of Bast," lion-shaped goddess; the two names are thus twins) are properly in the nome of Heliopolis. There is a site *Tell el-Yehudiyeh* ("Ruin of the Jews"), 13 kilometers North of Heliopolis, and the temple of Onias is in the vicinity, as an important Jewish necropolis has been found there; cf. William M. Flinders Petrie, *The Hyksos and Israelite Cities*, London, British School of Archaeology, 1906, p. 27; however, the whole is clearly posterior to the Maccabean crisis; cf. Gohei Hata, "Where Is the Temple Site of Onias IV in Egypt?" in: Jack Pastor, Pnina Stern, and Menahem Mor (eds.), *Flavius Josephus: Interpretation and History*, Leiden/Boston, Brill, 2011, pp. 177–91; Meron M. Piotrkowski, *Priests in Exile: The History of the Temple of Onias and Its Community in the Hellenistic Period*, Berlin/Boston, De Gruyter, 2019.

Antiochus IV Epiphanes, made an alliance with Egypt by marrying the daughter of Ptolemy VI at Ptolemais, and Jonathan, who went there, met the two kings and was showered with honors (1 Macc. 10:51-52). The prophecy sees things from afar and magnifies Israel's position. Other elements refer more directly to Onias' time (Isa. 19:18-19 and 21).

> On that day there will be five cities in the land of Egypt that speak the language of Canaan and swear allegiance to the LORD of hosts. One of these cities will be called the City of the disaster (MT ; versions and 1QIsa^a "City of the Sun" ; LXX "City of Justice"). On that day there will be an altar to the LORD [...] [people] will worship with sacrifice and burnt offering, and they will make vows to the LORD and perform them.

The lesson in *1QIsa^a*, the great Qumran manuscript of Isaiah,[18] is well attested by ancient versions and refers directly to Heliopolis. It is certainly original, but the variants are instructive: a disaster for the MT, glory for the LXX,[19] which strives to suggest another Hebrew name. There were traditions linking the Israelites to this place: the wife of Joseph the son of Jacob was the daughter of Potiphera, priest of On (Gen. 41:45 MT, LXX "Heliopolis"). According to Exod. 1:11, the Israelites enslaved in Egypt had built the warehouse cities of Pithom and Rameses, and the LXX adds a third, On, and immediately translates "Heliopolis," which is an allusion to the cult of Ra (Re); this suggests that the Israelites had a past in this place, mixed with the name of Onias.[20] Josephus says that Manetho, a priest of Heliopolis in the third century, claimed that a priest of the cult of Osiris in that same city had given the Jews a constitution and taken the name of Moses (*CAp* 1:250).

Furthermore, the expression "City of Justice" normally refers to Jerusalem (cf. Isa. 1:26), and that suggests that the translator indeed recognized Onias' work and was even a familiar figure in his temple.[21]

As for the name of Onias, which suddenly appears after Alexander in the succession of the high priests of Jerusalem, it has an Egyptian hue, because it can be considered as the combination of On, which is a transcription of *jwnw* "city-column," and a simple Yahwist suffix.[22] The dynasty of the Oniades would thus have Egyptian ties, and it must be suspected that the young Onias' interest in the ruins of Bubastis was guided by ancestral memories.

Later, there was a dynasty of high priests of Egyptian origin in Jerusalem: under Herod, we find a certain Simon son of Boethos, or more probably Simon Boethos (24–

---

[18] The paleography invites to date it between 125 BCE and 100 BCE; cf. Eugene Ulrich and Peter W. Flint, *Qumrân Cave 1. II, The Isaiah Scrolls* (DJD 32), Oxford, Clarendon Press, 2010, p. 61.

[19] MT ההרס, 1QIsa^a החרס, LXX πόλις ασεδεκ; this transcription assumes (or invents) in the original the Hebrew word הצדק, which is very common and which the translator cannot have ignored.

[20] It would then be little different from the original.

[21] Cf. Johann Cook and Arie van der Kooij, *Law, Prophets, and Wisdom: On the Provenance of Translators and Their Books in the Septuagint Version* (Contributions to Biblical Exegesis and Theology, 68), Leuven/Paris, Peeters, 2012.

[22] The LXX puts Ησαιας for ישעיהו "Isaiah," and likewise Ονιας must reflect אוניהו or אוניה; the Mishna knows the temple of Onias, and *m.Menahot.* 13:10 has חוני (for חוניהו).

5), then Joazar son (or brother) of Boethos (in 4 BCE); under Archelaus (4–6), Eleazar, his brother, was named twice; under king Agripa I (41–4), we find Simon Cantheras son of Boethos.[23] This family, though without an identifiable Judean origin, was thus of notable importance for at least two generations; and it is not imprudent to link it to the Egyptian oniads, for their legitimacy has never been disputed, at least according to Josephus.[24]

Although nothing is known about the communications between Heliopolis and Alexandria, the Jews of Egypt had a good reason for not accepting the Hasmonean regime, beginning with Jonathan. During the seven-year vacancy of the high priest in Jerusalem, the temple was inactive; this situation could have been considered provisionary, but Jonathan's promotion was unacceptable. Now, it is worth asking why.

3.3 Harmony Before the Crisis?

The situation before the crisis was quite different; there are in fact indications of peaceful coexistence. A joint case appears in the *Letter of Aristaeus*, a pamphlet commonly dated in the second half of the second century,[25] which, with a number of digressions, tells how the Greek translation of the Pentateuch was made more than a century earlier: Demetrios of Phalerus, the founder of Alexandria's famous library, had warned King Ptolemy II Philadelphus early in his reign that he had no satisfactory copy of the Law of the Jews. At the king's request, Eleazar, the high priest of Jerusalem, agreed to send seventy-two sages, six from each of the twelve tribes of Israel, to Alexandria to work on the text and translate it; he warned that this was "unnatural"[26] but, in his position as an Egyptian official of the cults, he was obliged to obey, just as the high priests appointed by the Syrian authority were later.

---

[23] Simon: *Ant.* 15:320-322; Joazar: *Ant.* 17:165; Eleazar: *Ant.* 17:339 and 18:3; Simon Cantheras *Ant.* 19:297; cf. *t.Menahot* 13:21.
[24] The rabbinic tradition, however, reproaches them for being attached to the calendar of Jubilees, like the Sadducees and the Essenes; cf. Moshe D. Herr, "Who Were the Boethusians?," in: *Proceedings of the Seventh World Congress of Jewish Studies*, Jerusalem, World Union of Jewish Studies, 1981, pp. 1–20. The objection is interesting, because it indicates a biblical frequentation far from the Babylonian circles: indeed, this calendar is as if buried in the Pentateuch; cf. Annie Jaubert, *La Date de la Cène. Calendrier biblique et liturgie chrétienne* (Études Bibliques), Paris, Gabalda/Leuven, Peeters, 1957, pp. 23–8. For his part, Josephus never discusses calendar conflicts.
[25] The dominant argument is still that of Elias J. Bickerman, "Zur Datierung des Pseudo-Aristeas," in: *Studies in Jewish and Christian History I*, Leiden, Brill, 1976, pp. 109-36. Also see André Pelletier, *Flavius Josephus adaptateur de la* Lettre d'Aristée, Paris, Klincksieck, 1962; Sylvie Honigman, *The Septuagint and Homeric Scholarship in Alexandria. A Study of the Narrative of the Letter of Aristeas*, London/New York, Routledge, 2003. The suspicion about the antiquity of the translation comes from an anomaly: one wonders why it was promoted so late by the Letter, with inaccurate or legendary details; it is possible that the Alexandrian conflict between Samaritans and Jews required a Greek text accepted by all, but the history of the Hebrew text need not be considered here; cf. Emanuel Tov, "Textual Harmonization in the Five Books of the Torah: A Summary," in: Magnar Kartveit and Gary N. Knoppers (eds.), *The Bible, Qumran, and the Samaritans*, Berlin/Boston, De Gruyter, 2018, pp. 31–56.
[26] Lettre § 44 παρὰ φύσιν; aux § 312–14, Ptolemy II is astonished that no historian or poet has ever pointed out the law of the Jews, and he is answered that it is because of its divine character and that a magic punishment protects it from any violation and in particular from any translation.

The *Letter*'s text is quite complex, and at the end it is not even certain that the translation reached the library. However, the point we want to stress here is a paradox: on the one hand, the twelve tribes were mobilized, which means that Samaritans and Jews worked together to produce a single text; but, on the other hand, everything is subordinated to a high priest in Jerusalem, and nothing is visible northward, neither a shrine nor any high priest, which before the Maccabean crisis would have been a major anomaly.[27] This paradox is significant at the time of the *Letter*, but it is entirely artificial under Ptolemy II. Indeed, it is difficult to situate a high priest Eleazar distinct from the son and successor of Aaron. For lack of other information, Josephus introduces him after Onias I and Simon I,[28] who are contemporaries of Ptolemy I but of whom nothing else is known. Next, the succession of high priests is very laborious (Figure 10). Since

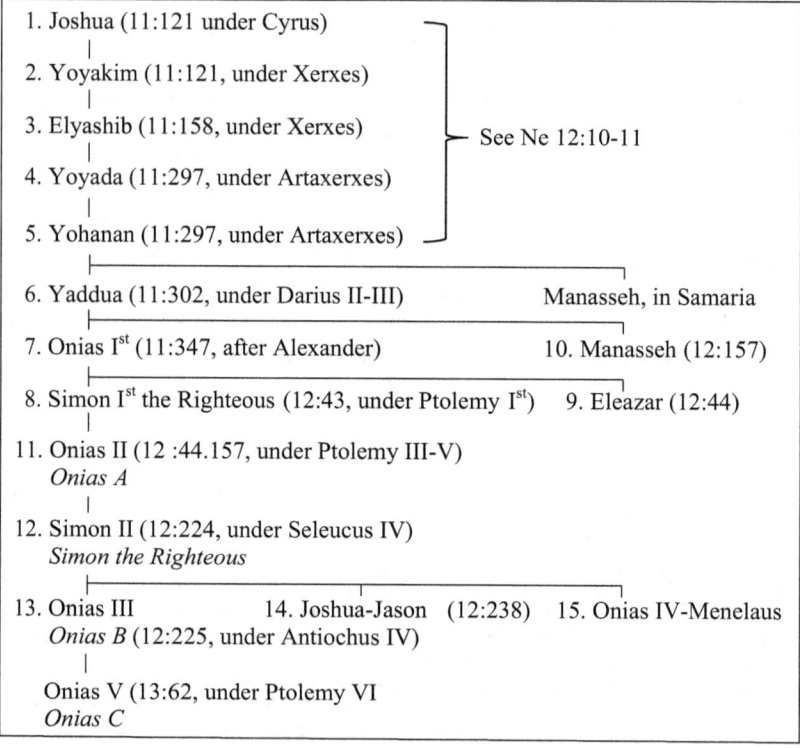

Figure 10 The high priests after the exile according to Josephus.

---

[27] Cf. Étienne Nodet, "Josephus and Aristeas' Letter: A Comparison," in: Christophe Rico and Anca Dan (eds.), *The Library of Alexandria: A Cultural Crossroads of the Ancient World*, Jerusalem, Polis Institute Press, 2017, pp. 89–120.

[28] Josephus calls him "Righteous," but Simon the Righteous, as known to rabbinic tradition, must be identified with the Simon son of Onias II (A) of Sir. 50:1, around 200 BCE; this is admitted since George Foot Moore, "Simeon the Righteous," in his *Jewish Studies in Memory of Israel Abrahams*, New York, Jewish Institute of Religion, 1927, pp. 348–64.

papponymy was a dominant custom, it is sufficient to assume that Josephus or his source created an Onias and a Simon to establish continuity from the Persian period and Alexander. For this reason, a simpler renumbering into Onias A, B, C is proposed here.[29]

The table shows that the succession of Hellenistic high priests according to Josephus remains very confused, with jumps in generations. Moreover, there is a major hidden discontinuity: the "temple of Onias," which was the only Jewish temple in activity for at least seven years. Yet, other circumstances of symmetry between Jews and Samaritans must now be highlighted.

The account in 2 Maccabees, which does not concern itself with the politics of Judea, reports that Antiochus IV, after having plundered the Temple under the high priest Menelaus, left for Antioch: "He left governors to oppress the people: at in Jerusalem, Philip [. . .] and at Gerizim, Andronicus"[30] (5:22-23). Then he sent Gerontius the Athenian "to pollute the temple in Jerusalem and call it the temple of Olympian Zeus, and to call the one in Gerizim the temple of Zeus-the-friend-of-strangers" (6:2). For the author, as well as for Antiochus IV, the Israelite nation had two temples.

Another detail confirms this. When Alexander Balas arrived, claiming to be the son of Antiochus IV, Demetrios (nephew of the same one), the king in place, saw himself threatened and sought the support of the high priest Jonathan, who had proven his military value. He offered him fiscal advantages and in particular three districts of the district of Samaria to attach them to Judea, that is, to the authorities of Jerusalem; 1 Macc. 10:38 specifies that the inhabitants should recognize the high priest, and Josephus also admits it (*Ant.* 13:54). It is not a question of a change of worship but only of a change of address for pilgrimages and for the legal benefits due to the cult (cf. Section 3.4, Figure 12).

Going back in time, we learn that a certain Joseph son of Tobias, skillfully maneuvering with a high priest Onias and then with the notables gathered in Alexandria, succeeded in receiving from King Ptolemy III Euergetes the farm taxes of Phoenicia, Judea, and Samaria, which he kept for twenty-two years (*Ant.* 12:224). Tobias had friends in Samaria as well as in Jerusalem (12:168), and his family's estate was east of the Jordan, in Ammanitide; the magnificent castle of Araq el-Emir remains.[31] A Tobiah will be found at the time of Nehemiah.

A similar image is given by the papyri of Zeno, secretary and treasurer of Apollonius, who was adviser to Ptolemy II Philadelphus and then to Ptolemy III Euergetes. His administrative activity lasted from 260 BCE to 239 BCE, but he began with a fourteen-

---

[29] Cf. Étienne Nodet, *La crise maccabéenne*, Paris, Cerf, 2005, pp. 267–76. James C. Vanderkam, *From Jeshua to Caiaphas: High Priests After the Exile*, Minneapolis, Fortress Press, 2004, pp. 112–239, as a good disciple of Josephus, tries to establish a continuity, but Alice Hunt, *Missing Priests. The Zadokites in Tradition and History*, New York/London, T&T Clark, 2006, rightly insists on the discontinuities and concludes that there is no identifiable Sadocide genealogy, either before or after the exile (cf. figure 13, Section 4.2.1).

[30] Several mss of the Vetus Latina and the Armenian dependent on it read argarizim (also in 6:2), which probably reflects the original; cf. Werner Kappler and Robert Hanhart, *Maccabaeorum liber II*, Göttingen, Vandenhoeck & Ruprecht, 1959, pp. 26, 69.

[31] Cf. Chang-Ho C. Ji, "A New Look at the Tobiads in 'Iraq al-Amir," *Liber Annuus* 48 (1998), pp. 417–40; François Larché et al., *Iraq al Amir, le château du Tobiade Hyrcan; restitution et reconsctruction* (BAH 172), Beyrouth, IFPO, 2005.

month stay in Syria-Palestine, which was under Lagid domination at the time. He oversaw transactions and semi-official interventions. He travelled throughout the country and in Transjordan, dealing with commercial and social issues on a daily basis.[32] The important point is that he did business with Judeans, signed contracts with them including oath formulas, but there is no reference to the Law of Moses, nor to specific customs, nor to official authorities in Jerusalem or elsewhere.

Finally, it is finally worth mentioning the island of Elephantine, in Aswan, although it is largely before Alexander; there, at the beginning of the twentieth century, archeologists fund a hundred papyri, dated by allusions to the Persian kings and covering a period from 495 BCE to 399 BCE.[33] They show that a garrison of Judean soldiers, with their families, was living on the island. One of the documents indicates that the group had built a shrine, which they claimed predated Cambyses, who had invaded Egypt in 525 BCE, although without touching the Judean shrine. A long document compiled from the table of capitations indicates that the proceeds of the collection were to be divided between Yaho (= YHWH), 'Ashim-Beth'el, and 'Anat-Beth'el, under the responsibility of Yedonyah son of Gemaryah. In the West-Semitic pantheon, 'Anat, a warrior goddess, was the sister of Baal, the storm god and principal divinity of the peoples of the Near East; he was the husband of Ishtar (or Astarte). A papyrus containing instructions for the feasts of Passover and unleavened bread is addressed by a certain Hananyah to the same Yedonyah, chief of the Judean garrison. He begins by invoking on them the protection of the gods. The proper names are Yahwist, and 'Anat is the goddess of Yaho, perhaps the Queen of Heaven mentioned in Jer. 44:17.[34] It is also noted that, despite the number of administrative documents collected (marriages, engagements), the name of Moses or a rule related to him never appears.

A group of documents makes it possible to follow an episode of the local Judaean shrine's destruction and its consequences. It took place in 410 BCE, at the end of a revolt apparently fomented by the Egyptian priests of Khnum—god of the nearby cataracts—who had a temple on the island. A supplication was then addressed by Yedonyah to Bagoas (or Bagawahi), governor of Judea; he invoked on him the favors of the "God of Heaven" and indicated that he had also addressed himself to the high priest Johanan and the notables of Judea. The aim was to put pressure on the local authorities, who did not allow the restoration of the shrine. This approach remained without result, probably because of a lamentable case situated by Josephus at the same time: the high priest Johanan had a brother Joshua to whom the governor Bagoses (Bagôhi) had promised to get him the same office. Armed with this assurance, Joshua provoked his brother in the temple of Jerusalem, so much so that the latter killed him during a service—a crime never seen before "either among the Greeks or among the

---

[32] Cf. Xavier Durand, *Des Grecs en Palestine au IIIe siècle avant Jésus-Christ. Le dossier syrien des archives de Zénon de Caunos (261–252)*, Paris, Gabalda, 1997.

[33] They were published with a French translation and a commentary by Pierre Grelot, *Documents araméens d'Égypte*, Paris, Cerf, 1972.

[34] The Elephantine excavations also yielded apparently non-Judean family correspondence; one of the letters begins, "Greeting (שלם) by the Temple of Beth-El and the Temple of the Queen of Heaven." Cf. Bezalel Porten, *Elephantine Papyri in English. Three Millenia of Cross Cultural Continuity and Change*, Leiden, Brill, 1996, pp. 89–92.

Neh. 12:10-11	Neh. 12:22	Neh. 12:23	Neh. 13:28	Ezra 10:6	Ant. 11:297-298
(Jehozadak)					(Jehozadak)
Jeshua					(Jeshua)
Joiakim					(Joiakim)
Eliashib	Eliashib	Eliashib	Eliashib	Eliashib	Eliashib
Joiada	Joiada	Johanan	Joiada +	Johanan	Joiada
Jonathan	Johanan		a son-in-law		Johanan + Jeshua
Jaddua	Jaddua		(Manasseh?)		Jaddua + Manasseh

Figure 11 High priests of Jerusalem in the Persian period.

Barbarians." Alerted, Bagoses forced his way into the temple and persecuted the people for seven years (*Ant.* 11:297-301). This account, which supposes that the Judaean high priest was subordinate to a Persian governor, has legendary amplifications, but it certainly did not come out of thin air.

Jehozadak was the high priest exiled in 587 BCE (1 Chron. 5:41), and Jaddua was Alexander's contemporary in 333 BCE (cf. Section 4.1.2). It is doubtful that the list is complete. Moreover, the confusion of names within the same chapter (Neh. 12) suggests intentional confusion rather than unbelievable carelessness (Figure 11).

3.4 The Maccabean Crisis and the Samaritans

The whole crisis has been presented through the accounts of Josephus (Section 1.2.6), but it is necessary to return to what specifically concerns the Samaritans. At the time of the persecution, the revolt was led by Mattathias, whom Josephus introduces briefly in his first account (*W* 1:36): "son of Hasmoneus, one of the priests of a village called Modin." This identification is surprising for two reasons: on the one hand, every priest is, by definition, a descendant of Aaron, and one would have to assume that a man of the priestly classes was domiciled there, but nothing indicates that; on the other hand, Modin was then in Samaria[35] (Figure 12). Indeed, according to 2 Macc. 13:13-14, in Judah's time, the Seleucid army camped near Modin *before* entering Judea,[36] and then there was a political change. When Alexander Balas arrived and appointed Jonathan as high priest, Demetrius wanted to outbid him: he offered him fiscal advantages, including a transfer of three *nomes* (districts) of Samaria to Judea, but Jonathan was suspicious and refused the offer (*Ant.* 13:58; 1 Macc. 10:46-47). After a series of events, his son Demetrius II granted a new statute, similar to that of his father, which this time was accepted (1 Macc. 11:30-37). He specified in particular the names of the

---

[35] The site is about 10 kilometer east of Lydda-Lod; cf. Joshua J. Schwartz, *Lod (Lydda), Israel: From Its Origins Through the Byzantine Period* (BAR International Series 571), Oxford, BAR, 1991, but the exact location has not yet been clearly identified. For the political situation in Modin, cf. Joseph Sievers, *The Hasmoneans and Their Supporters*, Atlanta, Scholars Press, 1990, p. 37.

[36] Cf. Gustav Beyer, "Die Stadtgebiete von Diospolis und Nikopolis im 4. Jahrh. n. Chr. und ihre Grenznachbarn," *ZDPV* 66 (1933), pp. 209–71 (234).

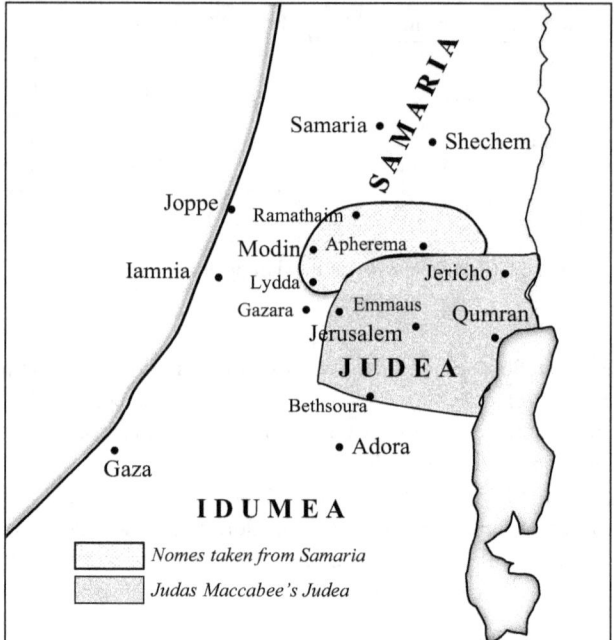

Figure 12 Enlarged Judea.

three districts[37] taken from the satrapy of Samaria-Galilee: Aphairema, Lydda, and Rathamin. The initial territory of Judea proper—roughly that of Nehemiah—was then limited in the North by Gibeon and Bethel, in the west by Emmaus (future Nicopolis), in the South by Bethsura (Bethzur), and in the east by the Jordan and Jericho. The added domain represents a notable extension to the North and northwest but does not include Gazara (Gezer), which was not conquered until later by Simon. The district Lydda (Lod) included Modin, the home of the Hasmoneans (Figure 12).

In addition to this territorial affair, it is necessary to note a maneuver of Jewish legitimacy. After the transfer of the three districts, when Jonathan was murdered, his brother Simon, who succeeded him, took the trouble to bury him solemnly in Modin and then had a huge monument of white polished stone built for his father and his brothers. "He raised it to such a height that it could be seen from everywhere, surrounded it with porticoes, and erected monolithic columns, an extraordinary scene. He also built seven pyramids for his parents and brothers, one for each, designed to amaze by their size and beauty and which have been preserved even to this day" (*Ant.* 13:211; 1 Macc. 13:27-30). It was thus the embellishment of a traditional family tomb, where Mattathias and his wife and Judas Maccabaeus were already buried (*Ant.* 12:432; 1 Macc. 9:19); everything was planned for Mattathias' five sons (but not for their wives).

---

[37] Josephus names the three districts "Samaria, Jaffa and Galilee" (*Ant.* 13:125-127). Earlier (§ 50), in the document of Demetrios I, he had put "Samaria, Galilee and Perea," which is hardly better, whereas 1 Macc. 10:30 says only "three nomes annexed from Samaria-Galilee." The corruption of the names is difficult to explain.

Mattathias' origin thus had an ambiguity that was masked. Moreover, his action was brief, since he died one year after the beginning of the persecution. It has been observed that his rebellion was not directed against Jerusalem and Judea but rather Samaria.[38] The episode that launched his revolt from Modin is described in some detail (*Ant.* 12:268-269; 1 Macc. 2:15-28): he had to go underground when he killed a Jew who wanted to observe an idolatrous custom *in public*. The problem was not obedience to a royal edict forbidding Judaism but the choice to accept a foreign cult. In other words, despite literary alterations that adapt the episode to the edict, the most natural circumstance of Mattathias' rebellion is the introduction of Hellenism as an option, and this began as early as the time of the high priest Jason, in 175 BCE. Thus, Mattathias was a rebel who was indiscriminately Jewish or Samaritan and therefore simply Israelite.

Even before the uprising led by Mattathias, Josephus inserts in his second account a supplication of the Samaritans addressed to King Antiochus IV[39] (*Ant.* 12:257-264). It is introduced by a comment from Josephus, who denounces their fickleness: "Seeing what the Jews endured, the Samaritans no longer regarded them as their brethren, and no longer recognized the temple on Mount Gerizim as the temple of the Great God." Then the supplication is quoted:

> To king Antiochus Theos Epiphanes, a memorial from the Sidonians of Shechem. After a series of draughts that desolated the land, our ancestors, following scrupulously an ancient superstition, began observing the day that the Jews call the "Sabbath." They had erected a nameless temple on the mountain called Gerizim, where they offered the proper sacrifices. Now that you have treated the Jews as their wickedness deserved, the royal officers, thinking that because of our kinship with them we must do the same things, cover us with the same accusations, although we are Sidonians by origin, as is clear from the public records. We therefore beseech you, our benefactor and savior, to order Apollonius, the governor of this district, and Nicanor, the royal agent, not to molest us by bringing against us the same accusations as against the Jews, who are foreign to us both by race and customs, and we ask that the anonymous temple bear the name of Zeus Hellenios. Thus, we will no longer be molested and, being able to safely go about our work, we will increase your income.

These Samaritans declared themselves "Sidonians," which is equivalent to "Phoenicians," a Greek term corresponding to "Canaanites." On coins minted at the time of Antiochus IV Epiphanes, Tyre is called "metropolis of the Sidonians," that is, "of the Phoenicians:" the term was detached from the city of Sidon, when it was supplanted by Tyre, and

---

[38] Cf. Joshua Schwartz and Joseph Spanier, "On Mattathias and the Desert of Samaria," *RB* 98 (1991), pp. 252–71.

[39] Elias J. Bickerman, "Un document relatif à la persécution d'Antiochus IV Épiphane," in: *Studies in Jewish and Christian History II*, pp. 105–35, removed the objections to the authenticity of the document, by examining the diplomatic formulas; Jonathan A. Goldstein, *II Maccabees: A New Translation with Introduction and Commentary* (The Anchor Bible, 41A), New York, Doubleday, 1983, p. 524.

applied to a wider Phoenician population.[40] Traces of Sidonians were found at the same time at Marissa in Idumea and at the port of Jamnia in Judea (see Figure 2), which suggests that these were Phoenician settlements or trading posts.[41] An ancient link is indicated in the biblical genealogies, where Sidon is the son of Canaan (Gen. 10:15). Therefore, the Samaritans, far from abjuring their traditional customs,[42] simply declare themselves to be Canaanites, but it is commonly assumed that there was reshuffling: they could not have presented themselves in this way, since the ancient Israelites had supplanted the nations of Canaan.[43] The Samaritans claim to have been there for a very long time, whereas the Jews in revolt are newcomers from Babylonia, as will become clearer later on: they are the ones who are "foreigners by race and customs."

As for the rededication of the anonymous temple to Zeus, it is only a label for external use. Such a concession on the part of the Samaritans is minimal, in contrast to the horrified language of 2 Macc. 6:2; it is by no means an outright Hellenization but a simple gesture of goodwill toward Antiochus.[44] In the *Letter of Aristaeus*, King Ptolemy II is told that he must emancipate the captive Judeans, for "the god who rules your kingdom is the one who established their laws . . . Indeed, the god who created all things, they and we worship in the same way, and we call him Zeus." Josephus, in his paraphrase, raises no objection (*Letter* § 16 and *Ant.* 12:22).

Herodotus is a useful witness to these names: followed by Strabo, he reports that in his time, in the fifth century, there were only a few primitive populations left who offered sacrifices to an anonymous god[45] and in particular in Syria-Palestine.[46] From the coast, along which he traveled from Egypt, one can indeed see Mount Gerizim but not Jerusalem. Herodotus' information shows that this is an exception concerning

---

[40] Cf. Catherine Apicella, "Sidon à l'époque hellénistique: quelques problèmes méconnus," in: Maurice Sartre (dir.), *La Syrie hellénistique* (Topoi, Suppl. 4), Paris, Gallimard, 2003, pp. 125–47. The king of Sidon had the title of "king of the Sidonians of Sidon."

[41] A funerary inscription mentions the leader of a Sidonian colony in Marisa; cf. Félix-M. Abel, "Tombeaux récemment découverts à Marissa," *RB* 35 (1925), p. 275. Another trace was discovered on the coast; cf. Benjamin Isaac, "A Seleucid Inscription from Jamnia-on-the-Sea: Antiochus V Eupator and the Sidonians," *IEJ* 41 (1991), pp. 132–44. Eusebius, *Praep. evang.* 9.17.8, quotes Eupolemus through Alexander Polyhistor, who states that Abraham left Ur of the Chaldees to come to Phoenicia (equivalent to Canaan).

[42] As many commentators believe, following the rhetoric of Josephus; cf. lastly Reinhard Pummer, *The Samaritans: A Profile*, Grand Rapids/Cambridge, Eerdmans, 2016, pp. 54–66.

[43] Cf. Richard J. Coggins, "The Samaritans in Josephus," in: Louis H. Feldman and Gohei Hata (eds.), *Josephus, Judaism, and Christianity*, Leiden, Brill, 1987, pp. 257–73.

[44] Antiochus IV had a great veneration for Zeus; he had contributed to the construction of the temple of Zeus Olympian in Athens. He founded or refounded several cities in his name, endowing them with Greek institutions. An inscription of Babylon dated September 166 BCE presents him as "savior of Asia and founder of the city." However, Babylon remained the city-temple of Bel. The astrologers were not molested, and a colophon indicates that traditional prayers were copied in 163 BCE on new tablets; cf. O. Mørkholm, *Antiochus IV of Syria*, København, Nordisk Forlag, 1966, p. 100.

[45] According to Acts 17:23, Paul argued in Athens from an "unknown god," that is, an anonymous one; to give him a name was to make him acceptable to the Greeks.

[46] Herodotus, 2.52; he specifies elsewhere that Phoenician rule extended to the Red Sea, thus including Canaan (5.58.1); he therefore knew the Syria-Palestine of his time, but he does not mention anything Israelite. That this deity is "anonymous" suggests that YHWH's name was not spoken in worship. In the burning bush passage, God gives Moses his name in the form "I will be" (Exod. 3:14 אהיה, LXX ὁ ὤν "the being").

populations far from the Mediterranean coast. Indeed, he does not mention the anonymous Phoenician deities, because they were given Greek names, commonly used in contacts with foreigners. The inhabitants of Tyre called their patron god "Heracles" in Greek, but among them he remained the "Master of Tyre" or "the King," that is to say the ancestral protector; Zeus and Heracles were simply the Greek names of Baal Shamen and Melqart.[47]

In the case of the Samaritans, there is no question of a change of worship that would imply more or less important architectural modifications; they continue to observe the Sabbath and to offer "suitable sacrifices." The etiological argument about drought presumably includes the Sabbatical year, which is a form of crop rotation.

The sacrifices offered in a sacred space imply a system of laws, but there is no reason not to link it to Moses. As for the site, recent excavations on the summit of Mount Gerizim have uncovered a vast Yahwist sanctuary with no visible syncretism: no statuette has been found, and the inscriptions are unambiguous. This sanctuary was built around the middle of the fifth century, the dating coming from many coins of the Persian period.[48] The high and steep place looks like a sacred mountain, and one can conjecture that there were previous cults, but nothing has been found so far, apart from prehistoric flints.

The structure that was excavated underwent two main phases: the most recent is a Hellenistic temple from the beginning of the second century, that is to say, from the time when Antiochus III, after several wars, finally conquered Coele-Syria. The oldest phase is a vast fortified space, where a very large quantity of bones has been found but no closed temple as such; there were certainly several altars, but their overall disposition has not been identified. In fact, all the rites of the Pentateuch presuppose only altars, except perhaps those of Atonement (Kippur), when the high priest enters the Holy of Holies (Lev. 16:3-4). For example, according to Ezra 3:3-6, the high priest Joshua and Zerubbabel returned from exile and rebuilt the holocaust altar and then reestablished the entire annual cycle of sacrifices, "but the foundation of the temple of the Lord of YHWH was not yet laid"; so, there was no closed temple.

In any case, the Samaritans' request was granted, and in his reply the king pretended to understand that the Samaritans were proposing a change of cult (§ 264): "Since they wish to live according to the customs of the Greeks." Josephus has indicated the date of the reply in the summer of 166 BCE, which corresponds to the year of the death of Mattathias, who is however not introduced until after the request and its consequences. This is perhaps a way of completely detaching his revolt from the Samaritan orbit.

---

[47] Cf. Corinne Bonnet, *Melqart, cultes et mythes de l'Héraclès tyrien en Méditerranée* (Studia Phoenicia, 8), Leuven, Peeters, 1988; Jessica L. Nitschke, "Interculturality in Image and Cult in the Hellenistic East: Tyrian Melqart Revisited," in: Eftychia Stavrianopoulou (ed.), *Shifting Social Imaginaries in the Hellenistic Period: Narrations, Practices, and Images*, Leiden/Boston, Brill, 2013, pp. 253–82.

[48] Cf. Yitzhak Magen, "The Dating of the First Phase of the Samaritan Temple on Mount Gerizim in Light of the Archaeological Evidence," in: Oded Lipschits, Gary N. Knoppers, and Rainer Albertz (eds.), *Judah and the Judeans in the Fourth Century B.C.E.*, Winona Lake, Eisenbrauns, 2007, pp. 157–212.

3.5 Conclusion

Whereas there were previously signs of harmony in the Israelite community, the Maccabean crisis represents a major break in several respects. Ultimately, the Hasmonean regime that resulted was accepted neither by the Jews of Egypt nor by the Samaritans. The former resisted for at least forty years, according to the letter in 2 Macc. 1:1-9; but it is not known how the tension was gradually resolved, since Onias' temple continued functioning until it was dismantled by Vespasian, around 73. Nevertheless, in Judea, there remained a current of hostility to the Hasmoneans, which is well attested by rabbinic tradition: the names of Judas Maccabeus and of his brothers are never mentioned, even in connection with the Dedication. Moreover, the Hebrew original of 1 Maccabees, entitled *Book of the Dynasty of God's Resisters*, has been discarded: Origen, who lists the biblical books with their Hebrew names, refers to it as an "external book."[49] A relatively well-preserved inscription discovered at Caesarea Maritima lists the twenty-four priestly classes.[50] The first name is Jehoiarib (cf. 1 Chron. 24:7), to which the priest Mattathias has been attached, and it is flanked by a very derogatory comment: "refusing the Most High." This severe judgment is not due to a lack of piety but more seriously to the fact of having made war.

As for the Samaritans, after their failed attempt in Alexandria, the very existence of the Gerizim temple was a threat to the Hasmonaeans' Jerusalem, even without hostile action, if only because of the biblical references. This is why John Hyrcanus son of Simon took care to destroy it as soon as the weakening of the Syrian suzerain left his hands free.

Now, regarding the reason for the symmetrical rejection, it could have been due to the low extraction of the Hasmoneans; but this is certainly too abstract, since they succeeded, as David once had. We must rather look at the customs, and there are two indications. The first is the matter of armed defense on the Sabbath. When, after a massacre of Jews on the Sabbath, Mattathias' entourage decided to authorize it (1 Macc. 2:41) in a situation that was serious; but no precedent is cited and this fact is remarkable, since the biblical accounts are studded with wars. Indeed, complete abstention from military activity on the Sabbath is inconceivable for a state, which must have a permanent defense system. It is conceivable only for a city or a district duly protected by a wall.[51] Now, Josephus makes it clear that the permission for armed defense on the Sabbath will be maintained during and after the Hasmonean regime (*Ant.* 12:277). Attacking will remain forbidden, and this is why the policy of territorial

---

[49] Quoted in Eusebius, *HE* 6.25.2, which gives Greek transcriptions of Hebrew names (βερεσιθ, σεμωθ, etc.); the restored Hebrew name is ספר בית סרבני אל. The expression "external books" appears in m.Sanhedrin 10:1 to designate forbidden books: whoever reads them is excluded from the "world to come."

[50] Cf. Michael Avi-Yonah, "The Caesarean Inscription of the 24 Priestly Courses," *Eretz Israel* 7 (1964), pp. 24–8: the expression מסרבי מרום "refusing the Most High," added to the name of Yehoyarib's class on the list of priestly classes, is very pejorative, disqualifying Mattathias and his posterity. According to t.Taanit 2:1, the class of Yehoyarib was removed from service, without further clarification.

[51] Cf. Moshe D. Herr, "The Problem of War on the Sabbath in the Second Temple and the Talmudic Periods," *Tarbiz* 30 (1961), pp. 242–56, 341–56.

expansion pursued by John Hyrcanus and his successors will require the recruitment of foreign mercenaries.[52]

The second indication is an allusion to the sacred library. In a second letter from the Jerusalemites to the Judeans in Egypt, we learn that Nehemiah, the Babylonian reformer, "founded a library and collected the books about the kings and prophets, and the writings of David, and the letters of the kings about votive offerings. In the same way Judas also collected all the books that had been lost on account of the war" (2 Macc. 2:13-14). Therefore, Judas is Nehemiah's heir, although it is not clearly stated that his library is the same. Nehemiah's library is difficult to reconstruct,[53] but the most remarkable fact is that neither the name of Moses nor his Law appears in it, which could only worry both the Samaritans and the Jews of Egypt, concerned about biblical legitimacy.

The next chapter will show that these two indications are intertwined and point to Babylonian customs and even more precisely to the Pharisees. For the time being, we can simply note a difference observed between 1 Maccabees and Josephus, which both depend on the same Hebrew source: the former introduces biblical allusions that the latter ignores. Consequently, the hypothesis to be made is that while the Hasmonean regime gradually made efforts to take up scriptural references,[54] it was already too late to recover the Samaritans.

A characteristic crisis at the court certainly contributed to this: according to *Ant.* 13:288-298, during a banquet, the high priest John Hyrcanus felt humiliated by the Pharisees, because he was suspected of being a bastard, which disqualified him for his priestly office. He then joined the party of the Sadducees, for whom only Scripture counts; this was a revolution, since the Hasmonean regime, heir to Nehemiah, was Pharisaic in style. A Talmudic parallel puts the episode under King Alexander Jonathan (Jannaeus), with much more verisimilitude, for there are good reasons to believe that he was indeed a bastard: since his birth he had been relegated to Galilee, and his father John Hyrcanus refused to see him until his death[55] (*Ant.* 13:321).

Now, a document from Qumran (4QMMT) is a letter addressed to an authority in charge that very cautiously suggests to him some rules regarding purity and Temple worship. The latter is always related to Scripture, whose three parts are mentioned: Moses, Prophets, David (beginning of the Writings, also see Lk 24:44). It has been recognized that these provisions are to be attributed to the Sadducees,[56] and furthermore that a fragment mentioning "King Jonathan" should be attached to the

---

[52] Cf. Emmanuelle Main, "Des mercenaires 'rhodiens' en Judée hasmonéenne? Étude du motif floral de monnaies de Jean Hyrcan et Alexandre Jannée," *REJ* 165 (2006), pp. 123-46.
[53] It may have included the Persian documents inserted in Ezra; cf. Giovanni Garbini, *Il ritorno dall' esilio babilonese* (Studi biblici, 129), Brescia, Paideia, 2001.
[54] Cf. Dongbin Choi, *The Use and Function of Scripture in 1 Maccabees* (The Library of Second Temple Studies, 98), New York, T&T Clark, 2020.
[55] Cf. *b.Qidushin* 66a and Emmanuelle Main, "Les Sadducéens vus par Flavius Josephus," *RB* 97 (1990), pp. 161-206; likewise, independently, Günther Stemberger, *Pharisäer, Sadduzäer, Essener* (SBS, 144), Stuttgart, Kathol. Bibelwerk, 1991, pp. 100-2.
[56] Cf. Yaakov Sussmann, "The History of the *Halakha* and the Dead Sea Scrolls," *Tarbiz* 59 (1989), pp. 11-76; also Lawrence H. Schiffman, "The New *Halakhic* Letter (MMT) and the Origins of the Dead Sea Sect," *BA* 52 (1990), pp. 64-73.

document,[57] which also gives the calendar of the *Jubilees*. A remarkable detail shows that the authors of this document proceed with humility, saying, "we think that," which means in particular that they do not rely on any precedent, at least explicitly. It must, however, be assumed that the cult prior to the Maccabean crisis was in some way related to the Law of Moses; but since the law is not monolithic, it certainly allows for great flexibility of interpretation. A typical case is the manner of celebrating the Passover, depending on whether one looks at Exod. 12:15-28 or at Deut. 16:1-8.

In any case, the people did not accept Jannaeus' reform, not because of cultic minutiae but because the change in the calendar upset their habits: the moon, visible to all, was no longer a reference point. Jannaeus understood this, and on his deathbed he advised his wife Alexandra, who was to succeed him, to return to the Pharisees in order to gain favor with the people (*Ant.* 13:401).

Finally, if we return to the conclusions of the previous chapter, the ancient religious divorce between Israel and Judah, which must have been very small, remains inexplicable.

---

[57] What has been shown for paleographic reasons; Annette Steudel, "4Q448 – The Lost Beginning of *MMT*?," in: Florentino García Martínez et al. (eds.), *From 4QMMT to Resurrection* (STDJ, 61), Leiden, Brill, 2006, pp. 247–63, but it would like to identify "King Jonathan" with the high priest Jonathan, attributing MMT to the Master of Justice of 1QpHab 8:8-13; but calling Jonathan, the brother of Judas Maccabeus, a king, seriously strains the meaning, and there is no reason to link this document to the Master of Justice; cf. Nodet, "Sadducéens, Sadocides, Esséniens," 186–212.

4

The Persian Period

Prior to the Maccabean crisis, very little is known about the Israelites during the Hellenistic period after Alexander, but in the preceding chapter small indications of peaceful coexistence between Jews and Samaritans were noted. Researchers have even surreptitiously gone back to the Persian period, with the findings of the small Judean colony of Elephantine, in Upper Egypt.

This period, from Cyrus to Alexander (538–332), must now be examined for itself. Field archaeology has revealed the sanctuary on Mount Gerizim, but for the Persian province of Yehud, analogous to Judas Maccabeus' Judea (Figure 12), it has so far yielded little. In contrast, the useful texts are of primary importance: mainly Ezra and Nehemiah for the return from exile that started with the decree of Cyrus and the traditions around the arrival of Alexander as reported by Josephus. Going back in time, we will first examine the latter.

4.1 Around Alexander

Josephus' account is complex; it is composed of two consecutive blocks, one under Darius III, the last Persian king, and the other linked to the arrival of Alexander the Great, who had just defeated him at Issus (*Ant.* 11:302-325).

4.1.1 The Expulsion of the Samaritan Women According to Josephus

The first ensemble deals with ethnic cleansing in Jerusalem and the construction of a Samaritan Temple. Three parts can be clearly distinguished:

1. (§ 302–3) The high priest Jaddua, son of Johanan, son of Joiada, son of Eliashib, had a brother named Manasseh who married Nicaso, daughter of Sanballat, the satrap of Samaria. The reason given for this marriage was that Sanballat, a Samaritan, wanted to get closer to Jerusalem and its reputation. These events took place in 336 BCE. at the time of the death of Philip II, the father of Alexander (§ 304–5). Having taken the control of all the Greek cities, Philip bequeathed a strong kingdom and a well-trained army to his son Alexander.

2. (§ 306–8) Afterward, Jerusalem's "elders," convinced that the misfortunes and the exile had been caused by marriages of this kind, came forward and commanded Manasseh either to divorce or not to approach the altar.
3. (§ 309–12) Manasseh then went to his father-in-law Sanballat, who, with the approval of King Darius III, began building for him a temple like Jerusalem's on Mount Gerizim. Manasseh thought that he would quickly obtain the pontificate, because Sanballat was very old. Many priests and laymen who had contracted similar marriages followed Manasseh, with the material help of Sanballat.

The initial policy of Sanballat, a Samaritan satrap and apparently also a high priest without a temple, was thus to move closer to Jerusalem; and this fact brings to mind the request of the "enemies of Judah and Benjamin" in Ezra 4:1-2, who wanted to join Joshua and Zerubbabel in restoring the temple in Jerusalem. In the dispute in Alexandria before Ptolemy regarding the true Temple, Jerusalem's reputation was emphasized by Josephus (Section 3.1).

The account must be compared with Neh. 13, a chapter that Josephus did not know. Nehemiah, having come to Jerusalem a second time, but without a mandate, continues an autobiographical account, in which he states that he criticized and sometimes struck Jews who had married foreign women, recalling that Solomon had fallen into idolatry precisely for this reason. Nehemiah even explains that he drove out a son of the high priest Joiada son of Eliashib, because he had married a daughter of Sanballat the Horonite (Neh. 13:28). This was during his second mission, after the thirty-second year of a King Artaxerxes (13:6), that is, one of the first two kings who bore that name, the third having reigned only twenty years (cf. Introduction, Figure 1). So, it was well before Darius III, and there is a chronological incoherence, doubled by a shift of two generations[1] (cf. Figure 14). There would thus have been two people named Sanballat whose daughter married a son of a Jewish high priest, a daring act that provoked similar reactions, first from Nehemiah, then from the "elders" of Jerusalem.

Now, the reform of the "elders" leads to the exodus of many priests and laymen to Samaria. These "elders" of Jerusalem give the impression that there was a sudden local initiative to counter a well-established situation, but at the same time their quality of elders gives them an authority which is not explained, but not discussed at all. Alongside the parallelism with Nehemiah 13, there is a great analogy with the main activity of Ezra, who attacked foreign wives but with the aim—as it is said—of driving them out. The two episodes can be compared in the light of Manasseh's case: the offenders had to choose between divorce and exile. The list of foreign wives given in Ezra 10:18-19, where all walks of life are affected, shows that the problem was very broad. Josephus did not make the connection between the "elders" and Ezra, for two reasons: on the one hand, he placed Ezra under Xerxes, that is, a good century earlier; and, on the other hand,

---

[1] Josephus, who does not have an absolute chronology, linked Yehozadaq to the exile of 587 BCE and Yaddua to the arrival of Alexander in 332 BCE, that is to say, six successions for some 255 years, which is not very likely, but some people are satisfied with it; cf. James C. Vanderkam, *From Jeshua to Caiaphas: High Priests after the Exile*, Minneapolis, Fortress Press, 2004, which identifies Zerubbabel with Sheshbazzar, which makes it possible to trace the chronology; cf. the discussion at Section 1.2.4.

Ezra expelled foreigners, more or less "Canaanites" (Ezra 10:38), whereas Josephus does not manage, despite notable efforts, to consider the Samaritans as ordinary foreigners.

The duplication of the same facts indicates two distinct traditions reporting the same events, and the references to Nehemiah and Ezra show that the "elders" were in fact Babylonian reformers.

These considerations highlight two major difficulties: on the one hand, there is a question regarding the reformers' time, which oscillates between Artaxerxes I and Darius III, with uncertainty about the identity of Sanballat, a high-ranking Samaritan figure, who acts as governor or high priest. On the other hand, the actual presence of such reformers, who make the Samaritans into a sort of refuse of Judaism, is practically invisible in Jerusalem for a century and a half, until the Maccabean crisis, according to the testimonies listed earlier (Section 3.3).

4.1.2 Alexander in Jerusalem?

Historians report that after his victory at Issos in 333 BCE, where he defeated the Persian army of Darius III, Alexander refrained from immediately pursuing the Persians toward the east. As a good strategist, he first wanted to secure control over the Mediterranean coast up to Egypt: to this end, he conquered Tyre, Gaza, and finally founded Alexandria. In the process, he sent Parmenion, his all-powerful deputy general, to conquer Damascus and install a governor of Coele-Syria in the ancient city of Samaria.[2] Incidentally, this shows once again that, between Tyre and Gaza, Jerusalem was not visible from the coast, contrary to what Josephus will assert.

It is in this context that Josephus places the second part of his narrative, which concerns the foundation of the temple on Mount Gerizim promised by Sanballat, a figure who ensures the link with the first part earlier. After a prologue about Alexander's unexpected victory at Issus, this part has two phases, in which the soldiers of Sanballat appear, but that are separated by a long account of Alexander's visit to Jerusalem.[3]

1. (§ 321–5) At the beginning of Alexander's siege of Tyre, Sanballat visited him with 8,000 men to announce that he was abandoning Darius and was ready to accept him as suzerain; this was after Issus. He told him about the affair concerning Manasseh and asked for permission to build a temple, in order to divide the power of the Jews, for in the past the unity of the nation had been harmful to the kings of Assur. Alexander agreed. Sanballat set about doing this, but he died nine months later, precisely when Alexander, after taking Tyre and then Gaza, was heading for Jerusalem with an aggressive intention, because the high priest Jaddua, alerted and wanting to remain faithful to Darius, had refused to pledge allegiance to him.

---

[2] The excavations confirmed the importance of the city of Samaria at the time; cf. Ron E. Tappy, "Israelite Samaria: Head of Ephraim and Jerusalem's Elder Sister," in: Bart Wagemakers (ed.), *Archaeology in the land of "tells and ruins"*, Oxford/Philadelphia, Oxbow Books, 2014, pp. 73–87.
[3] Amitay Ory, "Alexander and Caligula in the Jerusalem Temple: A Case of Conflated Traditions," in: Krzysztof Nawotka, Robert Rollinger, et al. (eds.), *The Historiography of Alexander the Great*, Wiesbaden, Harrassowitz Verlag, 2018, pp. 177–86.

2. (§ 326–39) A dream revealed to Jaddua that he would have nothing to fear, and he went out in procession to meet Alexander. When he arrived, Alexander prostrated himself before him, to the astonishment of those around him, beginning with his second-in-command, Parmenion. He explained that he recognized him in a vision or dream that he had had before leaving Macedonia, in which God revealed to him that he would defeat Darius. He went to offer a sacrifice in the Temple, and when he was shown a mysterious prophecy of Daniel in this respect (cf. Dan. 2:38 and 8:21), he believed that it applied to him. He then granted several requests: the high priest wanted a tax exemption during the sabbatical year, when nothing is sown (Exod. 23:10-11; 1 Macc. 6:49). Alexander granted it, and he also promised in advance that the Jews in Babylon could follow their own customs. Finally, he recruited a number of Jews as mercenaries to accompany him to Egypt.

3. (§ 340–6) After Alexander had granted these privileges, the Samaritans, "renegades of the Jewish nation," learned of it and decided to declare themselves Jews. They presented themselves before him, taking with them the soldiers offered by Sanballat. They invited him to visit their temple and asked him for the same tax exemption during the sabbatical year as he had granted to the Jews. However, learning that they were Hebrews and not Jews, he dismissed them until a future visit, but he did not neglect ordering the soldiers offered by Sanballat to accompany him to Egypt. Josephus concludes by reporting that, after Alexander's death, if anyone in Jerusalem was accused of transgressing the Law, and in particular of violating the Sabbath, he fled to the Samaritans saying that he had been treated unjustly; among them, the Law was more tolerant.

This account for the glory of Jerusalem is combined with Josephus' contempt for the Samaritans. Indeed, Alexander had no reason to come to Jerusalem; that would have been an unnecessary detour, especially after Gaza, which is much further South. Yet, in order to consolidate the later position of Alexandria's Jews, it was important to establish a tradition showing that Alexander was favorable to them.[4] However, the legendary features[5] cannot hide two contradictions concerning the temple on Mount Gerizim: on the one hand, it cannot have been built simultaneously under Darius and under Alexander, while the high priest of Jerusalem remained the same. On the other hand, it cannot have been both permitted and then ignored by Alexander.

In fact, two narrative lines can be discerned: on the one hand, the construction of the temple on Mount Gerizim with the approval of a king, in connection with the expulsion of priests married to Samaritan women, that is, local Israelites; on the other hand, a narrative with Alexander but without Sanballat, in which the Gerizim temple exists and the Samaritans are faithful to the Law. If we omit Alexander's legendary

---

[4] It is thus that the accounts of the campaigns of Alexander, due to his historian of court Callisthenes, were amplified, from where the name of Pseudo-Callisthenes or Alexander Romance; cf. Catherine Gaullier-Bougassas, "La fortune du Roman d'Alexandre: continuations et création d'un cycle (xiie-xve siècles)," *Anabases* 2 (2005), pp. 147–59.

[5] Cf. the historical discussion of Ralph Marcus, *Jewish Antiquities, Books IX-XI*, London, the Loeb Classical Library, 1966, pp. 512–26.

visit to Jerusalem, the bottom line is that he knew nothing about the Samaritans but recruited some. Thus, the construction of the temple on Mount Gerizim remains linked to Sanballat but is detached from Alexander.

Sanballat's dealings with Alexander are supported by an argument concerning the ancient power of the Jews that recalls another analogue circumstance: according to Ezra 4:11-12, Samaria's governor alerted the Persian king Artaxerxes about the danger of allowing Jerusalem to be rebuilt, since it was a rebellious city quick to rise up. In response, the king ordered the work to be stopped, because the records showed that powerful kings ruling in Jerusalem had dominated the whole of Transeuphrates, which is an exaggerated allusion to the empire of Solomon (cf. 1 Kgs 5:1).

The matter of Sanballat's temple is rapidly settled: it is built quickly, and Sanballat must disappear, for he has no place in the following episodes. He has no successor, and we lose sight of Manasseh and his plans. However, the Jews' power is indeed reduced by half since the Gerizim temple is built.

Jerusalem's population was unified only in appearance: the high priest who obtains a concession for the Sabbatical year, but he is not the one who asks for a guarantee of the status of the Jews of Babylonia, which is a curious anticipation since Alexander has not yet advanced toward the east. This Babylonian entity is represented in Jerusalem, and it must be linked to the "elders" or to Ezra and Nehemiah. However, they did not have a monopoly, and there is perhaps an anachronism, for Alexander's symmetrical recruitment of Jews and Samaritans to man garrisons in Egypt[6] implies that they have the same customs and will not be subject to the Sabbath ordinance; this coincides well enough with the Judean colony of Elephantine (cf. Section 3.3).

4.1.3 Conclusion

It has now been proven that the Gerizim temple certainly predates Alexander, and this is in fact implied by the last episode of his visit, when the Samaritans come to present themselves to him. The mention of Parmenion shows that the traditions reported by Josephus developed from the accounts of Callisthenes, Alexander's appointed historian.

The figure of Sanballat has several facets; their common feature is his desire to promote the Samaritan entity, and Jerusalem's fame anticipates the argument of the Jews during the conflict in Alexandria (Section 3.1). Sanballat's initial plan to move closer to Jerusalem implies that a Samaritan reality had already long existed without a temple and without a reputation but of the same culture as the Jews. This homogeneity predates the coming of the "elders," whose authority is not disputed, although its origin is unknown. It is also not known how Jewish priests and laymen could have blended in with the Samaritans, but apparently there could be no problem. This overall unity is recalled to Alexander by Sanballat, who by this time has lost sight of the division that

---

[6] Josephus reports other traditions, parallel or convergent: in *Ant.* 12:3-4 he indicates, quoting Agatharchides of Cnidus, that Ptolemy I Lagos, the successor of Alexander who conquered Egypt, had taken Jerusalem (ca. 312 BCE) and had taken many Jews and Samaritans captive. On the contrary, according to *CAp* 1:186, Hecataeus of Abdera states that many Jews then voluntarily emigrated to Egypt.

the "elders" introduced, and this indicates that they are an instable component in the tradition.

Indeed, the Samaritans' last recourse to Alexander, after the disappearance of Sanballat, shows a divided situation, at least according to Josephus: they are Hebrews and not Jews. Josephus thinks he has to call them renegades, but it is not known how their profiles differ, except on one essential point: there are now two temples, but this does not imply a different Yahwism. Elsewhere Josephus easily confuses Jews, Israelites, and Hebrews: for example, in *Ant.* 4:11 he speaks about Jews' revolt against Moses in the desert (cf. Num. 16:1); later, in connection with the struggles of the prophet Samuel against the Philistines, he manages to put all three denominations into a single sentence (*Ant.* 6:29-30).

4.2 Ezra and Nehemiah

These figures have given their names to two difficult books which, traditionally paired, are the only ones that propose a biblical anchoring in the Persian period, that is, between Cyrus' conquest of Babylon in 539 BCE and the defeat of Darius III at Issus in 333 BCE.

In spite of the numerous inscriptions collected,[7] the Persian period is poorly known in Judea, for the notion of "returnees from exile" is fairly complex, as the preceding considerations about the "elders" suggest. Apart from the temple on Mount Gerizim, archaeology shows almost nothing useful, except on one point: the figure of Sanballat is attested fairly well in written documents.

At the end of various conquests that culminated in the seizure of Babylon, Cyrus dominated the entire Near East. Inaugurating the Persian period, he established a new policy, properly imperial, which was based on the respect of the culture of the local populations, by means of a flexible, effective, and centralized administration. He gained from this attitude the prestige of an enlightened liberator, as attested by Greek historians and inscriptions, as well as the Bible (Isa. 45:3-4, where Cyrus is said to be "Anointed of YHWH"). He reestablished the gods dwelling in the vassal regions and rebuilt temples for them; he allowed the deported populations to return to their traditional homeland.[8]

In this context, the proclamation of Cyrus that opens the Book of Ezra seems simple and plausible, even if it is presented in biblical colors.

> *In the first year of King Cyrus of Persia, in order that the word of the* LORD *by the mouth of Jeremiah might be accomplished, the* LORD *stirred up the spirit of King Cyrus of Persia so that he sent a gerald throughout all his kingdom, and also in a written edict declared: "This says King Cyrus of Persia: The* LORD, *the God of heaven,*

---

[7] Cf. André Lemaire, "Unité et diversité des Judéens à l'époque achéménide d'après les données épigraphiques," *Transeuphratène* 49 (2017), pp. 163–86.
[8] Cf. Rahim Shayegan (ed.), *Cyrus the Great: Life and Lore* (Ilex Foundation, 21), Boston/Washington, DC, Center for Hellenic Studies, 2018.

has given me all the kingdoms of the earth, and he has charged me to build him a house at Jerusalem in Judah. Any of those among you who are of his people— may their God be with them!—are now permitted to go up to Jerusalem in Judah, and rebuild the house of the LORD, *the God of Israel—he is the God who is in Jerusalem."*

Cyrus takes charge of the restoration of the temple in Jerusalem and invites whoever is part of the whole people of YHWH to come up. This is the part in italics, which also constitutes the finale of 2 Chron. 36:22-23 and corresponds well to the perspective of this book: after the exile, which had become inevitable, all Israel, that is, all the tribes, will gather around the rebuilt temple of Jerusalem and observe the Law of Moses.[9]

However, the nonitalic ending of Ezra 1:3-4 gives an entirely different meaning: Cyrus invites only the deportees from Judah to return. In his paraphrase, Josephus perceived the nuance and regrets that few exiles heard the invitation (*Ant.* 11:133):

However, the entire people of the Israelites remained in the region. That is why only two tribes are now under Roman rule, in Asia and Europe, while the other ten are still beyond the Euphrates, forming endless myriads that cannot be properly counted.

The two tribes are Judah and Benjamin, without counting at least some of the priests and Levites; the other ten represent the ancient northern kingdom deported by Sargon II, which approximately corresponded to the regions of Samaria and Galilee (cf. Section 2.2). Josephus does not imagine for a moment that the Samaritans could, despite their fidelity to the Law, represent these ancient tribes.

4.2.1 Ezra

We have seen that the Book of Ezra is composed of two distinct parts (Section 1.2.4): the first goes from the Cyrus' decree ordering the restoration of the Temple to its actual inauguration (Ezra 1-6 // 1 Ezra 2-7); the second reports the mission of Ezra, the Babylonian reformer.

An Aramaic version of the decree, later found by King Darius, is quoted in Ezra 6:3-5. It does not speak of migration, but it indicates the dimensions of the sanctuary and specifies two points: the expenses will be covered by the king, and the cult utensils removed by Nebuchadnezzar in 587 BCE will be returned.[10]

---

[9] Cf. Jordan Guy, *United in Exile, Reunited in Restoration: The Chronicler's Agenda* (Hebrew Bible monographs, 81), Sheffield, Phoenix Press, 2019, which shows that the Chronicler wanted to convince all the tribes in diaspora to return. It is now recognized that this perspective is entirely different from that of Ezra-Nehemiah; cf. Sara Japhet, "The Relationship between Chronicles and Ezra-Nehemiah," in: John A. Emerton (ed.), *Congress Volume, Leuven 1989*, Leiden, Brill, 1991, pp. 298–313; James D. Newsome, "Toward a New Understanding of the Chronicler and His Purposes," *JBL* 94 (1975), pp. 201–17; Philippe Abadie, "Écrire l'histoire judéenne aux périodes perse et grecque: un défi identitaire," *RSR* 103 (2015), pp. 69–86.

[10] The two versions have been reconciled by Elias J. Bickerman, "The Edict of Cyrus in Esdras 1," in: *Studies in Jewish and Christian History I*, Leiden, Brill, 1976, pp. 72–108. Amélie Kuhrt, "The Cyrus Cylinder and Achaemenid Imperial Policy," *JSOT* 25 (1983), pp. 83–97, wonders whether the text of

The story seems simple: after issuing this decree, Cyrus had the Temple's furnishings delivered to Sheshbazzar, prince of Judah (1:8). Much later, Tattenai, governor of Transeuphrates, the region west of the Euphrates, came to inspect the work in Jerusalem and reported to King Darius to get his opinion about the legality of the undertaking. He explained that the builders cited the order of Cyrus, in accordance with which Sheshbazzar, who had become governor, had laid the foundations of the temple of God in Jerusalem; and he observed that the work was continuing (5:7-17). Thus, Cyrus' decree was later found in the Persian archives of Ecbatana and confirmed by Darius.

The work was therefore completed, although with a literary anomaly (Ezra 6:14-15): "They finished their building by command of the God of Israel and by decree Cyrus, Darius, and King Artaxerxes of Persia; and this house was finished . . . in the sixth year of the reign of King Darius." The mention of an order from Artaxerxes is surprising, since according to 4:21-22 he had the work in Jerusalem interrupted until the second year of King Darius. If one omits Artaxerxes, as most commentators do—beginning with Josephus (*Ant.* 11:106)—one understands that this is the sixth year of Darius I, and that the restoration was consequently completed in 515 BCE. This fits in quite well with the seventy-year exile announced by Jeremiah and beginning in 587 BCE,[11] as well as with the lamentations of elderly returnees who had known the old temple (Ezra 3:12). If, on the other hand, one respects the text, one must lower the date of completion of the temple; but the list of Persian kings leads to two solutions: either distinguishing between different Artaxerxes, which leads one to consider that the temple was completed under Darius III, or that Artaxerxes I may have changed his mind after having blocked the work, and one obtains the sixth year of Darius II, that is, 419 BCE. The first possibility (Darius III) could fit with the contest of Darius' pages related in 1 Ezra 3:1–5:6, but an intermediate solution is possible, considering that the author of the account is far from the events and has only a vague idea of the succession of the Persian kings.

The lower chronology remains difficult, but it seems to be confirmed by the fact that, in the Book of Ezra, many episodes are introduced between Cyrus and Darius, in particular interruptions of the construction under Cyrus, under Xerxes, and then under an Artaxerxes (Ezra 4). These interruptions need to be examined in detail, because the Samaritans are involved.

Looking at the narrative again from the very beginning, we first find a long list of returnees, defined as those "whom King Nebuchadnezzar of Babylon had carried captive" (2:1-2; 1 Ezra 5:7-8); this implies a very short exile, approximately forty-eight years (from 587 to 539). They arrived with twelve notables, including Zerubbabel, Jeshua, Nehemiah;[12] heads of families make important offerings for the restoration

---

this cylinder has not been overstretched, for Cyrus merely restores the cult of Marduk by dismissing the *neighboring* gods (but not the associated populations). One cannot therefore directly infer from it the order to reestablish the temple and the community of Jerusalem; one would then have to invoke more local reasons.

[11] Cf. 2 Chron. 36:21 citing Lev. 26:34 (acquitting the Sabbaths) combined with Jer. 25:11 (seventy years).

[12] This list, which recurs almost identically in Neh. 7, is probably composite, with twelve leaders supposedly representing all Israel. According to 1 Ezra 3:1–4:46, Zerubbabel was a page of King Darius, who won a wisdom contest; he would therefore largely postdate the convoy of Sheshbazzar.

of the Temple, but Sheshbazzar is no longer mentioned, although he was supposed to accompany this first convoy with the cultic utensils (1:11; 1 Ezra 2:11). However, Jeshua is the son of Jozadak, the last preexilic high priest, who was deported by Nebuchadnezzar (1 Chron. 5:40-41). Thus, a continuity appears to be ensured.

Then comes a resumption of the cult in the seventh month, with Zerubbabel and Jeshua; the repatriates, who have resettled in their cities of origin, come to Jerusalem. The altar was set up again on its foundations, and burnt offerings are offered to YHWH "as prescribed in the law of Moses." The Festival of Booths is celebrated, and then the prescribed sacrifices are made for all the solemnities of the annual cycle, "but the foundation of the temple of the LORD was not yet laid" (3:1-6). An altar of rough stones is a light structure (cf. Exod. 20:25), like the one quickly made by Judas Maccabeus and his companions after the Temple was regained (1 Macc. 4:59). It is possible to have a complete worship service without a closed temple, that is, without the Holy of Holies, but this presupposes that the rite of the high priest entering the temple on the day of atonement is not performed (Lev. 16:1-4), and that raises a question (also see Neh. 9:1).

A sentence draws attention (3:3): "They set up the altar on its foundations, because they were in dread of the neighboring peoples." One could try to correct "although they were in dread," which would be closer to the perseverance of the reformer Nehemiah, as we shall see. However, the logic of the passage would suggest that the resumption of worship to YHWH protects them, by assimilating them to the people of the land; in other words, if they had their own cult, they would no longer be considered as foreigners. On the contrary, in 4:4 the "people of the land" seek to prevent the work. In both cases, it could be the "inhabitants of the land" who were to be expelled from Canaan by Moses and Joshua.[13]

Then word of the work spread around, and "the enemies of Judah and Benjamin" came to Jeshua and Zerubbabel with a request (4:2; 1 Ezra 5:65): "Let us build with you, for we worship your God as you do, and we have been sacrificing to him since the days of King Essar-haddon of Assyria who brought us here." These "enemies" must refer to the ancient kingdom of Israel, for after Solomon there was a major secession, because the ten northern tribes with Jeroboam refused to accept Rehoboam son of Solomon as king, who ruled only over Judah and Benjamin; this led to a series of wars (1 Kgs 12:21-22.). However, this kingdom no longer exists, because Sargon II conquered it, and its population deported, according to 2 Kgs 17:6; then, colonizers were sent, but it is not clearly stated that this was done by the same king (cf. Section 2.1). There is thus a confluence between the ancient kingdom of Israel and the colonizers, which indicates that the two populations were assimilated or were perceived as assimilated.

Here, this successful fusion masks a chronological lag, for the "enemies" are indeed the colonizers sent by King Essar-haddon, who was the son of Sennacherib and the grandson of Sargon II. They are, therefore, people who adopted the same Yahwist cult that we will find later, but we do not know how their cult was organized, and they are merged into the ancient kingdom of Israel. In any case, their request is refused with a purely administrative argument (4:3): "We alone will build the house of the LORD, the

---

[13] Cf. François Langlamet, "Israël et 'l'habitant du pays'. Vocabulaire et formules d'Ex., XXXIV, 11-16," *RB* 76 (1969), pp. 321–50, 481–507.

God of Israel, as King Cyrus of Persia has commanded us." The argument is obviously specious, because Cyrus was not so precise, and it must be understood that, for the book's writer, these people cannot, in spite of their cult, really be part of Israel.

It should be noted that the "enemies" are not primarily the former Israelites of the North but settlers who, according to Josephus' version (Section 2.1), became Yahwists, perhaps by mixing with the local survivors of Israel. One can admit that they were sent by Essar-haddon and not by his grandfather, for it is enough to suppose an error regarding the king, without any further consequences.[14] On the other hand, there is no mention of either Bethel, Shechem, or Gerizim; and that corresponds to the situation of Sanballat, since he wanted to get closer to Jerusalem and had given his daughter to the brother of Jaddua, the high priest in office.

The difficulty that remains is the interest shown by these proto-Samaritans for a temple in Jerusalem, since they must have had a sanctuary somewhere where they sacrificed, that is, at least in Bethel. In any case, the request is denied. In fact, the wording of Cyrus' decree already quoted is broader (1:3): "Any of those among you who are of his people [...] are now permitted to go up." So there is the idea of an appeal to all Israel, but in the sequel only the heads of the families of Judah and Benjamin go (1:5). The discreet implication is that the true Israel is formed only by those who will come to rebuild the temple.

The fact to be underlined here is a religious rupture between the returnees and the heirs of the kingdom of Israel, seen as a whole. This new phenomenon seems isolated, but it must be connected with the anomaly that the colonizers who arrived in Samaria did not ask for information in Jerusalem about the appropriate way of worshipping YHWH (Section 2.2).

Nothing is said about the reaction of the "enemies" to the refusal to cooperate, or rather it is replaced by another intervention (4:4-5): "Then the people of the land discouraged the people of Judah . . . until the reign of King Darius of Persia." The consequence is that the "enemies'" claim of worshipping the same God is null and void; but the reason given—that is, that Cyrus' instructions concerned only the Jews (cf. Section 4.2)—is inaccurate. We shall likewise see that Nehemiah clashes with the local Israelites.

Then, the same "people of the land" address a complaint against the inhabitants of Judah and Jerusalem to King Xerxes (4:6); this episode, of which nothing else is known, is ignored in the parallel 1 Ezra 2:11 (and *Ant.* 11:20). Local authorities then warn King Artaxerxes that, with the reconstruction of the walls, Jerusalem's power will again become dangerous; in this way, they get it stopped "until the second year of the reign of King Darius of Persia" (Ezra 4:7-24). Alongside these authorities also appear the representatives of the peoples "whom the great and noble Osnappar deported and settled in the cities of Samaria and in the rest of the province Beyond

---

[14] The indifference to chronological accuracy is a constant biblical trait; it is particularly clear for the Persian period, where foreign kings are named. Thus, Daniel, a young page under Nebuchadnezzar (Dan. 1:6-7), was still living under Darius the Mede, son of Xerxes (9:1); after Darius, he still flourished under Cyrus (6:29). For the Jewish tradition, the Persian period is condensed into one generation; cf. Heinrich W. Guggenheimer, *Seder Olam Rabbah: The Rabbinic View of Biblical Chronology*, Lanham, MD, Rowman & Littlefield, 1998, pp. 247–56.

the River" (4:10). The parallel in 1 Ezra 2:12 refers only vaguely to the inhabitants of Samaria, without mentioning "the great and noble Osnappar," a king whose identity is moreover uncertain.[15] In the absence of any other indication of Assyrian deportations, it might suffice to identify these "inhabitants of Samaria" with the "enemies of Judah and Benjamin" mentioned in 4:1 and to see them reacting to the refusal addressed to them. However, this is difficult because here nothing is said about the temple but only the political-military strength of fortified Jerusalem is evoked. As for Josephus, who knows the historians and insists on a restoration under Darius I, he settles the question by replacing Artaxerxes by Cambyses, which is perfectly appropriate, at least with regard to the chronology (*Ant.* 11:21-22, cf. Figure 1).

This first part of the Book of Ezra leads to a solemn celebration of the Passover by the returned exiles, who are joined[16] by all "had separated themselves from the pollutions of the nations of the land" (Ezra 6:21). The overall narrative effect is an undeniable success, despite all sorts of harassment from the local populations and the Persian authorities; the Samaritans are mixed in with the various adversaries but in a diffuse way. Josephus, in his paraphrase, systematizes the Samaritan opposition far beyond his sources: the "enemies of Judah and Benjamin" are identified as Samaritans; in 11:97-98 and 114-119 it is the Samaritans who raise the accusations against the Jews. It is not certain, and indeed unlikely, that Josephus' sources are so explicit.

The second part of the book is devoted to the actions of Ezra himself. He is introduced as a prominent figure in the Aaronic line of high priests. However, the very brief genealogy of Ezra 7:1-5 has only five generations starting at David's time. It is very similar to that of 1 Chron. 5, which seems longer but has in fact been artificially lengthened, either by repeating sequences (vertical bars on the left) or by papponymy (bar on the right). Josephus obviously had more complete and more similar lists (Figure 13), most probably found in the Temple archives (cf. Section 1.2.3, #5).

It is to be noted that Ezra is described as an "agile scribe skilled in the Law of Moses" (Ezra 7:6), and that his genealogy makes him the brother of Jehozadak, exiled by Nebuchadnezzar. He is therefore Jeshua's uncle, which is certainly difficult to reconcile with the temple's restoration, which is narrated before him. This gives him the maximum of authority, at the cost of a certain unreasonableness, because he is placed above Jeshua, who had also reestablished the cult according to the Law of Moses. The continuity with the preexilic period is consequently expressed in two very distinct ways.

According to 7:6 and 7:27, God had inspired the heart of King Artaxerxes to glorify the temple of Jerusalem and to favor Ezra. This sudden favor is highly suspect, for two reasons: on the one hand, the king's motives are not expressed and the indication of a divine motion is certainly insufficient, since a king acts only out of interest, even if he is qualified as a "benefactor" (*everget*); on the other hand, Artaxerxes opposed

---

[15] The name is not otherwise known, and he is identified either with Assur-Banipal or with his father Essar-Haddon of Ezra 4:2; cf. Daniel Miller, "Objectives and Consequences of the Neo-Assyrian Imperial Exercise," *Religion and Theology* 16 (2009), pp. 124–49.

[16] Lit. "and"; the parallel 1 Ezra 7:13 omits "and," which gives "repatriated from the captivity, that is to say, those who have separated themselves from the abominations of the peoples of the land," and similarly Josephus, *Ant.* 11:110.

1 Chron. 5:30-41 (cf. 6:35-36)	Ezra 7:1-5 (1 Ezra 8:1-2)	Josephus Ant. 5:362 and 10:151-153	
Aaron	Aaron	Aaron	
Eleazar	Eleazar	Eleazar	Ithamar (1 Chron. 24:2)
Phinehas	Phinehas	Phinehas	
Abishua	Abishua	*Abiezer (Joseph)*	
Bukki	Bukki	Bukki	
Uzzi	Uzzi	Ozi	
Zerahiah	Zerahiah		Eli (at Silo)
Meraioth	Meraioth		Ahiah
Amariah	*Azariah*		
Ahitub	Ahitub		Ahitub
			Ahimelech
Zadok (David)	Zadok	Zadok	Ebiatar
Ahimaaz		Ahimaaz	
Azariah		Azariah	
Johanan		Joram	
Azariah		Isus (?)	
Johanan		Axioramus (Ahioram?)	
Azariah		Phideas (Pidiah?)	
		Sudeas (?)	
		Jeulus	
Amariah		Jotham	
Ahitub		Urias	
Zadok		Nerias	
		Odeas (Jehoiada? cf. 2 Kgs 12:8)	
Shallum	Shallum	Shallum	
Hilkiah (2 R 22:4)	Hilkiah	Hilkiah	
Azariah	Azariah	Azariah	
Seraiah (2 R 25:18)	Seraiah	Seraiah	
Jehozadak (exile)	**Ezra**	Jehozadak (exile)	
Jeshua (Zerubbabel)		**Jeshua** (Zerubbabel)	

Figure 13 The high priests until the exile.

the reconstruction of Jerusalem (5:21). With regard to this second point, one could distinguish between opposition by Artaxerxes I Long-Hand and the favors of Artaxerxes II Mnemon, which would place Ezra in the fourth century, after Darius II; but in this case, his very short genealogy would be even more absurd.

As for Ezra's action, it squarely goes against the Law of Moses that he is supposed to promote and observe: many had married women "from the peoples of the lands" (Ezra 9:1), in which we should recognize the seven nations of Canaan mentioned in Deut. 7:1-2. Ezra concludes that Israel is corrupt, and he organizes the dismissal of "foreign" wives and their children, regardless of the boys' circumcision, which means that Israelite identity comes strictly from the mother. A very edifying list of deviants is then given (10:18-19): sons and brothers of the high priest Jeshua son of Jozadak, priests, Levites, singers, porters, and Israelites. It is surprising that the cult ministers were not disqualified earlier. Yet, it is not expressly stated that they became idolaters. In the book's context, they clearly cannot be simply linked to the Canaanite nations of the time of Joshua son of Nun, but rather they are similar to the "enemies of Judah and

Benjamin" who worship YHWH. This action of Ezra coincides largely with that of the "elders" at the end of the Persian period, as recounted by Josephus (cf. Section 4.1.1); but Josephus did not make the connection, because it was a matter of forced divorces rather than the expulsion of couples and also because he situated Ezra's mission under King Xerxes, almost a century and a half before Darius III.

At first glance, it is difficult to see how to date such a reform, but the fact remains that Ezra is a strange figure: he has a prestigious but improbable genealogy, then legal competence regarding the Mosaic Law, which is immediately contradicted by his abusive action. Moreover, Artaxerxes' favors towards him remain unexplained (7:13-26): Ezra is authorized to lead a column of repatriates and to bring money for the cult; the Persian royal treasures will provide the useful complements; the cult ministers will be exempted from taxes; Ezra must appoint scribes and judges for the Jews in all of Transeuphrates, because the law of his God is the king's law, with the serious obligation of being faithful to it.[17]

These arrangements suggest a link with the charter granted to Jerusalem by the Syrian king Antiochus III the Great around 200 BCE (*Ant.* 12:138-146, see Section 1.2.2). After several wars between Syria and Egypt for the control of Coele-Syria, the region was finally conquered by this Antiochus. Since the Jews, who were very numerous in his kingdom—which included Mesopotamia—had helped him, he wanted to ensure their loyalty by granting them important privileges: repair, at the expense of the treasury, of the damage caused to Jerusalem by the wars; tax relief for the repopulation of the city; aid for worship; tax exemption for the cult ministers; and the obligation for the Jews to observe their ancestral laws.

The political interest of this observance appears in another decision of Antiochus III (*Ant.* 12:147-153): to prevent unrest in Asia Minor and counter Rome's growing influence, he sent civil colonizers there, precisely 2,000 Jewish families from Babylonia who volunteered. The decree includes a characteristic formula: "I am convinced that they will be well good guardians of our interests because of their piety towards their God." The link between civil loyalty and piety is the strict observance of the Sabbath, which forbids all hostility, as will be seen even more clearly in connection with Nehemiah (Section 4.2.2); in particular, an observant Jew is of no use in an enemy army. It was in view of this that, during the Maccabean crisis, Mattathias and his companions took the very novel decision to permit armed defense on the Sabbath[18] (1 Macc. 2:41-42), because it was a matter of urgency; this provision remained in force under the Hasmonean regime, which built a state.

Thus, Artaxerxes' order and the policy of Antiochus III are similar, but one does not discern the motivation of the first, whereas that of the second is obvious and

---

[17] Following Welhausen's documentary theory, it was believed that Ezra had brought a Pentateuch developed in Babylonia; cf. the synthesis in Gerhard von Rad, *Gesammelte Studien zum Alten Testament II*, München, Kaiser Vlg, 1973, pp. 9–86, but this is impossible because of the Samaritans and the atypical action of Ezra.

[18] Cf. Bezalel Bar-Kochva, *Judas Maccabaeus. The Jewish Struggle against the Seleucids*, Cambridge, Cambridge University Press, 1989, pp. 477–81. Later, for their policy of conquest, the Asmoneans will need mercenaries; cf. Gerasimos G. Aperghis, *The Seleukid Royal Economy: The Finances and Financial Administration of the Seleukid Empire*, Cambridge, Cambridge University Press, 2004, pp. 189–205.

coherent. Hence, there is good reason to conclude that the mission entrusted to Ezra is a reinterpretation of the much later stipulations of Antiochus III for the Jews.[19] Such a rearrangement is certainly not just fortuitous clumsiness, for it reveals a very precise profile of Ezra: a priest of high lineage in the Persian era, he was an expert in the Law of Moses, and his action must therefore be considered as an interpretation of this law,[20] when in fact he is opposed to it. A similar conclusion will be made about Nehemiah (Section 4.2.2). In short, the character of Ezra seems to be a fiction that combines the Law of Moses with Babylonian customs that are foreign to it.[21] In fact, there is a clue to this in Sirach's portrait gallery, which ends with Zerubbabel, Jeshua, and Nehemiah but which ignores Ezra (Sir. 49:13). From the point of view of the sources, the list of deviations in Ezra 10:18-44 must be compared with all those whom the "elders" of Jerusalem had driven away toward Samaria because of their marriages (Section 4.1.1).

In terms of dating, the second part of the book must therefore be placed after Antiochus III. However, Ezra's genealogy places him higher than Jeshua son of Jehozadak who, with Zerubbabel, had reestablished a cult according to the Law of Moses and then presided over the reconstruction of the temple, not without the help of Haggai and Zechariah (Ezra 5:1-2). In other words, we see the expression of a thesis: Ezra represents a reform coming from Babylonia, which by definition would be even more conformed to preexilic realities than Jeshua's restoration. However, there is a major difference concerning God's presence through his name: since Solomon, this name resided in the Temple, to which every prayer had to be addressed (1 Kgs 8:38). Then, Ezra, a priest who was never seen officiating in the Temple, inaugurated another arrangement: when he pronounced the name of God in blessing, the people responded: "Amen! Amen!" and then bowed down on the spot; the blessing pronounced made God present, independently of any sanctuary (Neh. 8:6 // 1 Ezra 9:46).

4.2.2 Nehemiah

The book presented as the "Memoirs of Nehemiah" is written in the first-person singular. Nehemiah, cupbearer of Artaxerxes, is given the mission of rebuilding the walls of Jerusalem. In spite of opposition from outside and inside the city, the undertaking was successful and the city was repopulated. In the meantime, Nehemiah was appointed governor. Then, Ezra comes to proclaim the Law of Moses in the presence of Nehemiah, and the people commit themselves to observing it, starting with a festival of booths in the seventh month. Later, Nehemiah returns for another mission under the same king and suppresses various disorders; he is then clearly a reformer, who like Ezra protests against the foreign wives.

---

[19] The identification is suggested by Sylvie Honigman, "Antiochus III's decree for Jerusalem and the Persian decrees in Ezra-Nehemiah and LXX 1 Esdras," *JSJ* (2021), pp. 303–29.

[20] This is precisely what most commentators do; cf. for example Sebastian Grätz, "The Second Temple and the Legal Status of the Torah: The Hermeneutics of the Torah in the Books of Ruth and Ezra," in: Gary N. Knoppers and Bernard M. Levinson (eds.), *The Pentateuch as Torah*, Winona Lake, Eisenbrauns, 2007, pp. 273–87; Bob Becking, *Ezra-Nehemiah* (Historical Commentary on the Old Testament), Leuven/Paris/Bristol (CT), Peeters, 2018.

[21] Cf. Already Charles C. Torrey, *Ezra Studies*, Chicago: University of Chicago Press, 1910, pp. 85–90.

Let us begin by examining the position of Ezra, who intervenes in the presence of Nehemiah. As a priest and an expert, it seems natural that he should proclaim the Law of Moses, and it is often thought that this episode (Neh. 8–10) should be placed at the time of Ezra's arrival in Jerusalem (Ezra 8 end), that is, before his reform of marriages. In this way, the expulsion of foreign wives could pass for a very strict interpretation of the written law. The parallel version of 1 Ezra, followed by Josephus, leans very slightly in this direction, putting the proclamation of the law at the end (1 Ezra 9:37-55); but it comes after the affair of the wives and not before, which hardly makes sense.

Moreover, the narrative is strange: according to 1 Ezra 5:46-52 (parallel to Ezra 3:1-6), Jeshua son of Jozadak and Zerubbabel restored the holocaust altar and set in motion the whole sacrificial cycle according to the Law of Moses, beginning with the festival of booths in the seventh month. In other words, there is a doublet, since the implementation of the written Law through a festival of booths appears twice in the same narrative,[22] but with completely different rites: the second, linked to Ezra and the Law of Moses, seems to supplant the first. There is a certain analogy with the way in which Ezra, from the very beginning, supplants the high priest Jeshua son of Jozadak by his genealogy (Ezra 7:1-5).

The accounts make Ezra and Nehemiah contemporaries, but the chronology is jumbled: according to Ezra 7:8, Ezra arrived in Jerusalem in the seventh year of King Artaxerxes of Persia, while Nehemiah remained there from the twentieth to the thirty-second year of Artaxerxes (Neh. 1:1) and later returned without a mandate (Neh. 13:6). Given the known reign lengths of the Achaemenids, King Artaxerxes can only be the first or second of that name; but in any case, Esdras and Nehemiah cannot have been contemporaries. However, the important thing is elsewhere: Ezra's intervention with the Law of Moses supports Nehemiah. But at this point, he has not yet been seen as a reformer.

Now, let us return to the beginning of the story. Nehemiah, the king's cupbearer, learns from his brother that the wall of Jerusalem is broken down and its gates have been burned (Neh. 1:3). The matter seems recent, but it is not otherwise explained.[23] Nehemiah gets an escort from the king and intends to make the repairs. Arriving in Jerusalem, he begins by secretly inspecting the walls at night. In fact, his path is limited to a small area (2:13) on Ophel Hill South of the Temple, between the Kidron

---

[22] In fact, the ending of 1 Ezra 9:55 stops abruptly just before the feast of tabernacles parallel to Neh. 8:14, which is strictly vegetal, as if the translator had felt the incongruity of a second feast of tabernacles so different, without sacrifices. On the contrary, Josephus, who has followed his source, mentions the feast briefly but without indicating its purely agrarian character (*Ant.* 11:157).

[23] At least in this place. For 1 Ezra 4:45.50, it may have been the misdeeds of the Idumeans (Edom), who burned the temple during the Chaldean attack. Thus, the ruin could be ancient (cf. Ab 9-18), and according to Ezek. 4:16-17 an Artaxerxes forbade the raising of the walls of the city. Ezek. 35:5 may allude to the participation of Edomites in the fall of Jerusalem, and similarly Jer. 49:7-22; cf. Bruce C. Cresson, "The Condemnation of Edom in Postexilic Judaism," in: James M. Efird, *The Use of the Old Testament in the New and Other Essays*, Durham, Duke University Press, 1972, pp. 125–48. Yet the account in 2 Kgs 25 (and 2 Chron. 36) ignores the Edomites, which casts doubt on their actual participation; cf. John R. Bartlett, "Edom and the Fall of Jerusalem, 587 B.C.," *PEQ* 114 (1982), pp. 2–13. After the fall of Jerusalem, the neighboring nations settled in Judea, the Edomites being only one of them but who could pass for the new chosen people; cf. Elie Assis, "Why Edom? On the Hostility towards Jacob's Brother in Prophetic Sources," *VT* 54 (2006), pp. 1–20.

Valley and the Tyropeon Valley, which roughly corresponds to the very first City of David (2 Sam. 5:9). Then, despite the extreme discretion of his inspection, Nehemiah succeeds in convincing the notables to rebuild the walls, and the vast operation begins, under the direction of the high priest Eliashib (Neh. 3:1-32), grandson of Jeshua son of Jozadak (12:10): each of the many gates of the whole city is repaired by the people of a neighboring villages or urban corporations, and all the names are given; such precision presupposes records. Two details are strange: first, Nehemiah is absent from the undertaking.[24] It is, therefore, hard to understand why work did not begin earlier, since the returnees were there.

Nehemiah's secret tour followed by his exhortation to the notables is thus a literary device to imply that he cares for the whole city and more generally for the entire people. In particular, it is stated that the work lasted fifty-two days, which is very short. On the contrary, Josephus puts in his paraphrase two years and four months (*Ant.* 11:179), which is less implausible. This discrepancy makes it possible to distinguish two construction sites of very different magnitudes: on the one hand, Eliashib's great undertaking, in which many collaborated, and that can be seen as a restoration of the walls of Jerusalem by the repatriates; on the other hand, the small district that Nehemiah inspected and then reorganized is quite singular. Indeed, the completion of the work gives it its full meaning: doorkeepers, cantors, and Levites are placed at the gates of the wall (7:1), which will constitute a sacred perimeter outside the temple; such an enclosure is specially designed for the strict protection of the Sabbath (also see Neh. 13:22). A second singularity is that this new neighborhood is sparsely populated, and Nehemiah will try to attract people to it (11:1-2).

So, it appears that Nehemiah is a reformer, and consequently that the *biblical* support of Ezra is essential. This profile is corroborated by the opposition he encounters. First, a series of notices indicate the extreme displeasure of "Sanballat the Horonite" when he learns and sees that the "sons of Israel" are being helped (2:10 and 19; 3:33-34; 4:1-2; 6:1-2). However, he is not the only adversary: he is most often found together with Tobiah the Ammonite—who has a Yahwist name—sometimes with a certain Geshem the Arab, and even with Ashdodites, in Philistine territory. There is in fact a communication network around Jerusalem, between the east (Tobiah), the South (Geshem), and the west (Ashdod); the North, represented by Sanballat, is located in Samaria (Neh. 3:34), as later largely confirmed by other sources. In fact, the most significant opponents are those of Jerusalem;[25] they include in particular Noadiah, a prophetess,[26] and other prophets (6:14).

After Ezra's service, the Law of Moses is present in various ways. At the festival of booths (8:17) it is said: "from the days of Jeshua son of Nun to that day the people of Israel had not done so. And there was great rejoicing." Then, on the 24th of the same seventh month, a sort of penitential liturgy takes place, with the separation of

---

[24] However, Josephus, for the sake of consistency, makes him head of the operation (*Ant.* 11:174); similarly, Sir. 49:13 makes Nehemiah the builder of the entire wall.

[25] These local oppositions against the reformer do not fit well with Nehemiah's position as governor and with the associated authority (5:1-2). In this connection, it is curious that it is not said that Artaxerxes had sent him as governor or satrap, since he had an escort and material means (2:9).

[26] A prophet in the LXX; opponents are implicitly called false prophets; cf. Ezek. 13:17.

all foreigners (9:2) and the confession of sins. As in Ezra 3, this supposes that the Day of Atonement as described in Leviticus 16 is not observed, but here it is for a simple reason concerning calendar. A special psalm is quoted at length that takes up the biblical story from the creation and Abraham to the gift of the law on Mount Sinai and emphasizes the failings of the people, first in the wilderness, then under the kings, and all that led to the exile despite the warnings of the prophets. The final touch denotes a servitude far removed from the joy of the festival of booths (9:36-37): "Here we are [. . .] slaves in the land that you gave to our ancestors [. . .] the kings you set over us [. . .] have power also our bodies and over our livestock." Again, this is not consistent with Nehemiah's position as a Persian governor, especially since he carried out an agrarian reform to correct injustices among Jews (Neh. 5:7-12). This domination by foreign kings is difficult to situate, apart from generalizations about the Babylonian and Persian eras.

The next passage represents a very particular communal commitment (Nehemiah 10): there is no ritual and God is not present, and the agreement is between two distinct entities, "us"[27] and "them" (v. 29): the former, with Nehemiah, include priests, Levites, and leaders; the latter (v. 28) are defined as "the rest of the people, the priests, the Levites [. . .], all those who have separated[28] themselves from the peoples of the lands." The agreement is to "walk in God's law, which was given by Moses." This is followed by a series of specific precepts, culminating in the temple fees and service, with some adjustments to the biblical rules.

This agreement leads to combining Nehemiah the reformer and his entourage with the rest of the people, among whom the ministers of the cult dominate, and everything is placed under the umbrella of the Law of Moses. This synthesis achieves the repair of the walls, while the redaction suggests that Nehemiah took charge of the whole operation. The literary effect is confirmed by an account of the dedication of Jerusalem's walls (Neh. 12:27-43): Nehemiah himself organizes two great choirs on the walls: both of them form a triumphal circuit leading to the Temple, where everything ends with important sacrifices; significantly, Ezra reappears in the ceremony. In Nehemiah's time as in the time of Zerubbabel, peace and harmony will reign thanks to a balanced cult (Neh. 12:44-47).

We must conclude that the stylistic clumsiness, which constantly impedes a simple reading, is in no way due to negligence, but rather it is a literary process that creates effects of meaning, with a precise aim:[29] Ezra and Nehemiah, though strangers to the Law of Moses, become its champions and are promoted as the beacons of true Israel, albeit they were only the guides of a minority attached to Babylonia. In this perspective, there is no space left for the local Israelites, let alone for the Samaritans.

Nehemiah's reforms are continued synthetically on a second trip to Jerusalem that he himself decided to make (Neh. 13:4-31): purification of the cult, observance of the Sabbath, and elimination of foreign wives. Even a high priest's son had married a daughter of Sanballat, but Josephus confirms that she was a Samaritan. In the prologue

---

[27] This group constitutes for the rabbinic tradition *The Men of the Great Assembly*; cf. Section 1.2.5.
[28] Cf. Nissim Amzallag, *Esau in Jerusalem* (CRB 85), Pendé, Gabalda (Peeters), 2015, pp. 62–78.
[29] Such a conclusion extends the analyses in John W. Rice, "The Diachronic Composition of the Shema-Reports in Nehemiah 1-6," *ZATW* 131 (2019), pp. 91–104.

to this final chapter, where Ezra or Nehemiah are no longer present, there is a kind of key for reading of the Law (13:1-3):

> On that day they read from the book of Moses in the hearing of the people; and in it was found written that no Ammonite or Moabite should ever enter the assembly of God, because they did not meet the Israelites with bread and water but hired Balaam against them to curse them—yet our God turned the curse into a blessing (Deut. 23:4-6). When the people heard the law, they separated from Israel all those of foreign descent.[30]

The "people" has grown from being limited to returnees, and the "mixture" refers to marriages with foreign women and possibly their children. The most remarkable thing about this short passage is that the verses quoted do not imply the conclusion drawn from them. A reminder of Deut. 7:1-2 prohibiting unions with the seven nations of Canaan would have been more appropriate, but even so it does not say to undo such marriages or to cast out circumcised children. In other words, the authority of Moses' law is affirmed, but it serves as a guarantee for customs that do not depend on it. Thus, we find the two elements of Ezra's personality: a priest who was an expert in the law of Moses and a practitioner of Babylonian customs.

Now, the question remains: How were Ezra and Nehemiah faithful to preexilic Yahwism? Before returning to this point, it is worth considering their posterity. We noted earlier that the strict observance of the Sabbath, demanded by Nehemiah and practiced at the time of the Maccabean crisis, blocked all military action and presupposed a protective wall for the Sabbath, creating a kind of sacred perimeter. This forms a major contrast with the preexilic period when the Sabbath never interfered with the conduct of warfare. Even more specifically, Judas Maccabeus is portrayed as Nehemiah's heir in a passage already evoked (2 Macc. 2:13-14, cf. Section 3.5):

> *The same things are reported in the records and in the memoirs of Nehemiah, and also that he founded a library and collected the books about the kings and prophets, and the writings of David, and letters of kings about votive offerings. In the same way Judas also collected books that had been lost on account of the war that had come upon us, and they were in our possession.*

The Book of Nehemiah is indeed presented as a *Memoir* in the first-person singular, but there is no reference to such a library; moreover, the composition is interesting because Moses does not appear in it. It is not known whether Judas' books were the same, but there is an indication in the Spartan correspondence of his brother Jonathan. Around 145 BCE, Jonathan replied to an ancient letter that Arius, king of the Spartans, had addressed to a former high priest named Onias. Jonathan recalls that Arius' message

---

[30] Ms. B of the LXX adds (cf. Dan. 3:72): "Light and darkness, bless the Lord. Sing to him, exalt him eternally."

clearly dealt with covenant and friendship,[31] and then he adds (1 Macc. 12:9-10): "Therefore, though we have no need of these things, since we have as encouragement the holy books that are in our hands, we have undertaken to send to renew our family ties and friendship with you, etc." Even if this letter is a forgery—as is readily assumed[32]—it has a raison d'être. In fact, this Onias is not mentioned elsewhere in the book and so, like Arius, he belongs to an indeterminate but prestigious past. Jonathan is thus presented as a legitimate successor of former high priests while being given sacred books that Onias did not have. This is well suited to 1 Maccabees, the founding story of the Hasmonean dynasty, which very quickly clashed with the Samaritans, as we have seen, and gradually came closer to Scripture.

4.2.3 Who Was Sanballat?

Josephus places the important figure of Sanballat at the hinge between the Persian and Hellenistic periods: on the one hand, he built a temple on Mount Gerizim at the time of Alexander's arrival; on the other hand, under Darius III, the last Persian king, he had welcomed Manasseh, the son of Jewish high priest who had married his daughter Nicaso and been expelled from Jerusalem. Another version of this last episode is reported in a passage of the *Nehemiah's Memoirs* that Josephus did not know (Neh. 13:28); hence there is a chronological difficulty.

Now, modern excavations have found two types of documents mentioning Sanballat. They are not explicit but very well dated, at least by comparison with the biblical texts.

The first case is an allusion found in the Aramaic papyri from Elephantine, near Aswan in Upper Egypt, which was presented earlier (Section 3.3). After the destruction of the Jewish sanctuary in the time of Darius II, a first letter sent to the high priest Johanan remained unanswered; then, in 407 BCE, a second letter was also sent to "Delayah and Shelemiah, sons (plur.) of Sanballat, governor of Samaria." The most immediate interpretation, given the chronological data, is that Sanballat, governor of Samaria in the time of Artaxerxes I (465-25, before Darius II), had a son named Delayah who inherited his office, for this makes it possible to imagine that he had a daughter who married a son of the high priest Joiada in the time of Nehemiah, and hence the latter's energetic reaction (Neh. 13:28). In these circumstances, Josephus' account of the construction of the Gerizim temple, in connection with the affair of Nicaso, would be a totally anachronistic version of the same event, which is acceptable, since in reality this temple dates back to at least the fifth century.

---

[31] Cf. Louis H. Feldman, "Parallel Lives of Two Lawgivers: Josephus' Moses and Plutarch's Lycurgus," in: Jonathan Edmondson et al. (eds.), *Flavius Josephus and Flavian Rome*, Oxford, Oxford University Press, 2005, pp. 209-43.

[32] Arius I of Sparta (309-265), the only notable king of this name, fought to preserve the independence of Sparta between the Macedonians, the Seleucids, and the Etolians; cf. Gabriele Marasco, *Sparta agli inizi dell'età ellenistica. Il regno di Areo I (309/8-265/4)*, Firenze, Cooperativa Libraria Universitatis Studii Florentini, 1980; Sylvie le Bohec, "Sparte et le royaume de Macédoine de Chéronée à Pydna (338-167)," *Ktema* 12 (1987), pp. 53-62. As for locating an Onias contemporary with Arius, one can only refer vaguely to the dynasty; cf. Section 3.3. It remains that the high priest Jason son of Onias, who had to escape from his successor Menelaus, fled to Lacedaemonia, disgraced by all, because of a common origin (2 Macc. 5:9).

The second case is taken from the Aramaic documents of the Wady Daliyeh, found in a cave in Samaria, not far from Jericho. They include two mentions of Sanballat: on the one hand a bull, dated between 375 BCE and 365 BCE, bears the inscription "...]yhw, son of [...]blṭ, governor of Samaria" (WD 22); the restoration of "Sanballat" is very likely, but the identity of the son is not assured. J. Dušek proposes restoring Delayahu, by analogy with Delayah son of Sanballat of Elephantine.[33] On the other hand, a sale contract (WDSP 11), written under Artaxerxes III (359–39) includes named witnesses, among them "...]w', son of Sanballat," without any other title. It thus appears, by comparison with the Elephantine letters, that the quality "son of Sanballat" is well defined, but the life span of Governor Sanballat seems unusually long. Moreover, in one of the documents it is said that the city of Samaria is the capital of the region of Samaria. It has therefore been assumed that there were several Sanballat, the grandson having received his grandfather's name by papponymy.[34]

Thanks to the ancient historians, it has been possible to specify the epoch's context: at the time of the conquest of Alexander, in 332 BCE, Parmenion, the all-powerful adjoint general, instituted a satrap of Coele-Syria in Samaria. The strategists had not failed to recognize that this narrow region formed only a thin barrier between the Arabs of the desert and the Mediterranean. This governor was killed during a revolt, and Alexander, on his return from Egypt in 330 BCE, punished the criminals and installed a Macedonian colony.[35] Many fled; in particular, a group of 205 people who, being pursued, sought shelter refuge in a cave in W. Daliyeh, where they were suffocated. The dryness of the climate allowed a good preservation of the archives they brought with them, including many slave sale or rent contracts. Most of the names found have theophoric prefixes or suffixes: Yah or Yahu (Yahwist, the most frequent); El (common); Baal (Phoenician); Isis (Egyptian); Qos (Idumaean); Shamash (Aramaic); Bel, Nabu, Sin (Babylonian). The Yahwist cult, long established at Samaria and in Samaria (cf. Section 2.4), did not exclude any other.

Hence, we can return to the name of Sanballat, for it is by no means Yahwist, and connect it with the god Sin. There are two spellings in the original Akkadian:[36] *Sin-uballit* "Sin made live (or 'begot')" and *Sin-ballit* "O Sin, make live!" Sin was a Semitic moon god, whose cult in Mesopotamia was centered around Ur in the South and Harran in the North. The last neo-Babylonian king, Nabonid (556–39), made Harran—where his mother had been a priestess—a stronghold of Sin's cult, while was Marduk was the primary deity in Babylon and in the South.[37]

The expressions in the texts of Elephantine and W. Daliyeh allow us to conclude that Sanballat designates an actual governor. Indeed, the locution "X, son of Sanballat,

---

[33] Cf. Jan Dušek, *Les manuscrits araméens du Wadi Daliyeh et la Samarie vers 450-332 av. J.-C.* (Culture and History of the Ancient Near East, 20), Leiden/Boston, Brill, 2007, pp. 227–31.

[34] Cf. Frank M. Cross, "Samaria and Jerusalem in the Persian Period," in: Hanan Eshel and Ephraim Stern, *The Samaritans*, Jerusalem, Magnes, 2002, pp. 45–70; Philippe Abadie, "Sânballat," *DBS* 11 (1991), col.1102–4. Before the discoveries of W. Daliyeh, the thesis of a papponymy had been suggested by Torrey, *Ezra Studies* (réimp. New York, KTAV, 1970), p. 330.

[35] Cf. Schürer-Vermes, II:160.

[36] Corresponding respectively to סנאבלט (Elephantine and W. Daliyeh texts) and סנבלט (Neh); the LXX puts Σαναβαλλατ and Josephus Σαναβαλλέτης.

[37] Cf. Cyril J. Gadd, "The Harran Inscriptions of Nabonidus," *Anatolian Studies* 8 (1958), pp. 35–92.

governor of Samaria," without a declination suffix, is perhaps a double qualification of X.[38] In the letters exchanged between Elephantine and Samaria, we read "Delayah and Shelemyah, son of Sanballat, governor of Samaria," it is Delayah who is governor, since he is the one who replies; Shelemyah may be either a coregent or more likely a predecessor of Delayah, the author of the letter no longer being sure. Likewise, the abovementioned bull from W. Daliyeh contains ". . .]*yhw* son of [. . .]*blṭ*, governor of Samaria." It must be concluded that it is the first, yahwist, name that designates the governor.

Therefore, it suffices to consider that the expression "son of Sanballat" qualifies the governor of Samaria in association with a Semitic god. In these circumstances, it is not necessary to ask whether these documents attest the existence of one or two persons with the same name, and the chronological difficulty noted earlier is thus resolved.[39] As one was looking for a specific person, the identity of Sanballat "the Horonite" remained unclear. The connection with Beth-horon,[40] a small town and a sanctuary in Ephraim (Josh. 10:10-11 and 16:3-11) is very approximate, for "Beth" is missing (cf. 1 Macc. 3:24).[41] It has also been observed that Horon is a Phoenician protective deity, that is, a "Sidonian" one as well.[42]

However, the term of geographical origin is written defectively and can quite well be vocalized as "the Harranite,"[43] thus opening up other perspectives. Hence, a much better hypothesis,[44] which takes into account the importance of the lunar deity Sin in Harran, consists in restoring "Sanballat the Harranite." Now, we know that Harran and Samaria were in the same satrapy of Transeuphratene (Abraham left from Harran, according to Gen. 12:4). Given these facts, it must be concluded that the author of Nehemiah 2 and 13 preserved the trace of a real link between Sanballat and Harran but at the same time made Sanballat a Samaritan individual so that he became a specific adversary. Josephus, or rather his source, retained the same transformation, which made Sanballat a neighbor of Jerusalem. All this indicates that the writers were already quite far from the facts.

---

[38] A similar case is reported by Nahman Avigad and Benjamin Sass, *Corpus of West Semitic Stamp Seals*, Jerusalem, Israel Exploration Society, 1997, n° 28, pp. 59–60: the inscription on the bull reads "of Ḥanân son of Ḥilqiyahu, the priest," where the priest is Ḥanân.

[39] An additional clue in this sense is provided by a fourth-century coin of Sidonian type, which bears an inscription reading [ש]סנאבל; cf. Ya'akov Meshorer and Shraga Qedar, *Samarian Coinage* (Numismatic Studies and Researches, 9), Jerusalem, Israel Numismatic Society, 1999, pp. 26–7, 93; according to Dušek, *Les manuscrits*, pp. 323–4, the term would rather be an abbreviation סנאב, designating the (divine) patron of a local governor.

[40] Suggested by Yohanan Aharoni and Anson F. Rainey, *The Land of the Bible*, London, Burns and Oates, ²1979, p. 432.

[41] Other proposals have been made: Ḥoronaim in Moab (Isa. 15:5 חורנים, Αρωνιμ), but this does not fit, since by symmetry Sanballat should then be "the Moabite," and besides it is only a village, not a region; Ḥawara, a village at the foot of the Gerizim, but this remains a tiny reference; Ḥaurân, the volcanic plateau in southern Syria, a poor region; cf. Siegfried Mittmann, "Tobia, Sanballat und die persische Provinz Juda," *Journal of Northwest Semitic Languages* 26.2 (2000), pp. 1–50.

[42] Cf. Isidore Lévy, *Recherches esséniennes et pythagoriciennes*, Paris, Minard, 1965, pp. 65–9; according to an inscription, the god Horôn was part of the pantheon of Iamnia, with Heracles.

[43] We read in Neh. 2:10.19 סנבלט החרני, LXX ὁ Αρωνι, and similarly in Neh. 13:28 חרני, LXX τοῦ Σαναβαλλατ τοῦ Ωρωνίτου.

[44] Already suggested by Samuel I. Feigin, "Etymological Notes II: *mmzr*," *American Journal of Semitic Languages* 43 (1926), pp. 56–60. Oded Tammuz, "Will the Real Sanballat Please Stand Up?," in: Menachem Mor and Friedrich V. Reiterer (eds.), *Samaritans: Past and Present. Current Studies*, Berlin/ New York, De Gruyter, 2010, pp. 51–8, adopts this solution but believes that Sanballat was born in Ḥarrân and thus bears the name of his city.

The question of Sanballat's duration or posterity being thus settled, there remains the odd fact that the expulsion of the Jewish high priest's son married to a daughter of Sanballat is reported twice. We cannot assume that the same thing happened twice in two episodes separated by a century, and so it is necessary to choose. In order to do this, we must return to Nehemiah's story. For his first stay in Jerusalem, he had the approval of Artaxerxes, but he played two roles: as governor he reduced a social injustice, and as reformer he established, in spite of the notables of Jerusalem, a small sacred perimeter to protect the observance of the Sabbath. The literary mixture of the two functions gave Nehemiah a posthumous authority. On the contrary, the second stay seems artificial, devoid of chronology: he has no mandate, but he acts as if he were an authorized reformer, protecting the cult, imposing the observance of the Sabbath, and supervising the question of foreign wives. An additional element is that the version of the Hebrew-Aramaic book used by Josephus ignores this second stay, which in fact adds nothing to Nehemiah's work, except on a point that is very poorly explained, the dismissal of Sanballat's son-in-law. One can even add a characteristic clumsiness of the writer, who says that Nehemiah obtained a leave of absence from Artaxerxes, "King of Babylon" (Neh. 13:6) and not, as elsewhere, "of Persia."

We must therefore conclude that Nehemiah's second stay is an artificial composition added to consolidate his work. Consequently, the tradition reported by Josephus, with the proper name Nicaso, must be taken as primary, and its relationship to Nehemiah is a purely chronological fiction. This does not imply that it is more accurate, since one cannot identify Sanballat as a real character. Yet it is he who appears as the principal adversary of Nehemiah, from the moment of his arrival; but his name is not at all Israelite, and he is only weakly attached to Samaria. In his paraphrase, Josephus speaks of an overall opposition of Ammonites, Moabites, and Samaritans (11:174), without naming leaders.

The combination of Nehemiah's narratives with Josephus' accounts has given rise to hypotheses of increasing complexity, depending on the archaeological discoveries which hardly confirm the texts:

1. Josephus' solution is simple: he expressly indicates the Samaritans among Nehemiah's opponents, but he does not name Sanballat until the time of Darius III and Alexander, with the affair regarding Nicaso and the construction of the temple on Mount Gerizim.
2. Torrey, taking into account the Elephantine papyri and observing that the Sanballat who was Nehemiah's adversary and that of Josephus cannot be contemporary, proposes papponymy. This makes it possible to distinguish two Sanballat, the grandfather and his grandson. However, this distinction, far from usefully resolving the tension between Nehemiah and Josephus, tends to uncritically immobilize contradictory data;[45] this solution is interesting because it situates Nehemiah toward the end of the Persian period, given his second journey and Nicaso.

---

[45] Cf. Lester L. Grabbe, "Josephus and the Reconstruction of the Judean Restauration," *JBL* 106 (1987), pp. 231–46; Daniel R. Schwartz, "On some Papyri and Josephus' Sources and Chronology for the Persian Period," *JSJ* 21 (1990), pp. 175–99, shows that the papyri of W. Daliyeh do not confirm Josephus' statements but explain how he could have been mistaken.

The Persian Period

Kings of Persia	"Sanballat" as a figure				"Sanballat" as a divine attribute
	Josephus	Torrey (1910)	Cross (1974)	Dušek (2007)	
Artaxerxes I 465–425 (Eliashib)	Samaritans Néhémie		Sanballat I Nehemiah Nicaso I	Sanballat Nehemiah	(Two temples)
Darius II 425–405 (Elephantine)		Sanballat I		Sanballat Nicaso Gerizim	Son of Sanballat
Artaxerxes II 405–359		Sanballat II Nehemiah Nicaso Gerizim	Sanballat II		Son of Sanballat Nehemiah Nicaso
Artaxerxes III 359–339					
Darius III 339–331 (Josephus) (W. Daliyeh)	Sanballat, Nikaso, Gerizim		Sanballat III Nicaso II Gerizim		
Alexander 333–323	(Onias I)		W. Daliyeh		Son of Sanballat

Figure 14 Some ways to situate Nehemiah and Sanballat.

3. Cross, who also takes into account the findings of W. Daliyeh, merely connects all the data, which further develops the Sanballat papponymy. Like Josephus, he places Nehemiah under Artaxerxes I, but he is then obliged to suppose two Nicasos, and so his view becomes entirely unreasonable.[46]
4. Dušek, who adds the dating of the Gerizim, takes the opposite direction and logically enough refuses any papponymy, because this drowns out the questions without really solving them. He situates Nehemiah like his predecessors, and for him there was only one Sanballat. Thus, he merely dates Josephus' account of Sanballat, Nicaso, and Gerizim a century earlier and detaches the whole from Alexander.
5. The last hypothesis consists in separating "Sanballat," a prominent Samaritan mentioned in the Jewish sources, and the expression "son of Sanballat" provided by epigraphy, where it is a theophore quality attached to a general Yahwistic proper name. It is, therefore, no longer useful for the chronology, but Nehemiah can then without difficulty be situated at the end of the Persian period.

The fact that this confusion over the meaning of "Sanballat" added to the wavering of the books of Ezra and Nehemiah over the nomenclature of the Persian kings proves that the editors were far from the facts. Their purpose was certainly not to inform about the past but to establish a thesis about the real Israel: only exile returnees can belong to it.

---

[46] Cf. Geo Widengren, "The Persian Period," in: J. H. Hayes and J. M. Miller (eds.), *Israelite and Judean History*, London, SCM Press, 1977, pp. 506–9.

4.2.4 Conclusions

In spite of editorial effects which seem to be due to a certain carelessness, it appears that the character of Ezra is a skillful creation that combines three not very coherent elements in order to derive a new definition of Israel: continuity with the royal period, the promotion of the Law of Moses, and the decisive contribution of Babylonian customs, which must be linked to the later Pharisees; thus, Jewish identity comes from the mother, and the local Israelites, Samaritans or others, are excluded. This synthesis, which overshadows the work of Zerubbabel and Jeshua, must be situated before the Maccabean crisis, somewhere in the second century. As for the reformation itself, it would probably have taken place at the end of the Persian period, before Alexander.

The restoration of the temple should be situated earlier, but there is a doubt: after Cyrus' decree ordering the work, the utensils taken from the temple by Nebuchadnezzar are given to Sheshbazzar, "prince of Judah," and later it is reported to King Darius that he has begun to rebuild the sanctuary on its former site (Ezra 5:15), and then it is lost sight of. In the meantime, Zerubbabel and Jeshua, having arrived and settled with a column of returnees, rebuilt the altar on its site and offered all the sacrifices "prescribed in the Law of Moses" (3:2). Later, the same Zerubbabel and Jeshua, encouraged by the prophets Haggai and Zechariah, finished the work (6:14).

At this point, it should again be noted that, according to 1 Ezra 3:1–4:46, Zerubbabel was a page of Darius III (cf. Section 1.2.4), for this will make it possible to turn Josephus' accounts regarding Alexander and Jerusalem's reputation: the Gerizim temple was of notable antiquity, whereas that of Jerusalem was struggling to emerge from the ground in the Persian period. This would represent the continuation of the ancient superiority of Israel over Judah since the royal period,[47] but Judah ends up answering by advancing a royal historiography.

As for Nehemiah, he does not lead a column of returnees but cares about those "who had escaped the captivity"[48] (Neh. 1:2), and it is as a builder that he is a reformer, since he creates a new district, whose enclosure creates a sacred space independent of the Temple and there seeks to attract people from the surrounding area. His position as governor, ignored by Josephus and Sir. 49:13, highlights two peculiar facts: on the one hand, it is not clearly linked to his formal dismissal by King Artaxerxes, although he had received an official escort (Neh. 2:9); on the other hand, the agrarian reform that he undertakes as governor consists above all in cancelling debts (5:2-3), but at this point he seems to ignore one of the stipulations of the subsequent community commitment,

---

[47] Cf. Ralk Heckl, "The Composition of Ezra-Nehemiah as a Testimony for the Competition Between the Temples in Jerusalem and on Mt. Gerizim in the Early Years of the Seleucid Rule over Judah," in: Magnar Kartveit and Gary N. Knoppers (eds.), *The Bible, Qumran, and the Samaritans* (Studia Judaica, 104), Berlin/Boston, De Gruyter, 2018, who concludes that since the Torah was common to both temples, the Ezra-Neh books represent an effort by Jerusalem in the Hellenistic period to resist Samaritan supremacy.

[48] The expression הפליטה אשר נשארו מן השבי may be understood to mean either "those who had escaped from captivity" (remaining in Judea) or "who had remained in captivity" (after the departure of the repatriates left with Zorobabel), but the first meaning is better; cf. Hubertus C. M. Vogt, *Studie zur nachexilischen Gemeinde in Esra-Nehemia*, Kommissionsverlag Dietrich Coelde, 1966, pp. 45–7; Hugh G. M. Williamson, *Ezra, Nehemiah* (Word Biblical Commentary, 16), Waco, Word Books, 1985, pp. 171–2.

that is, forgoing the exaction of every debts in the seventh year (10:31), which in fact goes beyond the biblical precept of the sabbatical year. It must be concluded that this office of governor is a mere artifice intended to give Nehemiah authority, for the literary presentation of his building activity suggests that he reconstructed Jerusalem entirely, and hence that the reform concerns the whole city and not just one district. It is this half-civil, half-religious authority that gives substance to his second mission (Neh. 13).

Hence, it appears that Ezra and Nehemiah are complementary: they successfully bring to Jerusalem a Babylonian reform, by cloaking it in a submission to the written Law of Moses. In fact, this is exactly what occurred during the Maccabean crisis and the subsequent establishment of the Hasmonean dynasty. Of course, it remains that Nehemiah may have established a small reformed district much earlier, even before Alexander.

One question remains: the clashes between the Babylonian traditions and the Law of Moses are still unexplained, since both should be linked to preexilic Yahwism. We can put the problem in the following terms, since the Samaritans, not having experienced exile, stick to the written Law: How did the exile transform the beliefs of the deportees from Judah? Or again, why did the repatriated Judeans want to call themselves Israel?[49]

---

[49] Israel Finkelstein and Neil A. Silberman, "Temple and Dynasty: Hezekiah, the Remaking of Judah and the Rise of the Pan-Israelite Ideology," *JSOT* 30 (2006), pp. 259–85, assume a strong migration to the South, hence the birth of a pan-Israelite identity, but there is no clear evidence, hence the criticism of Nadav Na'aman, "When and How Did Jerusalem Become a Great City? The Rise of Jerusalem as Judah's Premier City in the Eighth-Seventh Centuries B.C.E.," *BASOR* 347 (2007), pp. 21–56; Philip R. Davies, *The Origins of Biblical Israel* (JSOTSup 485), London, T&T Clark, 2007, pp. 30–41, places the case after the fall of Samaria; Nadav Na'aman, "The Israelite-Judahite Struggle for the Patrimony of Ancient Israel," *Biblica* 91 (2010), pp. 1–23, thinks that Judah wanted to recover the prestige of ancient Israel, just as Assyria had wanted to recover that of Mesopotamia. For Anton van der Lingen, *Comment gérer une crise religieuse majeure? Réactions prophétiques et théologiques après la chute de Samarie*, Saint-Denis, Edilivre, 2020, it is the intervention of prophets that has kept alive a hope.

5

Pause

This study of the origin of the Samaritans, who have always been local "Canaanites," must now be concluded, since we believe we have shown that they steadily lived around Shechem. Yet, many questions remain unanswered. Therefore, after summarizing the path we have followed—which in reality concerns the formation of Judaism—we shall propose some avenues of research, especially biblical ones.

5.1 Conclusions

Here, it will suffice to draw some conclusions from the approach taken through the four chapters:

1. In New Testament times, the divorce between Samaritans and Jews is an accomplished fact. Flavius Josephus shows this through various episodes. Above all, as a witness of authorized Hebrew writings, he highlights two things: on the one hand, the regime of the Hasmonean high priests that originated during the Maccabean crisis had its roots in the proto-Pharisaic traditions coming from Babylonia; on the other hand, this regime gradually acclimatized the Bible, and this evolution was favored by a momentary promotion of the Sadducees, who only wanted to acknowledge the Scriptures. This happened during a crisis around 100 BCE, associated with the name of Alexander Jannaeus, the first recognized Hasmonean king.

   Messianism, as a movement of national emancipation inspired by King David, has existed in various, more or less violent, forms. In the early days of Christianity, it took on a special form, announced by the prophets: weakly political, it was the culmination of the hope of all Israel, that is, of all the tribes, considered symbolically between the Jordan River and the Mediterranean Sea. Samaria, situated between Galilee and Judea, represented the ancient kingdom of Israel, or the central tribes. Paul, little concerned about symbolic geography, ignores it; but the Fourth Gospel and Acts make it an essential theme.
2. The examination of the famous passage of 2 Kings 17, which shows the origin of the Samaritans as more or less acclimatized Assyrian settlers after the fall of the kingdom of Israel in 721 BCE, reveals some surprises. First of all, even if one is not very sure of the identity of the king who sent them, there is nothing

pagan about them; on the contrary, they mingled with the surviving ancient Israelites to the point of later becoming indistinguishable: all of them claimed to be related to their ancestor Jacob, much more than to Moses. Second, it is clear that the kingdom of Israel united at the time of David and Solomon was only a parenthesis in an indiscriminate Yahwist whole. However, the lasting royal dynasty attributed to these founders leads to a reversal: Judah, the smallest entity, becomes preponderant around Jerusalem, a modest locality that is transformed into a capital, magnified by prestigious reforming kings, such as Hezekiah and Josiah. Apart from the indeterminacy of the "place where YHWH chose to put his name" and a foretelling of the exile, the Pentateuch knows only the realities of the North around Shechem, beginning with Mount Gerizim.

This specifically Judaean upheaval, developed by the Deuteronomist narratives in 1-2 Samuel and 1-2 Kings, and energetically confirmed by the Chronist, leads to an exile in Babylonia, whereas the ancient, or not-so-ancient, Israelites living in the North stably remained there, with an infinitesimal diaspora, despite what Josephus says. This major difference, which will have lasting consequences, is first of all political, for it is difficult to see any appreciable differences within the Yahwist entity; even Jeroboam's choice of Levites and priests from outside the tribe of Levi is not very significant, for we know nothing about the genealogies during the royal period. Yet, in spite of a common Yahwism, there is no evidence for the origin of a single Pentateuch at such an early period; a tradition claims in various ways that it was forgotten during the entire royal period, thus maintaining its antiquity. The traditional hypothesis of linking Deuteronomy to King Josiah runs up against impossibilities; in particular, it bears marks of having been rooted in the North, which had disappeared a century earlier.

3. The Maccabean crisis finally sheds some light on the situation: first, there was Israelite religious unity, then came the split between Jews and Samaritans. The cause was the political and social emergence of the Hasmonean high priests, a dynasty that originated in a Babylonian Judaism independent of Moses, which then tried to give itself a more biblical profile. The Samaritans, presenting themselves as "Sidonians of Shechem," simply say that they are of local origin, and allusion to a mixture between Israelites and assimilated settlers has disappeared. Contrariwise, the Jews claim a more complex movement, with at least partial exile and repatriation in several waves and under several colors.

However, the Hasmonean policy of territorial expansion, especially under John Hyrcanus and Alexander Jannaeus, has never been represented as a return to the kingdom of David, although there are obvious analogies. After a major reduction with Pompey in 63 BCE, Herod managed to reconstitute the whole domain as a "great Judea" but not as "Israel." His desire to make the Temple of Jerusalem a sumptuous edifice did not stem from a desire to imitate Solomon but rather from the need to erase the previous building, which was certainly more modest than the shrine on Mount Gerizim, even in ruins. After his death in 4 BCE, Augustus divided his kingdom distributing parts to his three surviving sons: around Jerusalem, from Samaria to Idumea, to Archelaus, promoted to

ethnarch; Galilee and Transjordan to Herod Antipas; and the territories east of the Lake of Galilee to Philip.
4. Between the exile and the Maccabean crisis, there was a period of gestation in which we can distinguish two phases, separated by Alexander's victory over Darius III, in 333 BCE, that inaugurated the Hellenistic period. Prior to that, the Persian period had begun for Jerusalem and the province of Yehud with the edict of Cyrus in 538 BCE. Two important events are presented by the books of Ezra and Nehemiah: on the one hand, a substantial repatriation of exiles that led to the reestablishment of the Temple in Jerusalem; on the other hand, a reform linked to the names of Ezra and Nehemiah, whose pillars are the strict observance of the sabbat in community, as well as a genealogical purity of the repatriates, which excludes any mixing with the local Israelites and in particular with the Samaritans. The texts are awkward and, so, they are often overlooked; but they are in fact produced by literary devices that converge toward an essential aim, that is, that of presenting these reformers as both heirs of the preexilic period and faithful to the Law of Moses; thus, the Samaritans are excluded.

After Alexander, the control of Coele-Syria (or Syria-Palestine) was the subject of long conflicts between Syria and Egypt. At the end of a century-long Egyptian domination, around 200 BCE, during a fifth war, Antiochus III managed to reverse the situation permanently. The Samaritans were little affected, but the links between Jerusalem and the many Jews of Mesopotamia became clearer, under the same umbrella of a Syrian suzerainty. This period is poorly documented until the Maccabean crisis, but no tension between Jews and Samaritans is discernible; the papyri of Zeno bear witness to this and even earlier the documents of the Jewish colony of Elephantine.

These observations led to a paradox: during the entire early Hellenistic period, the divorce between Jews and Samaritans would have become invisible, only to reappear after the Maccabean crisis. This would be very illogical and really improbable; yet, the solution is very simple: one only needs to consider that the clever literary maneuvers of Ezra-Neh have the effect of dating back to the Persian period the divorce that took place in the aftermath of the Maccabean crisis.[1] We have seen that the character of Ezra is an essential literary fiction that makes it possible to place the Syrian policy of Antiochus III under a Persian Artaxerxes. This literary effect was then projected further back, to the period of the Syrian settlers: at the time of the affair with the lions, teaching on the proper way to worship YHWH was not sought in Jerusalem but from a priest deported from the kingdom of Israel, as if Yahwism was different there.

5.2 Pending Questions

The ancient Israelite history certainly is very different from the biblical presentation, especially with regard to the evolution of Yahwist monotheism. The ancient kingdom

---

[1] Cf. Benedikt Hensel, "On the Relationship of Judah and Samaria in Post-Exilic Times: A Farewell to the Conflict Paradigm," *JSOT* 44 (2019), pp. 19–42.

of Israel in the North was more prosperous than Judah, but there were transfers that finally lead to a Samaritan decline in the face of a major evolution of Judea. Here are some aspects that deserve further investigation:

1. Biblical historiography is not a journal, for it is always motivated. In the case of the Books of Kings, the MT is certainly later than the source of the LXX; moreover, Josephus attests to the most ancient form, at least of 2 Kings 17, since it is consistent with Ezra 4:2 (colonizers assimilated to Yahwism). However, the redactional history is complex. In the case of Joshua to 2 Kings, many passages are in the style proper to Deuteronomy; hence, M. Noth introduced the notion of "Deuteronomistic history."[2] However, a distinction must be made:[3] the books Joshua and Judges extend Deuteronomy or even the entire Pentateuch, with regard to all the tribes, but then 1-2 Samuel and 1-2 Kings focus on Judah (and a bit on Benjamin), with a certain appropriation of the North, within the framework of monarchical continuity. The story finally leads to the promotion, in Babylon, of an exiled king, Jehoiachin, a king of Judah without a kingdom: it is a total failure, presented ironically. Indeed, Judah is not and cannot be Israel, but at the same time Israel has disqualified itself since Jeroboam. This seems definitive, since Jeremiah, the prophet of the return from exile, is not mentioned in this book. According to this perspective, the alliance of the high priest Jeshua son of Jozadak and Zerubbabel, of Davidic descent, on the contrary represents a major effort to return to the preexilic realities in Jerusalem. However, this is the extreme opposite of the reformers Ezra and Nehemiah, who disregard the idea of royalty and rebuild Israel in a different way.[4] It is therefore necessary to ask who—Jeshua or Ezra—is more faithful to preexilic Yahwism. Moreover, in spite of the opprobrium attached to Jeroboam's dissidence, the name of Israel remains firmly attached to the North, and various indications show that this is indeed its origin, whereas the beginnings of a very ancient cult of YHWH seem to be linked to the South.[5]

2. The Chronicler reinterprets the story more optimistically:[6] Judah takes on the magnitude of all Israel, and in the end the edict of Cyrus opens a future. In fact, the destruction of the Gerizim temple by John Hyrcanus, after the Samaritan threats, made Jerusalem the unique pole of all Israel, with perceptible literary consequences. First, the *Letter of Aristaeus* relates a matter regarding the revision and translation into Greek of the Pentateuch by sages from the twelve tribes of Israel, under the authority of the high priest Eleazar of Jerusalem who sent them to Alexandria (cf. Section 3.3).

---

[2] Cf. Léo Laberge, "Le Deutéronomiste," in: Michel Gourgues (dir.), *"De bien des manières". La recherche biblique aux abords du XXIᵉ siècle*, Paris, Éditions du Cerf, 1995, pp. 47–77.

[3] As already suggested by Heinrich Ewald, *Geschichte des Volkes Israel. Einleitung in die Geschichte des Volkes Israel*, Göttingen, Dieterichschen Buchhandlung, ³1863.

[4] Some would lower the date to the Hellenistic period; cf., for example, Ingrid Hjelm, *Jerusalem's Rise to Sovereignty. Zion and Gerizim in Competition* (JSOTSup, 404), London/New York, T&T Clark International, 2004: Rejecting the usual biblical historiography, based on the work of Hezekiah and Josiah, it focuses on the work of J. Van Seters, Th. Thompson, and N. Lemche, who seek a theological interpretation rooted in history. Lemche to search for a theological interpretation that is anchored in history; it ends up proposing a second-century dating for 1-2 Kings.

[5] Cf. Nissim Amzallag, *La forge de Dieu*, Paris, Cerf, 2020, pp. 29–46.

[6] Cf. Ehud Ben Zvi, "Memories of Kings of Israel and Judah within the Mnemonic Landscape of the Literati of the Late Persian/Early Hellenistic Period: Exploratory Considerations," *SJOT* 33 (2019), pp. 1–15.

There are only two possibilities: either this representation of all Israel is a purely Jewish artifice, which deliberately ignores Mount Gerizim and the Samaritans, or the *Letter* must be dated after the destruction of the shrine on Mount Gerizim, and the high priest of Jerusalem is the representative of all Israel; the second hypothesis is more realistic. Now, this way of representing all Israel around Jerusalem is precisely an essential characteristic of the Chronist, who for that same reason is likely to draw the same conclusion.[7] The dating to the Persian period, commonly accepted,[8] seems to be a residue of the old consensus that the Chronicler was the common author of the collection which includes 1-2 Chronicles, Ezra, and Nehemiah.[9]

3. The Samaritan woman whom Jesus met considered Jacob as her ancestor. This incidentally indicates full assimilation of the Assyrian settlers to the surviving Israelites of the ancient northern kingdom and so to Yahwism. Such a development raises two questions: on the one hand, with regard to the nature of the commandments given to the sons of Jacob (2 Kgs 17:34), since Moses is not mentioned; while, on the other hand, the notion of tribe becomes indistinct, at least for the North. These two questions appear together at the final assembly convened by Joshua at Shechem (Josh. 24:1-27): the people seem to arrive in mass from Mesopotamia, as did the Assyrian colonizers,[10] and Joshua, after having asked for free adherence to YHWH, makes a covenant and sets down in writing "a statute and a law." He is thus positioned as a legislator and Moses' successor in the strongest sense of the term.[11] As for the people, it is not clear how the tribes were formed in Egypt, and there is even an allusion to a mixture of the sons of Israel with a "rabble" (Num. 11:4; cf. Exod. 12:38). The origin of the tribes and the formation of the territories proper to each one were certainly complex: for example, Dan, close to the sea before its migration, perhaps came from Greece[12] (Daneans); but, by a great anachronism, we hear about it since Abraham's time (Gen. 14:14).

---

[7] See too Israel Finkelstein, "The Historical Reality Behind the Genealogical Lists in 1 Chronicles," *JBL* 131 (2012), pp. 65–83, which considers geography: the places indicated do not coincide with Persian Yehud, because the domain is both too large (with Hebron, Lowland, Bethel, Gezer, Lod, Ono) and too small (ignoring En Gedi, Ramat Rachel, Beit ha-Kerem); on the other hand, one sees a good correspondence with the territories governed by the first Asmoneans, Jonathan and Simon, from which a dating is possible; also see Gary N. Knoppers, "Intermarriage, Social Complexity, and Ethnic Diversity in the Genealogy of Judah," *JBL* 120 (2001), pp. 15–30.

[8] The genealogy of the Davidic kings after the exile (1 Chron. 3:17-24) has six generations in the MT but eleven in the LXX, counting from 587 BCE.

[9] Cf. Hugh G. M. Williamson, "Sources and Redaction in the Chronicler's Genealogy of Juda," *JBL* 98 (1979), pp. 351–9; Id., *Israel in the Books of Chronicles*, Cambridge, Cambridge University Press, 1977; Yigal Levin, "Who Was the Chronicler's Audience? A Hint from His Genealogies," *JBL* 122 (2003), pp. 229–45.

[10] Cf. William G. Dever, *Beyond the Texts; An Archaeological Portrait of Ancient Israel and Judah*, Atlanta, Society of Biblical Literature, 2017, pp. 119–247; Konrad Schmid, "Overcoming the Sub-Deuteronism and Sub-Chronicism of Historiography in Biblical Studies: The Case of the Samaritans," in: Magnar Kartveit and Gary N. Knoppers (eds.), *The Bible, Qumran, and the Samaritans* (Studia Judaica, 104), Berlin/Boston, De Gruyter, 2018.

[11] According to Thomas Römer and Marc Zvi Brettler, "Deuteronomy 34 and the Case for a Persian Hexateuch," *JBL* 119 (2000), pp. 401–19, the assembly at Shechem in Joshua 24, which echoes Gen. 35:2 for the suppression of the oriental idols, is a key to the coherence of the Hexateuch.

[12] Cf. Yigael Yadin, "And Dan, Why Did He Remain in Ships? (Judges, V,17)," *Australian Journal of Biblical Archaeology* 1 (1968), pp. 9–23.

4. In connection with the Onias high priests, an Egyptian connection has been highlighted (cf. Section 3.2). In the process of legitimizing the new Hasmonean dynasty, 1 Macc. 12:2-23 speaks of the correspondence between the high priest Jonathan and Arius, a Spartan king. Jonathan's letter is quoted, with a copy of the one sent by Arius to the high priest Onias attached, so well before the Maccabean crisis:

> *King Arius of the Spartans, to the high priest Onias, greetings. It has been found in writing concerning the Spartans and the Jews that they are brothers and are of the family of Abraham. And now that we have learned this, please write us concerning your welfare; we on our part write to you that your livestock and your property belong to us, and ours belong to you. We therefore command that our envoys report to you accordingly.*

This closeness of the flocks attracts attention, since it implies proximity, and in his paraphrase Josephus omits them, given the distance between Peloponnesus and Judea, but adds the name of the courier who delivered the letter, Demoteles, specifying rather realistically (*Ant.* 12:226-227): "The writing is square, the seal is an eagle that has seized a serpent in its claws." In addition to the oddity of the flocks, one might think that a document in which Greeks claim kinship with Barbarians is a forgery due to Hasmonean vanity.[13] However, the fiction of an ancient document is a useful precedent, for later, when Simon, Jonathan's brother, was confirmed as high priest, "the rulers and the city of the Spartans" sent him a letter renewing the friendship that envoys had come to request but without further details; the preceding one is sufficient (1 Macc. 14:20-23). Moreover, Sparta itself is not mentioned but only of Spartans, and there were in fact Spartan mercenaries in Egypt, perhaps with villages,[14] which may explain the flocks.

Another element suggests a more precise link with the Oniad dynasty: in 175 BCE, Antiochus IV became king of Syria and, needing money, he sold the office of high priest to Jason (Jesus), who thus ousted his own brother Onias, then assassinated. Three years later, Menelaus bought the office in his turn, and this led to a civil war; while Jason finally fled, first to the Nabateans and then to Egypt, and ultimately "embarked to go to the Lacedaemonians (Spartas) in the hope of finding protection because of their kinship" (2 Macc. 5:9). The narrator has not gone into detail: the origin was in Egypt, and earlier in Sparta. Regarding the possible relationship between the Spartans and the Law of Moses, a nonbiblical tradition, reported by Hecataeus of Abdera, says that the legislator had left instructions for the military training of the young so that they would

---

[13] According to Elias J. Bickerman, "A Question of Authenticity: The Jewish Privileges," in his *Studies in Jewish and Christian history: A New Edition in English*, Leiden/Boston, Brill, 2011, pp. 295–314; likewise, Jan N. Bremmer, "Abrahams and Jews: Abrahamic Cousins?" in: Martin Goodman et al. (eds.), *Abraham, the Nations, and the Hagarites*, Leiden/Boston, Brill, 2010, pp. 47–59, refuses after many others any authenticity but does not ask himself the raison d'être of such fictions.

[14] Cf. Maurice Sartre, *D'Alexandre à Zénobie. Histoire du Levant antique, IVe siècle av. J.-C. – IIIe siècle ap. J.-C.*, Paris, Fayard, 2001, pp. 275–6; Joseph Mélèze-Modrzejewski, *Les Juifs d'Égypte de Ramsès II à Hadrien*, Paris, PUF, ^{2}1997, pp. 109–17.

be courageous, enduring, ready to overcome any difficulty and to resist mixing with neighboring nations;[15] there is a Spartan analogy.[16]

5. These Egyptian rumors are vague, but they invite us to consider the formation of the Pentateuch in a new light, after the exile.[17] We note first of all that it did not originate in Babylonia, nor in Coele-Syria, because it would have to be linked to Shechem or Samaria,[18] and it is very doubtful that the oriental documentation, which was clearly used, could have been found there: the Code of Hammurabi, Gilgamesh, Enuma-Elish, and so on; by elimination, we are thus directed toward Egypt. Moreover, it is certain that there are variations in style, but we have not been able to isolate source documents that could have had an independent existence[19] and clear legal authority,[20] hence a second remark: the whole was published at once. Indeed, a rabbinic tradition (*b. Qidushin* 30a) has observed that the center of the Torah, or its key, is found in Lev. 10:16a, between the words *darosh* (infinitive) and *darash* (perfect), which are two forms of the same verb, meaning "search, scrutinize," the result of the operation being a midrash; the turn of phrase consisting in splitting a root to mark an emphasis is frequent in the Bible. Basically, it is difficult to believe that this very significant verb has appeared in the center by chance. Here is the verse:[21]

Moses, seeking the goat of the sin offering, inquired, and—it had already been burned.

A small detail of the Hebrew draws our attention: instead of the normal passive form "was burned," we find an intensive "was completely burned," which never occurs elsewhere and here adds nothing useful to the meaning. At this point, one can read

---

[15] Hecateus, contemporary of Alexander, is known only through Diodorus of Sicily; cf. Menahem Stern, *Greek and Latin Authors on Jews and Judaism*, Jerusalem, Israel Academy of Sciences, 3 vol., 1974–84, I:20-24.

[16] Cf. Erich S. Gruen, *Heritage and Hellenism: The Reinvention of Jewish Tradition*, Berkeley, University of California Press, 1998, p. 261; Louis H. Feldman, "Parallel Lives of Two Lawgivers: Josephus' Moses and Plutarch's Lycurgus," in: Jonathan Edmondson et al. (eds.), *Flavius Josephus and Flavian Rome*, Oxford, Oxford University Press, 2005, pp. 209–43.

[17] The classical theories on the formation of the Pentateuch, and their collapse, are summarized in Philippe Wajdenbaum, *Argonauts of the Desert: Structural Analysis of the Hebrew Bible*, Sheffield/Oakville, Equinox, 2011, pp. 22–37.

[18] Archaeology shows that Jerusalem was only an unfortified village; cf. Israel Finkelstein, "Jerusalem in the Persian (and Early Hellenistic) Period and the Wall of Nehemiah," *JSOT* 32 (2008), pp. 501–20.

[19] On the contrary, Joel S. Baden, *The Composition of the Pentateuch: Renewing the Documentary Hypothesis*, New Haven, London, Yale University Press, 2012, judges that one must maintain the hypothesis, but by seeking the documents themselves, and not their literary evolution; he concludes curiously that it is not directly useful for the history.

[20] Except perhaps for something concerning the Day of Atonement (Kippur), the 10th of the seventh month: according to Ezra 3:1-6 the whole annual cycle of sacrifices is reestablished on the altar of burnt offering, but there is no sanctuary, and therefore it is impossible to perform the rite of the entry of the high priest into the Holy of Holies for the Day of Atonement (Kippur, cf. Lev. 16:3-4); in Neh 8:13-18 after the proclamation of the Law on the first day of the seventh month, the people prepare and then celebrate the Feast of Tabernacles from the 15th to the 22nd of the month, ignoring the Atonement on the 10th of the month, but on the 24th of the same month an atonement ceremony takes place (Neh. 9:1-2, cf. Joel 1-2). But Ezekiel is never precise about the Law of Moses, as can be seen in Neh. 10:30: the community commitment is according to "the Law of God, given through the ministry of Moses, the servant of God," but the details given afterward are approximate.

[21] ואת שעיר החטאת דרש משה והנה שרף; an exact count falls two verses later, but textual tradition after the writing may have created a small gap.

the verse in a purely formal way, by centering our research on the word for "goat," and so we obtain a key to the Hebrew numerical system.²² Now, two suggestions can be extracted from this verse: on the one hand, one will have to search under the apparent meaning, and on the other hand, there will be numerical codings of the scribes.²³

6. The *Letter of Aristaeus* has been briefly examined in connection with the translation of the Pentateuch (cf. Section 3.3). This is only spoken of in a small part of the story: in § 28–51, Demetrios, the Library's founder, notifies the king that he has no good copy of the Law of the Jews, and that he must ask the high priest Eleazar for amended books, as well as seventy-two translators, six per tribe; after various digressions, including a long philosophical banquet, we read in § 301–22 that the translation is effectuated after textual comparisons between specialists and then read to the Jews and the king; but curiously it is not clearly said that it was indeed deposited in the Library; finally, the translators are sent home loaded with gifts. The operation however must be considered strange: Why make so many people come, when a few trained scholars could work efficiently in Jerusalem? In reality, the task of the seventy-two was twofold: to finalize the text by discussion and compromise, before translating it. In these conditions, Alexandria was obviously the best place, given all the Library's documentation that allowed completing the oral traditions and the ancient Israelite texts, which are sometimes quoted: the *Book of the Covenant* (Exod. 24:7); the *Book of the Wars of the* LORD (Num. 21:14); the *Law* (Deut. 17:18, etc.; Josh. 1:8, etc.) Moreover, at the beginning of the Hellenistic period, the Syrian Berossus and the Egyptian Manetho wrote, in Greek, official histories of their nations, that is, of the two principal kingdoms that were Alexander's heirs; both were priests with access to the sacred archives.²⁴ In particular, in 278 BCE, Berossus exploited the ancient cuneiform sources to compose a story very similar to the biblical proto-history (Gen. 1–11), with accounts of creation, paradise, Cain and Abel, the flood, Nimrod, the Tower of Babel, and so on, but without anything that announces Israel. The ancients believed that Berossus had known the Bible and had mistreated it, but the opposite hypothesis is much simpler, because it avoids assuming multiple sources. Biblical Hebrew differs little from Phoenician, which was spoken in Alexandria. In any case, it is not excessive to imagine that the Pentateuch has kept traces of seventy-two different hands.

---

²² The *pual* שֹׂרַף draws attention; the normal form should be the nifal נִשְׂרָף. If Moses' search is not for a lost goat, but for the word שֵׂעִיר, the result immediately reads, "And this is שׂרף." In other words, שׂרף = שֵׂעִיר; removing the similar letters leaves פ = ע. This gives us the key to the numerical value of the letters: the letters ע and פ are consecutive and are separated by י, the tenth letter which is worth ten; everything else is deduced from this. Sometimes ע and פ are in reverse order (cf. Ps. 10:7-8); cf. Mitchell First, "Using the *pe-ayin* Order of the Abecedaries of Ancient Israel to date the Book of Psalms," *JSOT* 38 (2014), pp. 471–85.

²³ Cf. François Langlamet, "Arithmétique des scribes et texte consonantique: Gen 46,1–7 et 1 Sam 17,1–54," *RB* 97 (1990), pp. 379–409. In many villages, excavations have collected numerous schoolbooks (ostraka) from the royal period; cf. Aaron Demsky, "The Interface of Oral and Written Traditions in Ancient Israel: The Case of the Abecedaries," in: Christophe Rico and Claudia Attuci (eds.), *Origins of the Alphabet*, Newcastle, Cambridge Scholars Publishing, 2015, pp. 17–48.

²⁴ Cf. Russell E. Gmirkin, *Berossus and Genesis, Manetho and Exodus. Hellenistic history and the Date of the Pentateuch* (JSOTSup, 433), New York/London, T&T Clark, 2006; Id., *Plato and the Creation of the Hebrew Bible*, London/New York, Routledge, 2017.

With regard to time and place, the synagogue can also be considered a place of study and prayer. Field finds indicate that the oldest known synagogues do not go back much further than 250 BCE and are located in Egypt but not in Alexandria.²⁵ It was perhaps this multiplicity of places of worship that Onias, fleeing Judea, wanted to unite around a temple in the region of Heliopolis (cf. Section 3.2). Moreover, the name of Moses is interesting, for it is given by the Pharaoh's daughter, who explains it by linking the name *Moshe* to the verb *masha* "to draw" (Exod. 2:10): "because I drew him out of the water." Yet, this is very approximate, because *moshe* means "drawing" and not "drawn," and water is not mentioned. There is a better explanation, which is consistent with the form *Moüses* in the LXX: in Coptic, *mou* means "water" and *uzai* "save." Previously, in the demotic Hellenistic period, *mw* meant "water" and *hsy* "exalted, favored." Thus, the name of Moses was Egyptian and not Hebrew, and moreover it was given by an Egyptian woman.²⁶

7. It is surprising that the Samaritans lost sight of the prophets of the ancient kingdom of Israel, typically Elijah, Elisha, Amos, Hosea, or even Jonas. In contrast, Sirach brushes a wide range of biblical portraits, from Enoch to Nehemiah; he even adds the high priest Simon son of Onias. In these eulogies, he calls different people "prophets:" Samuel, Elijah, Isaiah, Jeremiah; in reference to the "twelve prophets" he says "may their bones flourish again"—certainly in reference to the individuals and not to the books with their names. The author's grandson, who translated the work around 132 BCE, has shifted the terminology, for in his prologue he speaks of "the Law, the Prophets, and the other books," and he indicates that the translations differ from what the original expresses. There is now a formally defined three-part library, and the whole has been translated. A century later, Philo presents a different view: apart from the Pentateuch, his biblical allusions are minimal, perhaps because of his lack of interest in history, prophecy, and eschatology. However, the silence of the Samaritans after Joshua remains difficult to understand, unless the status of the prophets and other writings was promoted after their separation from the Jews, around 150 BCE. In this regard, it is notable that the psalms' allusions to biblical history hardly go beyond the Pentateuch and never take it in its entirety.²⁷

In a word, the Bible buries its commentators, but they keep reemerging!

---

²⁵ Cf. Étienne Nodet, "La synagogue et l'autorité scripturaire," *Semitica et Classica* 10 (2017), pp. 59–80.

²⁶ The classical Egyptian etymology is based on a suffix *-mses* (like *Ramses* "son of Ra"); the most complete study in this sense is due to J. Gwyn Griffiths, "The Egyptian Derivation of the Name Moses," *JNES* 12 (1953), pp. 225–31, who endeavors as an Egyptologist to justify the received explanation, so as to connect Moses with Ramses II. This theory must be abandoned, because רעמסס "Ramses" appears elsewhere in the Bible (Exod. 1:11; 12:37), and the suffix מסס- clearly has nothing in common with משה "Moses." Other explanations are proposed par Francis Breyer, *Ägyptische Namen und Wörter im Alten Testament*, Münster, Zaphon, 2019, pp. 57–8.

²⁷ Cf. Thomas Römer, "Extra-Pentateuchal Biblical Evidence for the Existence of a Pentateuch. The Case of the 'Historical Summaries', Especially in the Psalms," in: Thomas B. Dozeman, Konrad Schmid, and Baruch J. Schwartz (eds.), *The Pentateuch: International Perspectives on Current Research* (Forschungen zum Alten Testament, 78), Tübingen, Mohr-Siebeck, 2011, pp. 471–88.

Appendix

Status Quæstionis

Work on the origin of the Samaritans has been revived by the recent excavations on Mount Gerizim, which revealed a huge shrine that is much older than Josephus says. In the absence of other written evidence, it was previously assumed that this temple was erected around the time of Alexander.

A.1 The First Modern Studies

Before these recent discoveries, we must mention the first classic modern investigation by J. Montgomery,[1] who spoke of a Jewish sect. Then, the ordinary opinion, represented by G. Wenren and R. Coggins, was that the separation of the Samaritan was gradual and crystallized at the time of the construction of the temple on Mount Gerizim.[2] J. Purvis' synthesis should be considered; taking into account all the archaeological work around Shechem and in the desert of Judah, he concluded that the postexilic schism highlighted by Josephus could be followed. He proposed a global sketch based on 2 Kings 17 MT[3] (cf. Section 2.1):

1. Shechem was rebuilt by the dissident leaders of Samaria, after the expulsion that followed their revolt against the Macedonians, a fact known from the classical sources and confirmed by W. Daliyeh's findings. Since their settlement by the Assyrians, they already had a long tradition of independence from Jerusalem and an inveterate antipathy, as shown by their opposition to the returning exiles in Persian times. Inversely, they were despised by at least part of the Judeans because of their ethnically and religious hybrid origin. The Samaritans who rebuilt Shechem were, however, attached to the Hebrew God, even though their ancestors had revered other gods.

---

[1] James A. Montgomery, *The Samaritans: The Earliest Jewish Sect. Their History, Theology and Literature*, Philadelphia, Winston, 1907; cf. ch. I, n. 2.

[2] Geo Widengren, "Israelite-Jewish Religion," in: C. Jouco Bleeker and Geo Widengren (eds.), *Historia Religionum*, Leiden, Brill, 1969, I:225–317; Richard J. Coggins, *Samaritans and Jews: The Origins of Samaritanism Reconsidered*, London, Blackwell, 1975.

[3] Cf. James D. Purvis, *The Samaritan Pentateuch and the Origin of the Samaritan Sect*, Cambridge (MA), Harvard University Press; Id., "The Samaritans and Judaism," in: Robert A. Kraft and George W. E. Nickelsburg (eds.), *Early Judaism and Its Modern Interpreters*, Philadelphia, Fortress Press, 1986, pp. 81–98, complété par Id., "The Samaritans," in: William D. Davies and Louis Finkelstein (eds.), *The Cambridge History of Judaism*, Cambridge University Press, 1984–9, II:591–613.

2. When the Samaritans restored Shechem, they built a shrine to YHWH on nearby Mount Gerizim, thus deliberately establishing a connection with ancient Israelite traditions in order to keep the local population in favor, much as Jeroboam I had done by creating a shrine at Bethel to stabilize the northern secession (1 Kgs 12:26-29). This is consistent with other places in the eastern Mediterranean where, in response to the founding of a Greek colony, we find the local population gathering around an ancestral shrine.[4]

3. Contrary to what Josephus suggests, it is not proven that the priesthood of Mount Gerizim derived from that of Jerusalem. The dominant opinion is to accept the independence of the Samaritan priesthood, considering that Sanballat could easily find an Aaronic family endowed with the desired pedigree.[5] Others keep to Josephus' dissenters,[6] or combine the two, suggesting that, after the service of a few dissenting high priests, a proper Samaritan dynasty was installed.

4. The building of the temple on Mount Gerizim was therefore an independent activity, not a schism from Jerusalem, though it certainly constituted a counterweight, another place of loyalty within the whole of Judaism but without any claim to sole legitimacy.

5. It was only later, in the second century, that relations deteriorated to the point of a real schism: first because of political tensions due to rivalries between Seleucids and Lagids for control of Coele-Syria and then because of a difference in attitude during the Hellenization crisis, the Jews rebuking the Samaritans for their submission to Antiochus IV. These difficulties culminated in John Hyrcanus' expansionism, until the destruction of the Gerizim shrine around 111 BCE and Shechem shortly afterward, events which are known from Josephus (*Ant.* 13:254-281).

6. At a time difficult to specify, but at the earliest in the second century, the Samaritans edited a Pentateuch, with some manipulations[7] tending to establish their exclusive legitimacy. It was this claim, confirmed by the rejection of "Judean" literature (Prophets, Writings), and not the mere fact of the Gerizim Temple that made the gulf between Jews and Samaritans unbridgeable.

7. Finally, if one views Judaism in a very broad sense as the collection of groups that legitimately claim to represent the Israelite tradition, then the Samaritans can be considered a Jewish sect, as does the rabbinic tradition. On the other hand, traces of divergence within the sources show that the Samaritans did not form a single bloc: as evidenced in particular by the Dosithean movement, identifiable as early as the

---

[4] Cf. Elias J. Bickerman, *From Esdras to the Last of the Maccabees: The Historical Foundations of Post-Biblical Judaism*, New York, Schocken, 1962, pp. 43–6.

[5] As supposed by Hans G. Kippenberg, *Garizim und Synagogue: Traditionsgeschichtliche Untersuchungen zur Samaritanischen Religion der aramäischen Periode*, Berlin, De Gruyter, 1971, pp. 60–8; and Coggins, *Samaritans and Jews*, pp. 142–4.

[6] For example, John Bowman, *The Samaritan Problem: Studies in the Relationships of Samaritanism, Judaism, and Early Christianity*, Pittsburgh, Pickwick, 1975, pp. 33–56.

[7] On this point, it is necessary to follow the updates d'Emanuel Tov, "The Samaritan Pentateuch and the Dead Sea Scrolls," in: Shani Tzoref and Ian Young (eds.), *Keter Shem Tov: Memorial Alan Crown*, Piscataway, Gorgias Press, 2013, pp. 59–88.

second century and with an anti-sacerdotal tendency, which is reminiscent of what the Pharisees were in relation to the Sadducees.[8]

This overall view gives a permanent impression of uneasiness, of assertions immediately retracted. The following are just a few examples of this fragility: Why believe the Samaritan sources when they affirm that the Gerizim priesthood is of old Levitical stock and does not come from Jerusalem and at the same time reject them when they declare that the Samaritan tradition is of old Israelite stock? How can one simultaneously understand an inveterate antipathy between Jews and Samaritans, with an ethnic-religious basis and dating back to the royal era, and the non-schismatic erection of the Gerizim Temple? The low dating of the Samaritan Pentateuch is obviously problematic, but is it reasonable to compare it with a Jewish (or Judean) Pentateuch that was supposedly fixed centuries ago? As for the "whole of Judaism" as the repository of the Israelite tradition, the least we can say is that it is an ill-defined notion.[9]

A.2 Some Recent Works

Many studies deal with biblical questions, ranging from the formation of the Pentateuch to the historiography of 1-2 Kings and 1-2 Chronicles. The question of the relationship of the Samaritans to the ancient kingdom of Israel or even to King Josiah always comes up,[10] but here we shall confine ourselves to the main studies dealing specifically with their origins.

M. Kartveit[11] observes that the many attempts to synthesize the Samaritans' origin that have recently been proposed remain imprecise or very conjectural: the authors oscillate between foreign colonizers who were gradually acclimatized (cf. 2 Kings 17) or Jewish dissidence in the Persian period with a forged Torah, which is surprising for a "sect" because the term suggests something more strict. He proposes to take up all the known data on the Samaritans, since some have hardly been exploited. He goes through a network of allusions in many Jewish and Christian sources, from the Jewish poet Theodotus, at the time of John Hyrcanus, to Epiphanius of Salamis. He gives a detailed inventory of Samaritan inscriptions and avatars of Paleo-Hebrew writing (Gerizim, Qumran). Two Greek inscriptions from Delos, dated to the second century, report that the Israelites sent taxes to ΑΡΓΑΡΙΖΙΜ, a transcription of the typical one-word expression הרגריזים; the Aramaic equivalent still appears on the map of Madaba in the transcribed form ΤΟΥΡΓΑΡΙΖΙΜ (for טור-גריזים). Finally, he examines in detail

---

[8] Cf. Kippenberg, *Garizim und Synagogue*, pp. 128–71; Stanley J. Isser, *The Dositheans: A Samaritan Sect in Late Antiquity* (SJLA, 17), Leiden, Brill, 1976, cf. Section 1.3.2.
[9] Morton Smith, *Palestinian Parties and Politics That Shaped The Old Testament*, New York, Columbia University Press, 1971, pp. 148–92, simplifies: he judges that Josephus did not know anything precise about the Samaritans before Antiochus IV Epiphanes, and that he projects into the past later conflicts.
[10] Or is completely ignored; cf. for example John J. Collins, *The Invention of Judaism. Torah and Jewish Identity from Deuteronomy to Paul*. Oakland, University of California Press, 2017.
[11] Magnar Kartveit, *The Origin of the Samaritans* (VTSup, 128), Leiden/Boston, Brill, 2009.

the singularities and corruptions of the Samaritan Pentateuch, whose importance has been renewed by the Qumran finds. He questions the absence of the prophets among the Samaritans, especially those of the North. He considers that the divorce with the Jews began during the Maccabean crisis, when the Samaritans, wanting to separate themselves from the Jews, addressed a supplication to Antiochus Epiphanes in which they declared themselves to be "Sidonians of Shechem" (cf. Section 3.4). In conclusion, he judges that the appearance of the Samaritans must be linked to the construction of the sanctuary on Mount Gerizim, which according to recent excavations dates back to at least the fifth century. He must then admit, albeit hesitantly, that the repatriates of Ezra-Nehemiah were only a minority, and that in and around Jerusalem there were Yahwist populations, perhaps of foreign origin, and who unlike the reformers accepted exogamy.

This conclusion is sound, and it is enough to reinforce it by turning the usual paradigm upside down: the second wave of returnees from exile, who correspond to Josephus' "elders," are indeed intruders in a traditional Israelite whole, and there is no reason to attribute the arrival of the Pentateuch to them. Even the rabbinic tradition indirectly admits this, as we have seen (Section 2.1). In fact, the author is hampered by his implicit assumption of Hebrew biblical texts set in the Persian period and centered entirely on Jerusalem. He does not really explain why the Samaritans took on a new identity when they built their temple on Mount Gerizim, or more precisely he goes back more than a century in Josephus' explanation, which has a strong flavor of dissent.

R. Pummer,[12] rightly believing that Josephus' writings constitute the best source on the Samaritans, focuses on his testimony and carefully reviews all the episodes reported, in chronological order: the settlement of Assyrian colonizers and their adoption of Yahwism; the resistance of the Samaritans to the project of reestablishing the Temple in the time of Zerubbabel; the erection of the Gerizim Temple in Alexander's time; Josephus' romanced account of the Tobiad, nephew of a high priest Onias, who obtained the farm tax of a vast domain including Samaria; the supplication of the Samaritans "Sidonians of Shechem" addressed to Antiochus IV Epiphanes to separate themselves from the Jews, a step from which one cannot conclude that they became "Hellenized"; the dispute in Alexandria between Jews and Samaritans, which is strange, since Ptolemy no longer has jurisdiction over Coele-Syria; moreover, the Samaritans have a similar account, under Nebuchadnezzar or under a pharaoh, and they win; the expansionism of John Hyrcan, who annexes Samaria and destroys the Gerizim Temple, but recently collected coins make it possible to rectify the chronology given by Josephus. Finally, the case of Malthace, one of Herod's wives, attracts attention, for she was a Samaritan, and her sons Antipas and Archelaus received from Augustus most of the government of the vast Herodian Judea without anyone contesting their legitimacy, while Ezra and Nehemiah would certainly have been scandalized.

The same author[13] takes up with all the erudition that is desirable an examination of all the texts subsequent to the Hebrew Bible that mention the Samaritans: Sir. 50:25-

---

[12] Reinhard Pummer, *The Samaritans in Flavius Josephus* (Texts and Studies in Ancient Judaism, 129), Tübingen, Mohr-Siebeck, 2009.

[13] Reinhard Pummer, *The Samaritans: A Profile*, Grand Rapids/Cambridge, Eerdmans, 2016.

26, which calls them a "stupid people"; 2 Macc. 5:22-23 and 6:1-2, where Jerusalem and Mount Gerizim are mentioned symmetrically; the fragments of Qumran and Masada in Paleo-Hebrew script; the writings of Josephus, where his antipathy toward the Samaritans is not absolute, for it is expressed only in *Antiquities*; the supplication of the Samaritans to Antiochus IV; the dispute in Alexandria before Ptolemy VI; John Hyrcanus' conquest of Samaria and the destruction of the Gerizim Temple; various incidents between Jews and Samaritans during the Roman period; the case of a prophet summoning all the people to Gerizim, thus triggering a violent repression by Pontius Pilate, who was then dismissed; the New Testament; rabbinic literature, which from century to century treats the Samaritans more and more as pagans. Then the results of the archaeological excavations are presented in detail: the temple and the city on top of Mount Gerizim and the different synagogues found in the country and as far as Delos.

After a review of different modern opinions, especially of biblical scholars, the author holds that Yahwism never disappeared from the ancient kingdom of Israel after the Assyrian deportation. The Books of Chronicles prove this, now that they are detached from Ezra-Nehemiah: there was never any real religious difference between the North and the South. Thus, one cannot speak of the Samaritans as a sect, and the Pentateuch must be considered a common Israelite work. The divorce from the Jews resulted from the destruction of the Mount Gerizim temple, not from its construction. The case of the reformers Ezra and Nehemiah must be considered marginal, and they had little influence.

The author concludes that the account of Samaria's repopulation by foreigners (2 Kings 17 MT) cannot be the founding account of the Samaritans, since they are portrayed as pagans practicing a rather bizarre syncretism. Unfortunately, he ignores the LXX and Josephus, which offer a different perspective, not to mention the similarity between the Assyrian settlers and the people of Israel as represented in Joshua's testament in Joshua 24.

G. Knoppers wants to take the whole issue up again.[14] First, he wonders why Jews and Samaritans are so far apart when they have so much in common. Yet, the foundational narrative in 2 Kings 17 MT firmly separates them: they arrived as strangers and converted to Yahwism out of fear of lions. That may be so, but one should ask what became of the ten tribes of the kingdom of Israel, since it is proven that Sargon II's deportation was only partial. The author proposes looking for local traces in order to reconstruct a history of Samaria. Indeed, modern discoveries open up new perspectives, including large-scale excavations (Samaria, Shechem, and Gerizim), surface surveys (on the Hills of Manasseh and Ephraim), texts and inscriptions (Qumran, coins).

Around the fall of Samaria, archaeology shows both continuity (e.g., pottery remains stable) and discontinuity (many sites have a layer of destruction). Transjordan and Galilee were severely affected by the campaign of Teglath-Phalasar III against the

---

[14] Gary N. Knoppers, *Jews and Samaritans: The Origins and History of Their Early Relations*, Oxford/New York, Oxford University Press, 2013; Id., "Mt. Gerizim and Mt. Zion: A Study in the Early History of the Samaritans and Jews," *Studies in Religion/Sciences Religieuses* 34 (2005), pp. 309–38; Id., "Aspects of Samaria's Religious Culture During The Early Hellenistic Period," in: Philip R. Davies and Diana V. Edelman (eds.), *The Historian and the Bible: FS Lester L. Grabbe*, New York/London, T&T Clark, 2010, pp. 159–74.

Philistines (in 734 BCE, cf. 2 Kgs 15:29), but the region of Samaria was less devastated by Salmanasar-Sargon. Subsequently, the majority of the population remained Israelite.

The Deuteronomistic account shows a development of the North after the deportation. 2 Kgs 17:24-41 is composite: there is a discontinuity, but it appears that the ancient Yahwism was continued. In particular, King Josiah, a century after Sargon, extended his reform to the North; and this implies an Israelite population that had absorbed the Assyrian settlers. The Chronicler loses sight of the rupture and clearly indicates that the northern tribes kept their customs and listened to the prophets. They thus regained a Yahwist brotherhood with Judah.

During the Persian period, the city of Samaria was certainly more prosperous than Jerusalem, and the temple on Mount Gerizim was probably more important than that in Jerusalem. Ezra and Nehemiah focused on refounding Judah, but they are probably not representative: apart from their reform and ethnic cleansing, there was no schism between two Yahwisms. The documents of Elephantine confirm this.

The crisis around Hellenism and the Maccabean led to the separation, because of growing mistrust on both sides. The destruction of Gerizim had a lasting, but not definitive, effect, judging by a later parallel development that becomes increasingly clear in the Byzantine period, with the synagogue, mezuza, miqveh. However, it is still strange that the Samaritans stayed out of the wars of 66–70 and 132–5, totally disregarding Israelite solidarity.

The author is obviously biased in favor of an immemorial Yahwist unity, and this leads him to simplifications. If we start at the end, we do not see why the Samaritans, whose temple had been destroyed by Jews, would have joined the wars against the Romans: the first was due to the Jewish zealots, a movement of Galilean-Pharisee origin; the second, very similar to the Maccabean crisis, was the result of a desecration of the Holy of Holies by the emperor Hadrian. On the other hand, the label "Yahwist" can cover a wide range of realities, from obscure monolatry to wide-ranging scriptural monotheism. The books of Ezra-Nehemiah are certainly repulsive, but it would be a mistake to underestimate their importance.

D. Nocquet takes a quasi-rural approach,[15] for the Pentateuch considers both the territoriality of the Promised Land and the relationship with the other nations neighboring Samaria and Judea: the countries of Transjordan, Edom, Egypt, and Philistia were first of all lands where Israel was welcomed or places conducive to the cult of YHWH. Then, a redefinition of the cult centrality, after Joshua's conquest and well before Jerusalem, highlighted Shechem, Bethel, and Mount Gerizim. These specific places, including the covenant with Joshua at Shechem (Josh. 24), should be seen as representing a Samaritan contribution to the origin of the Torah, which complemented the priestly stratum; this is contrary to Judean historiography, which wholly challenges Samaritan legitimacy. The author places this editorial work in the fifth or fourth century, in reaction to the strictly Judean Yahwism of Ezra and Nehemiah. The Hexateuch, completed in the Persian period, thus opens the possibility

---

[15] Dany R. Nocquet, *La Samarie, la diaspora et l'achèvement de la Torah: territorialités et internationalités dans l'Hexateuque* (OBO 284), Fribourg, Academic Press Fribourg/Göttingen, Vandenhoeck & Ruprecht, 2017.

of a cult to YHWH outside of Canaan, strictly limited to the west of the Jordan. Thus, Israel's secular enmities toward Edom, Moab, or Midian are put into perspective, by distinguishing between cultic purity and ethnic purity; this would, therefore, represent the beginning of an international history of salvation.

This very thorough study is full of judicious observations, but it spontaneously gives priority to Judah. Yet, it is difficult to see how Ezra and Nehemiah could have accepted a Pentateuch reworked by Samaritans in the Persian period.

Index of Modern Authors

Abadie, Philippe   95 n.9, 108 n.33
Abel, Félix-Marie   30 n.46, 84 n.41
Aharoni, Yohanan   109 n.40
Albertz, Rainer   xvi n.17, 21 n.34, 85 n.48
Alt, Albrecht   63 n.52
Amphoux, Christian-Bernard   72 n.2
Amzallag, Nissim   26 n.39, 105 n.28, 118 n.5
Anthonioz, Stéphanie   64 n.56
Aperghis, Gerasimos G.   101 n.18
Apicella, Catherine   84 n.40
Arnold, Bill T.   63 n.53
Artus, Olivier   19 n.31
Assis, Elie   103 n.23
Attuci, Claudia   122 n.23
Auwers, Jean-Marie   32 n.54
Aviam, Mordechai   13 n.13
Avigad, Nahman   109 n.38
Avi-Yonah, Michael   7 n.3, 86 n.50

Babota, Vasile   33 n.56
Baden, Joel S.   121 n.19
Barkay, Gabriel   64 n.57
Bar-Kochva, Bezalel   101 n.18
Barthélemy, Dominique   15 n.21
Bartlett, John R.   103 n.23
Becking, Bob   102 n.20
Ben Zeev, Miriam Pucci   33 n.58
Ben Zvi, Ehud   118 n.6
Berlin, Adele   xvii n.21
Berthelot, Katell   32 n.52
Beyer, Gustav   81 n.36
Bickerman, Elias J.   34 n.61, 36 nn.63, 68, 72 n.4, 77 n.25, 83 n.39, 95 n.10, 120 n.13, 126 n.4
Bikerman, Élie   27 n.49
Binger, Tilde   64 n.54
Bird, Michael F.   23 n.35
Bleeker, C. Jouco   125 n.2
Böhler, Dieter   23 n.35, 25 n.37
Bonnet, Charles   65 n.62
Bonnet, Corinne   85 n.47

Borchardt, Francis   34 n.59
Bourgel, Jonathan   xii n.11, xv, xv n.14
Bowman, John   44 n.97, 126 n.6
Bremmer, Jan N.   120 n.13
Brettler, Marc Zvi   119 n.11
Briggs, Charles A.   32 n.54
Briggs, Emilie G.   32 n.54
Bromiley, Geoffrey William   xiv n.12
Brooke, George J.   34 n.61
Bruneau, Philippe   72 n.2
Bultmann, Rudolf   43 n.96

Cadbury, Henry J.   39 n.78
Carbonaro, Paul   40 n.80, 42 n.88
Cazelles, Henri   49 n.2
Chalmers, Matthew J.   46 n.103
Charlesworth, James Hamilton   vii n.1, xx
Choi, Dongbin   87 n.54
Cogan, Mordechai   50 n.5
Coggins, Richard J.   84 n.43, 125, 125 n.2
Collins, John J.   127 n.10
Columbus, Christopher   xx
Cook, Johann   76 n.21
Costa, Jose   15 n.19
Cresson, Bruce C.   103 n.23
Cross, Frank M.   108 n.34
Crown, Alan D.   ix n.4, 7 n.2, 8 n.5
Cullmann, Oscar   45 n.100

Dahmen, Ulrich   32 n.54
Dan, Anca   78 n.27
Davies, Philip R.   113 n.49, 129 n.14
Davies, William D.   125 n.3
Day, John   65 n.63
de Geus, Cornelis H. J.   67 n.73
de Hoop, Raymond   67 n.74, 68 n.76
Delcor, Matthias   8
de Miroschedji, Pierre   58 n.32, 66 n.69
de Moor, Johannes C.   67 n.73
Demsky, Aaron   122 n.23
Dentzer, Jean-Marie   36 n.68

de Pury, Albert   56 n.23
De Robert, Philippe   9 n.6
de Troyer, Kristin   16 n.23
Dever, William G.   64 n.54, 119 n.10
de Vos, J. Cornelis   67 n.74
Diebner, Bernd Jørg   5 n.1
Do, Toan   43 n.93
Doran, Robert   35 n.62
Dozeman, Thomas B.   21 n.33, 123 n.27
Dubberstein, Waldo H.   30 n.48
Dubovský, Peter   49 n.1
Duggan, Michael W.   35 n.62
Dunn, James D. G.   38 n.73
Durand, Xavier   80 n.32
Dušek, Jan   53 n.13, 108 n.33, 109 n.39

Echols, Charles L.   67 n.71
Edelman, Diana V.   129 n.14
Edmondson, Jonathan   107 n.31, 121 n.16
Efird, James M.   103 n.23
Egger, Rita   52 n.7
Egger-Wenzel, Renate   35 n.62
Einstein, Albert   xx
Elayi, Josette   55 n.20
Eliot, T. S.   xx
Emerton, John A.   95 n.9
Eshel, Hanan   xi n.8, 44 n.97, 108 n.33
Ewald, Heinrich   118 n.3

Fabien, Patrick   41 n.84
Feigin, Samuel I.   109 n.44
Feldman, Louis H.   84 n.43, 107 n.31, 121 n.16
Field, Eugene   xx
Fiensy, David A.   13 n.13
Finkelstein, Israel   57 n.28, 63 n.50, 70 n.82, 113 n.49, 119 n.7, 121 n.18
Finkelstein, Louis   125 n.3
First, Mitchell   122 n.22
Flint, Peter W.   76 n.18
Ford, Josephine Massyngbaerde   44 n.97
Foster, Paul   39 n.78
Frei-Stolba, Regula   28 n.41
Frerichs, Ernest S.   15 n.19
Frevel, Christian   50 n.5
Frey, Jörg   vii n.1, 39 n.77
Fried, Lisbeth S.   25 n.37

Friedrich, Gerhard   xiv n.12
Fritz, Volkmar   66 n.69
Frolov, Serge   66 n.69

Gadd, Cyril J.   108 n.37
Galil, Gershon   49 n.2
Garbini, Giovanni   87 n.53
Gaster, Moses   x, 5 n.1, 9 n.8, 16 nn.22, 25, 17
Gaullier-Bougassas, Catherine   92 n.4
Geoltrain, Pierre   40 n.83
Gertz, Ian C.   19 n.30
Gex, Kristine   28 n.41
Giambrone, Anthony   11 n.9
Giuntoli, Federico   21 n.34
Gmirkin, Russell E.   122 n.24
Goldstein, Jonathan A.   36 n.64, 83 n.39
Goodman, Martin   120 n.13
Gourgues, Michel   39 n.75, 118 n.2
Grabbe, Lester L.   50 n.3, 110 n.45
Grätz, Sebastian   102 n.20
Green, Peter   36 n.66
Green, W. Scott   12 n.13
Gregory, Andrew   39 n.78, 40 n.81
Grelot, Pierre   80 n.33
Griffiths, J. Gwyn   123 n.26
Groh, Dennis E.   12 n.13
Gruen, Erich S.   36 n.66, 121 n.16
Guggenheimer, Heinrich W.   98 n.14
Guy, Jordan   95 n.9

Haar, Stephen   39 n.76
Halpern, Baruch   50 n.3
Hanhart, Robert   79 n.30
Hasegawa, Shuichi   50 n.5
Hata, Gohei   75 n.17, 84 n.43
Haudebert, Pierre   39 n.75
Hayes, Andrew   39 n.77
Hayes, J. H.   111 n.46
Heckl, Ralk   112 n.47
Hensel, Benedikt   xii n.11, 117 n.1
Herr, Moshe David   46 n.102, 77 n.24, 86 n.51
Hill, Charles E.   39 n.78
Hjelm, Ingrid   8, 39 n.77, 118 n.4
Honigman, Sylvie   77 n.25, 102 n.19
Hunt, Alice   79 n.29
Hurst, Lincoln D.   37 n.71
Hyrcan, John   16 n.23, 44 n.97

Isaac, Benjamin 84 n.41
Isser, Stanley J. 42 n.88, 127 n.8

Japhet, Sara 95 n.9
Jaubert, Annie 77 n.24
Jeremias, Joachim xiv n.12
Ji, Chang-Ho C. 79 n.31
Jokiranta, Jutta M. 63 n.49
Jones, F. Stanley 40 n.83
Joseph Aviram 7 n.3

Kahle, Paul 16 n.24
Kampen, John 32 n.53
Kappler, Werner 79 n.30
Kartveit, Magnar xii n.11, xvii n.23,
 9 n.8, 53 n.13, 72 n.2, 77 n.25,
 112 n.47, 119 n.10, 127, 127 n.11
Kelle, Brad E. 64 n.59
Kelso, James L. 54 n.15
Kennedy, James 16 n.26
Kippenberg, Hans G. 126 n.4, 127 n.8
Kittel, Gerhard xiv n.12
Knauf, Ernst A. 50 n.3
Knohl, Israel 66 n.69
Knoppers, Gary N. xvi n.17, 9 n.8,
 77 n.25, 85 n.48, 102 n.20,
 112 n.47, 119 nn.7, 10, 129,
 129 n.14
Kochva, Bezalel Bar 30 n.49
Koopmans, William T. 19 n.29
Kraft, Robert A. 125 n.3
Kuhrt, Amélie 95 n.10

Laberge, Léo 118 n.2
Lang, Peter 21 n.32, 28 n.41
Langlamet, François 58 n.39, 97 n.13,
 122 n.23
Larché, Francois 79 n.31
le Bohec, Sylvie 107 n.32
le Boulluec, Alain 40 n.83
Lefebvre, Philippe 58 n.37
Lemaire, André 64 nn.55, 59, 67 n.72,
 94 n.7
Lemche, N. 118 n.4
le Rider, Georges 28 n.41
le Roux, Jurie H. 69 n.80
Levin, Christoph 50 n.5
Levin, Yigal 119 n.9
Levine, Lee I. 75 n.14

Levinson, Bernard M. 102 n.20
Lévy, Isidore 109 n.42
Levy, Thomas E. 50 n.3
Lichtert, Claude 59 n.44
Lieberman, Saul 15 n.17
Lipschitz, Oded xvi n.17, 85 n.48
Loewe, Raphael 45 n.98
Lohfink, Norbert 63 n.53

Mccarter, P. Kyle 64 n.54
Macchi, Jean-Daniel 53 nn.13, 14,
 55 n.22, 62 n.46
Macdonald, John x, 5 n.1, 16 n.22,
 43 n.95
Mcglynn, Moyna 36 n.63
Maeir, Aren M. 58 n.32, 59 n.44
Magen, Yitzhakh xvi nn.17, 18, xvii
 n.22, 7 n.1, 85 n.48
Maier, Aren M. 66 n.69
Main, Emmanuelle 87 n.52, 87 n.55
Mannati, Marina 32 n.54
Mantel, Hugo D. 46 n.102
Marasco, Gabriele 107 n.32
Marcus, Ralph 92 n.5
Margalit, Baruch 66 n.66
Marguerat, Daniel 41 n.86
Markl, Dominik 49 n.1
Martinez, Florentino Garcia 88
Meier, John P. 37 n.69
Mélèze-Modrzejewski, Joseph 120 n.14
Meshorer, Ya'akov 109 n.39
Meyers, Carol L. 49 n.2
Meyers, Eric 12 n.13
Miller, Daniel 99 n.15
Miller, J. M. 111 n.46
Miller, Patrick D. 64 n.54
Mittmann, Siegfried 109 n.41
Montgomery, James A. 7 n.2, 125,
 125 n.1
Moore, George Foot 78 n.28
Mor, Menahem 75 n.17, 109 n.44
Mørkholm, Otto 28 n.41, 84 n.44
Murphy-O'Connor, Jerome 15 n.19,
 42 n.89

Na'aman, Nadav 57 n.29, 63 nn.51, 53,
 113 n.49
Nawotka, Krzysztof 91 n.3
Neusner, Jacob xiv n.13, 15 n.20

Index of Modern Authors

Newsome, James D.   95 n.9
Nickelsburg, George W. E.   125 n.3
Nicolle, Christophe   66 n.66
Nihan, Christophe   62 n.46
Nisula, Timo   72 n.4
Nitschke, Jessica L.   85 n.47
Nocquet, Dany R.   59 n.44, 130, 130 n.15
Nodet, Étienne   vii, x, xii–xvi, xviii–xx,
    5 n.1, 11 n.9, 12 n.12, 13 n.14,
    14 n.16, 30 nn.44, 50, 32 n.53,
    40 n.83, 57 n.30, 62 n.46,
    74 n.13, 78 n.27, 79 n.29,
    88 n.57, 123 n.25
Noll, Kurt L.   63 n.53
Norton, Gerard J.   24 n.37
Noth, M.   118
Novotny, Jamie   55 n.20

Orthmann, Winfried   36 n.68
Ory, Amitay   91 n.3

Packer, John E.   11 n.9
Parker, Richard A.   30 n.48
Parvis, Sara   39 n.78
Pastor, Jack   75 n.17
Pelletier, André   77 n.25
Penwell, Stewart   xv n.14
Petrie, William M. Flinders   75 n.17
Pfoh, Emanuel   59 n.42, 59 n.44
Phillips, Thomas E.   40 n.81
Piotrkowski, Meron M.   75 n.17
Pitkin, Ronald E.   xiv n.12
Porten, Bezalel   80 n.34
Powels, Sylvia   44 n.97
Pritchard, James B.   64 n.58
Proctor, Mark A.   37 n.70
Prudký, Martin   5 n.1
Puech, Émile   64 nn.54, 55
Pummer, R.   44 n.97
Pummer, Reinhard   xv n.16, 8 n.5, 9 n.8,
    72 n.2, 73 n.6, 84 n.42, 128,
    128 nn.12, 13
Purvis, James D.   125, 125 n.3

Qedar, Shraga   109 n.39

Radner, Karen   50 n.5
Rahlfs, Alfred   23 n.35
Rainey, Anson F.   109 n.40

Rajak, Tessa   34 n.61
Reif, Stefan C.   35 n.62
Reiterer, Friedrich V.   109 n.44
Revell, E. J.   16 n.26
Reymond, Sophie   39 n.75
Riaud, Jean   39 n.75
Rice, John W.   105 n.29
Richter, Sandra L.   62 n.48
Rico, Christophe   78 n.27, 122 n.23
Roat, Alyssa   x n.6
Rollinger, Robert   91 n.3
Römer, Thomas   19 n.30, 21 n.33,
    62 n.46, 119 n.11, 123 n.27
Ross, William   54 n.16
Rothschild, Jean-Pierre   8 n.4

Sachs, Abraham J.   30 n.47
Sartre, Maurice   65 n.61, 84 n.40,
    120 n.14
Sass, Benjamin   109 n.38
Scheffler, Eben   67 n.73
Schenker, Adrian   24 n.37, 25 n.37,
    56 n.23, 63, 63 n.49
Schiffman, Lawrence H.   53 n.12, 87 n.56
Schmid, Konrad   21 nn.33, 34, 119 n.10,
    123 n.27
Schnocks, Johannes   32 n.54
Schwartz, Baruch J.   21 n.33, 123 n.27
Schwartz, Daniel R.   38 n.74, 110 n.45
Schwartz, Joshua J.   81 n.35, 83 n.38
Selavan, Barnea Levi   44 n.97
Sergi, Omer   50 n.3, 64 n.60
Servais-Soyez, Brigitte   65 nn.62, 64
Shayegan, Rahim   94 n.7
Sievers, Joseph   33 n.57, 81 n.35
Silberman, Neil A.   57 n.28, 63 n.50,
    113 n.49
Simon, Marcel   15 n.18
Singer, Itamar   58 n.32
Sixdenier, Guy Dominique   8 n.4
Ska, Jean-Louis   49 n.1, 59 n.44
Skehan, Patrick W.   44 n.97
Smith, Mark S.   65 n.63
Smith, Morton   127 n.9
Smithuis, Renate   34 n.61
Sonnet, Jean-Pierre   49 n.1
Spanier, Joseph   83 n.38
Spencer, F. Scott   41 n.87
Staples, Jason A.   32 n.52

Stavrianopoulou, Eftychia 85 n.47
Stemberger, Günther 87 n.55
Stenhouse, Paul 8 n.5, 9 n.7
Stern, Ephraim xi n.8, 108 n.33
Stern, Menahem 121 n.15
Stern, Pnina 75 n.17
Steudel, Annette 88
Steymans, Hans Ulrich 69 n.80
Stoops, Robert F., Jr. 40 n.83
Strange, James F. 12 n.13
Strange, James Riley 13 n.13
Sugimoto, David T. 64 n.56
Sullivan, Sharon xii n.9
Sussmann, Yaakov 87 n.56

Tadmor, Hayim 50 n.5
Tal, Abraham 8 n.5
Talmon, Shemaryahu xi n.8
Tammuz, Oded 109 n.44
Tangberg, K. Arvid 66 n.65
Tappy, Ron E. 91 n.2
Tate, Marvin E. 32 n.54
Taylor, Joan E. 75 n.16
Taylor, Lily R. 45 n.99
Tekoniemi, Timo 50 n.5
Thompson, Th. 118 n.4
Tobolowsky, Andrew 66 n.68, 67 n.71
Torrey, Charles C. 102 n.21
Touati, Charlotte 41 n.85
Tov, Emanuel 77 n.25, 126 n.7
Tsedaka, Benjamim xii n.9
Tucci, Pier Luigi 11 n.9
Tzoref, Shani 44 n.97, 126 n.7

Ulrich, Eugene 76 n.18

van der Horst, Pieter W. 72 n.2

Vanderkam, James C. 79 n.29, 90 n.1
van der Kooij, Arie 76 n.21
van der Lingen, Anton 113 n.49
van Henten, Jan W. 34 n.61
van Oorschot, Jurgen 65 n.63
van Ruiten, Jacques 67 n.74
van Seters, John 70 n.82, 118 n.4
Vaughn, Andrew G. 64 n.57
Villeneuve, François 33 n.55
Vogt, Hubertus C. M. 112 n.48
Voitila, Anssi 63 n.49
von Rad, Gerhard 101 n.17

Wagemakers, Bart 91 n.2
Wajdenbaum, Philippe 121 n.17
Weber, Beat 32 n.54
Weinfeld, Moshe 63 n.53
Wenren, G. 125
Weyde, Karl W. 66 n.65
White, L. Michael xii n.10, 72 n.2
Widengren, Geo 111 n.46, 125 n.2
Wifall, Walter R. 70 n.81
Williamson, Hugh G. M. 112 n.48, 119 n.9
Wilson, Robert R. 66 n.68
Wilson-Wright, Aren M. 66 n.66
Wise, Michael O. 33 n.56
Wiseman, Donald 30 n.47
Witte, Markus 65 n.63
Wright, Jacob L. 66 n.69
Würthwein, Ernst 50 n.5

Yadin, Yigael 119 n.12
Yahuda, Abraham S. 16 n.24
Yeivin, Israel 16 n.26
Young, Ian 126 n.7

Zollschan, Linda T. 33 n.57

Index of References

Gen.
- 1–11   122
- 1:1   13 n.15
- 4:4   xiii, 13 n.15
- 8:20   xiii
- 10:15   58, 84
- 12:4   109
- 12:6   55
- 12:6b   62 n.45
- 12:8   54
- 14:14   119
- 14:18   xiii
- 15:13-16   66 n.67
- 22   xiii
- 28:10-17   42 n.88
- 28:17   55
- 28:17-19   65
- 28:19   55
- 29–30   66
- 31:13   55
- 32:28   66
- 34   68
- 35:1-7   55
- 35:2   119 n.11
- 35:22   68
- 38   68
- 38:29   57 n.31
- 41:45   76
- 48:22   59 n.41, 68
- 49:1-27   68
- 49:8-18   68
- 50   68
- 50:20   68

Exod.
- 1:7   66
- 1:11   123 n.26
- 2:10   123
- 3:14   43, 84 n.46
- 6:16-17   67
- 6:20   66
- 12:15-28   88
- 12:37   123 n.26
- 12:37-38   67
- 12:38   119
- 17:6   41
- 20:25   97
- 23:10-11   92
- 23:24   55 n.17
- 24:1   56 n.24
- 24:7   122
- 28:41   59 n.43
- 32:4   54
- 33:7-8   56 n.24

Lev.
- 4:3-4   59 n.43
- 4:3-16   43 n.94
- 6:15   43 n.94
- 10:16a   121
- 11:38   43
- 13:43-46   37
- 14:1-32   37
- 16   105
- 16:1-4   97
- 16:3-4   85, 121 n.20
- 18:12   66
- 26:1   55 n.17
- 26:33-35   70
- 26:34   96 n.11

Num.
- 1:46   67
- 3:43   67
- 4:48   67 n.75
- 6:1-21   68 n.78
- 6:24-26   64
- 9:12-28   67
- 11:4   67, 119
- 16:1   94
- 21:8-9   61
- 21:14   122
- 25–36   21
- 26:51   67

26:62	67	7:1	17
35:6	18	7:2-3	17
		7:16	17
Deut.		7:26b	17
1:2	66 n.70	8	63 n.53
4:34	19	8:30-32	62 n.48
5:1	41	8:30-35	18, 62
7:1	56 n.24	9:2	62
7:1-2	100, 106	9:3-27	18
10:5	61	10:1-11	18
11	19, 63 n.53	10:10-11	109
11:27-28	62	10:12-14	18
11:29	62	11:1-14	18
11:30	7 n.1, 55	11:8	67
12–26	62	11:15-23	18
12:13-14	73 n.5	11:23	62
16:1-8	88	12	18, 62
16:21	65	13–21	18
17:14-15	63	15	19
17:14-20	47, 58 n.36	15:27	31 n.51
17:18	122	16:3-11	109
18:18	38, 42 n.88, 43	18:1	58, 68 n.77
20	32	18:1-2	56 n.24
23	52 n.8	18:1-10	18
23:4	58	18:22	54
23:4-6	106	19:1	68
26–29	68	20:7	18
27	63 n.53	21:41	56 n.24
27–28	18, 19	23:1–24:28	19
27:1-13	71	24	xxii, 21, 62, 63 n.53,
27:2	62 n.47		119 n.11, 129, 130
28:47-68	63, 70	24:1	19, 58 n.35
30:4	62	24:1-27	119
33:1-5	68	24:13	46
33:2-3	66 n.70	24:25	19
33:7	68	24:25-26	19
33:13-18	68	24:31a	19
		24:32	42 n.88
Josh.	8, 118		
1:4	58 n.32	Judg.	
1:8	122	1:26	55
2:1	17	2:13	61
2:24	17	3:31	67
3:10	56 n.24	5:3-5	66
4:19	7 n.1, 55	5:6	67
5:2-8	17	13:5	68 n.78
5:9	17	18:29	54
5:10-12	15	18:30	56 n.24
7–8	54		

Index of References

Ruth
- 4:17   57
- 4:18   57 n.31

1 Sam.
- 1:3   56 n.24
- 1:22   68 n.78
- 3:20   58
- 4:3-4   56 n.24
- 8:1-18   58
- 9:2   59 n.41, 68
- 10:20-21   58
- 10:23   59 n.41
- 11:1-11   58 n.34
- 13:1   58
- 14:47-48   58
- 22–29   60
- 22:3-4   57
- 24:7-8   59
- 26:11-12   59

2 Sam.
- 1:14-15   59
- 1:18-27   18
- 2:4   59
- 5:3   59
- 5:9   104
- 5:12   57
- 6:2   60
- 6:5   59
- 11–20   60
- 11:3   57
- 12:24   64
- 15:12-13   57
- 15:24   61
- 23:34   57
- 25:25   60

1 Kgs
- 1:39   57
- 2–5   60
- 2:3   59
- 2:46   57
- 3:1   61
- 3:4-14   60
- 5:1   93
- 5:5   54
- 5:15 LXX   57
- 6:37-38   57
- 6:38   57 n.27
- 8:2.65   73 n.4
- 8:16   63
- 8:38   102
- 9:11-14   57 n.29
- 9:20-21   56 n.24
- 11   60
- 11:7   58
- 11:27-39   56
- 11:42   58
- 12:1   56
- 12:19   56
- 12:21-22   97
- 12:24a LXX   58 nn.33, 34
- 12:25–14:23   60
- 12:26-29   126
- 12:28   65
- 12:28-32   56
- 13:32   50 n.4
- 14:21   58, 61
- 16:23-26   50, 64
- 16:32-33   65
- 18:19   65
- 18:29-33   51
- 18:30   73 n.5
- 18:31   51
- 19:2   65
- 19:16   65

2 Kgs
- 8:26   65
- 10:14   65
- 10:28-29   61
- 10:29   65
- 12:8   100
- 12:29   54
- 15:29   56 n.24, 130
- 17   ix, xiv, xxi, xxii, 3, 21, 49, 60, 115, 118, 125, 127, 129
- 17:1-4   50 n.5
- 17:3-6   50
- 17:5   19
- 17:5-6   50 n.5
- 17:6   97
- 17:7-23   54
- 17:19   54
- 17:24   xi, xii, 45
- 17:24-41   50, 130

17:28	52	34:9	xi
17:29-33	52	34:33	60
17:29-34a	50	35	23
17:34	51, 52, 119	35–36	23, 24
17:34-36	19	35:18	61
17:34-40	53	35:19a-d	23
17:34b-40	50	35:22	23
17:35-39	52	35:25	23
17:40	52	35:27	60
18	53 n.14	36	103 n.23
18:4	61	36:2a-c	23
18:6	70	36:5a-d	23
18:9-11	57	36:8	60
18:9-12	53	36:21	23, 96 n.11
21:7-8	59	36:22-23	23, 95
22–23	61	36:23	60
23:15	54		
23:19	54	Ezra	x, 14, 111, 117, 128–31
23:22	61	1–6	25, 95
23:28	60	1:1-3	24
25	103 n.23	1:1-3a	23
		1:3	98
1 Chron.		1:3-4	95
3:17-24	119 n.7	1:4-5	24
5	99	1:5	60, 98
5:30-41	100	1:6	24
5:40-41	97	1:7-8	24
5:41	81	1:8	96
6:35-36	100	1:9-11	24
7:5	73 n.4	1:11	97
8:28	57	1:104	60
10:1	60	2–3	26
11:1	60	2:1-2	96
13:6	60	2:1-70	24
16:13	66	3	105
21:30	60	3:1-6	24, 97, 103, 121 n.20
24:2	100	3:2	112
24:4	31 n.51	3:3	97
24:7	74, 86	3:3-6	85
		3:7-13	24
2 Chron.	8	3:12	96
1:3	60	4	96
6:6	63	4:1	99
11:14-15	56 n.24	4:1-2	90
12:33	63	4:1-3	24
30:1	xi	4:2	50 n.6, 97, 99, 118
30:1-2	60	4:3	97
34	61	4:4	97
34:3-7	60		

4:4-5	24, 98	2:19	104
4:6	98	3:1	14
4:7-23	24	3:1-32	27, 104
4:7-24	98	3:33-34	104
4:10	99	3:34	104
4:11-12	93	4:1-2	104
4:21-22	96	4:1-17	27
4:24	24, 26	5	27
5:1-2	24, 102	5:1-2	104 n.25
5:3-17	24	5:2-3	112
5:7-17	96	5:7-12	105
5:15	112	6:1-2	104
5:21	100	6:1-11	27
6:1-13	24	6:12-14	27
6:3-5	95	6:14	104
6:14	112	6:15	14
6:14-15	96	6:16	27
6:14-22	24	7	96 n.12
6:21	99	7:1	14, 104
7:1-5	99, 100, 103	7:4	27
7:1–8:14	24	7:5–9:37	27
7:6	99	8–10	103
7:8	103	8:1-2	25
7:13-26	101	8:1-13a	24
7:27	99	8:1-18	23
8	103	8:6	102
8:15-36	24	8:13-18	121 n.20
9:1	100	8:13b-18	24
9:1–10:44	24	8:14	103
10:18-19	90, 100	8:17	25, 61, 104
10:18-44	102	9:1	97
10:38	91	9:1-2	121 n.20
		9:2	105
Neh.	x, 13, 111, 117, 128–31	9:36-37	105
		10	27, 105
1:1	103	10:28	105
1:1-3	27	10:29	105
1:1-3	14	10:30	121 n.20
1:2	112	10:31	113
1:3	103	11:1	27
1:4-11	27	11:1-2	104
1:9	62	11:174	110
2	109	12	81
2:1-9	27	12:10	104
2:9	104 n.25, 112	12:27-43	27, 105
2:10	104	12:44-47	27, 105
2:10.19	109 n.43	13	27, 90, 109, 113
2:13	103	13:1-3	106
2:17-18	27	13:4-31	105

13:6	90, 103, 110	Hos.	
13:22	104	12:5	66 n.65
13:28	90, 107, 109 n.43		
		Joel	
Ps.	8	1-2	121 n.20
10:7-8	122 n.22		
45:3	15	Amos	
74	32 n.54	7:13	54
79	32 n.54		
79:2-3	32	Obad. (Abd.)	
110:1	41 n.84	9-18	103 n.23
137:7	26 n.39	18	26 n.39
Isa.		Hag.	
1:26	76	1:12-14	25
15:5	109 n.41	2:9	26
19:16-24	75		
19:18-19	76	Zech.	
19:21	76	4:9	26
40:3	42		
44:28	24	New Testament	
45:3-4	94		
45:14	38	Mt.	
		9:35	viii
Jer.		10:5-6	37
25:11	96 n.11	19:28	38
44:17	80	26:64	41 n.84
49:7-22	103 n.23	27:54	45
		28:19	41
Ezek.			
4:16-17	103 n.23	Mk	
13:17	104 n.26	6:8	viii
16:46	xi		
16:51	xi	Lk	
35:5	103 n.23	1:15	68 n.78
		3:14	42
Dan.		3:38	45
1:6-7	98 n.14	4:43-44	viii
2:33-34	14	9:51-53	ix
2:38	92	9:52	viii, 37
6:29	98 n.14	10	vii
7:13	41 n.84	10:33	37
7:25	28	17:11	viii
8:21	92	17:11-12	37
9:1	98 n.14	22:69	41 n.84
9:25	43	24:21	38
9:27	28	24:44	87
11:27-30	29 n.43, 34 n.60		

Index of References 143

Jn
1:29	43
1:37	46
1:45	42 n.88
1:51	42 n.88
3:22-23	42
3:26	45
3:28-29	46
4	46
4	51
4:12	xi
4:19	43
4:21	44
4:25	43
4:36	46
4:38	46
4:42	44
8:48	45
10:34-35	45
11:51-52	43 n.96
19:7-8	45
21:2	42 n.88

Acts 115
1:6	38
1:8	38
1:23	40 n.82
2:38	41
5:36-37	42 n.88
7:55	41 n.84
8	viii
8:1-2	41
8:5-6	38
8:10	40
8:12.37	41
8:14-17	viii
8:39	41
9:31-32	38
10:1-2	37
10:27	41
10:48	41
13:21	58 n.38
15:7	37
17:23	84 n.45
19:5-6	41
21:8-9	42
21:28-29	38

1 Cor.
| 1:13 | 41 |

Apocryphal and Deuterocanonical Books

1 Macc. 34, 47
1:10-15	35
1:41-42	36
1:59	30
2:1	30, 74
2:15-28	83
2:41	60, 86
2:41-42	101
2:51-64	32
3:3-9	32
3:24	109
3:47-49	32
4:59	31, 97
6:49	92
7:5-6	74 n.10
7:16	32
8:2-11	33
9:19	82
10:30	82 n.37
10:38	79
10:46-47	81
10:51-52	76
10:51-58	72
11:30-37	81
12	33
12:2-23	120
12:9	33
12:9-10	107
12:26	30 n.50
13:27-30	82
13:51	35
13:52a	31
13.52b	31
14:1-4	31
14:4-15	31, 32
14:16-24	31
14:20-23	120
14:25-49	31
15:1-14	31
15:15-24	31
15:16-23	xii n.10
15:25–16:10	31

16:2	32	4:45.50	103 n.23
16:11-24	31	4:45b.50	24
		4:47–5:6	24
2 Macc.	34	5:7-8	96
1:1-9	86	5:7-45	24
1:1-10a	72	5:46-52	24, 103
2:13-14	87, 106	5:47-48	25
3:1-4	35	5:53-62	24
3:2-3	71 n.1	5:63-68	24
4:9	35	5:65	97
4:13-15	36	5:69-70	24
4:19-20	35	6:1-2	24
4:22	36	6:3-21	24
5:1	29 n.43	6:22–7:1	24
5:1-14	75	7:2-15	24
5:9	107 n.32, 120	7:13	99 n.16
5:15-16	36	8:1-2	100
5:22-23	79, 129	8:1-40	24
5:22–6:2	36	8:5-6	23 n.36
5:24-26	29 n.42	8:41-64	24
6:1-2	129	8:65–9:36	24
6:2	79, 84	9:37-55	24, 103
6:9	30	9:38-39	25
9:1-17	36 n.65	9:46	102
11:16-37	30	9:55	23, 103 n.22
13:13-14	81		
14:3-4	74 n.10	4 Mac.	34 n.61
15:37	35		
		Sir.	
1 Ezra	13, 21	49	27
1:23, 24		49:7-10	26
1:25	23	49:11-12	26
1:30	23	49:13	14, 26, 102, 112
1:47-52	23 n.36	50	ix
2–7	25, 26, 95	50:1	78 n.28
2:1-3	24	50:25-26	128–9
2:4-5	24		
2:6	24	Testament of Judah	
2:7-8	24	3-7	68 n.79
2:9-11	24		
2:11	23 n.36, 97, 98	**Dead Sea Scrolls**	
2:12	99		
2:12-25	24	1QIsa^a	76
2:26	24	1QpHab	
3:1–4:46	24, 96 n.12, 112	8:8-13	88
3:1–5:6	96	1QS	
3:2-3	25	1:16	43 n.91
4:1–5:6	26	5:7-9	43 n.91
4:45	26 n.38	6:7-8	43 n.92

8:14	42 n.90	m.Sota	
4QMMT	87	7:5	62 n.47

4QPesher Nahum
    1:6-8   xvi
4QSam^a   68

Cairo Document (CD)
    5:2-5   61

Pseudo-Clementine writings

Hom.
    1.15   40
    2.14   40
    2.22-23   40
    2.23-24   42 n.88
    2.33   41

Rec.
    1:57.1   41
    1.12   40
    1.27-71   40 n.83
    1.60.5   40 n.82
    2.7   40
    2.8-11   42 n.88

Pseudepigrapha

Jubilees   88
    34:2-8   68 n.79
    45:14   68 n.79
Letter of Aristaeus   73, 77, 118
    16   84
    28–51   122
    44   77 n.26
    264   85
    301–22   122

Rabbinic Literature

Mishna

m.Abot
    1:1   53 n.9
m.Sanhedrin
    6   xvi n.20
    10:1   86 n.49
m.Menahot.
    13:10   76 n.22

Tosefta

t.Menahot
    13:21   77 n.23
t.Pesahim
    1.15   52
t.Taanit
    2:1   86 n.50
Sifre Num.
    70   73 n.5

Talmud of Jerusalem

j.Megila
    1:11   15
    1:71c   15
j.Pesahim
    6:1   13, 15
    33a   15

Talmud of Babylon

b.Pesahim
    53a-b   15
b.Qidushin
    30a   121
    66a   87 n.55
b.Rosh ha-Shana
    31a-b   46 n.102
b.Sanhedrin
    21b   53
b.Kuthim
    2:7   x, 52 n.8

Greco-Roman Literature

Arrien
Anabase
    7.4.6   26 n.38

Epiphanius
Panarion
    10.5.1   44 n.97

Eusebius
Demonst. evang.

10.1.12	32 n.54	61	18
Eccl. Hist. (HE)		68	18, 24
3.9	11	69	24
4.22.7	44 n.97	75–77	24
6.25.2	86 n.49	76–79	18
Praep. evang.		78–79	24
9.17.8	84 n.41	81–87	18
9.17.13	44 n.97	88	24
9.21	66 n.67	91	18
9.33	57 n.29	98–103	24
		99–103	24
Hippolytus of Rome		115–16	19
Refutatio		120	23
9.18.2	44 n.97	184–296	23
		363	11
Homer		418	11
Iliad		422	14
6:290	64 n.61	*Jewish Antiquities (Ant.)*	9, 12
23:743	64 n.61	2:213	15
Odyssey		2:268-269	83
4:84	64 n.61	2:347	18
		3:248	15
Irenaeus		3:401	88
Adv. Haer.		4:11	94
1.30.15	40	4:203	73 n.5
4:10	68 n.77	5:2	17
		5:69	62
Josephus, Flavius	1–3, 5, 7, 9–10	5:81-87	16
Against Apion (CAp)	9	5:362	100
1:34	14	6:29-30	94
1:106-107	57 n.29	7:6	18
1:186	93 n.6	7:95	57 n.31
1:250	76	7:365	31 n.51
2:39-41	13, 30	8:141-142	57 n.29
2:39-41	29	8:230	57
2:77	14	9	52
2:193-195	14	9:96	13 n.15
Autobiography (Life)	9, 12	9:291	xv, xviii
2	31 n.51	10:76	23
4–5	15	10:151-153	100
5	17	10:184	xv, xviii
6–14	17	10:210	14, 18
15	17	11	27
34	17	11:20	98
35	17	11:21-22	99
43	17	11:97-98	14, 99
44	17	11:106	96
54	13	11:110	99 n.16
55–57	18	11:114-115	14

11:114-119	99	15:15-24	33
11:133	95	15:320-322	77 n.23
11:157	14, 23, 103 n.22	16:174	33
11:174	104 n.24	17:20	xv, xviii
11:179	14, 104	17:23-28	13
11:297-301	81	17:165	77 n.23
11:302-325	89	17:339	77 n.23
11:341	xv, xviii	18:3	77 n.23
12–13	28	18:85	xv, xviii
12:3-4	93 n.6	18:85-86	45 n.101
12:4	29 n.42	18:116-119	42
12:22	84	19:297	77 n.23
12:136	71 n.1	20	xviii
12:136-144	12	20:235-238	74
12:138-146	101	*Jewish War* (W)	9, 10, 14
12:147-153	101	1:31-53	27
12:168	79	1:32-33	74
12:224	79	1:36	81
12:226-227	120	2:128	43 n.92
12:257-264	83	2:137-140	43
12:265	30	3:35-43	13
12:277	86	3:141-288	xvii
12:285	74 n.8	3:307-315	xviii, 11
12:300	32	4:449	12, 53 n.10
12:325	29	5:367	11
12:387-388	74 n.11	6:288-315	11
12:414	33	7:150	11
12:432	82	7:162	11
13	31	7:423-432	74
13:54	79	11:302–3	89
13:58	81	11:304–5	89
13:61	72	11306–8	90
13:62-73	74 n.11, 75 n.14	11:309–12	90
13:74-79	71	11:316ff	xvii
13:80	72	11:321–5	91
13:125-127	82 n.37	11:326–39	92
13:167	33	11:340–6	92
13:175	30 n.50		
13:211	82	Justin	
13:215	31	*I Apol.*	
13:227	33	26.1-8	39
13:254-281	126	*Dial.*	
13:256	73 n.6	120	40
13:257	73	120:3-4	68 n.77
13:288-298	87		
13:321	87	Pliny the Elder	
14:163-184	13	*Hist. Nat.*	
14.213-16	xii	5.15.73	44
14.231-32	xii		

www.ingramcontent.com/pod-product-compliance
Lightning Source LLC
Chambersburg PA
CBHW051526230426
43668CB00012B/1755